Ethics and the Limits of Philosophy

Bernard Williams was born in 1929 near London. He was educated at Chigwell School and at Balliol College, Oxford, and after National Service as a pilot in the RAF became a Fellow of All Souls College, and then of New College, Oxford. He taught for eight years in the University of London, first at University College, and subsequently as Professor of Philosophy at Bedford College. In 1967 he went to Cambridge as Knightbridge Professor of Philosophy; since 1979 he has been Provost of King's College. He is a Fellow of the British Academy. He has served on a number of Government committees, including the Committee on Obscenity and Film Censorship, of which he was Chairman.

His books include *Morality; Problems of the Self; Descartes: the Project of Pure Enquiry;* and *Moral Luck.*

Ethics and the Limits of Philosophy

BERNARD WILLIAMS

FONTANA PRESS/COLLINS

170.42
W67e

For Jacob

First published in 1985 by Fontana Paperbacks
and William Collins, 8 Grafton Street, London W1X 3LA

Copyright © Bernard Williams 1985

Printed and bound in Great Britain by
William Collins Sons & Co. Ltd, Glasgow

Hardback ISBN: 0 00 197171 9
Paperback ISBN: 0 00 686001 X

Preface

T HIS BOOK is principally about how things are in moral philosophy, not about how they might be, and since I do not think they are as they should be, some of it consists of criticism of present philosophy. Some of it, further, raises the question of how far any philosophy could help us to recreate ethical life. As I shall try to show, it can at least help us to understand it. In the course of saying what the present state of affairs is, and complaining about it, I hope to introduce a picture of ethical thought and a set of ideas that apply to it, which could also help us to think about how it might be.

There are two points I should like to make briefly at the beginning. It may seem surprising that a study of contemporary moral philosophy spends some time, particularly in the first three chapters, considering some ideas to be found in ancient Greek thought. This is not just the piety of philosophy toward its history. There is a special reason for it, which I hope will emerge in the course of the book (I try to make it explicit in the Postscript). The idea is certainly not that the demands of the modern world on ethical thought are no different from those of the ancient world. On the contrary, my conclusion is that the demands of the modern world on ethical thought are unprecedented, and the ideas of rationality embodied in most contemporary moral philosophy cannot meet them; but some extension of ancient thought, greatly modified, might be able to do so.

The second point is a matter of style. The philosophy of this book can no doubt be called, on some broad specification, "analytical," and so is much of the recent philosophy it discusses. I take this to be, indeed, a matter of style, and the limitation it introduces comes only from the fact that style must to some extent determine subject matter. There is no distinctive subject matter of analytical moral philosophy, as compared with other kinds of moral philosophy. What distinguishes analytical philosophy from other contemporary philosophy (though not from much philosophy of other times) is a certain way of going on, which involves argument, distinctions, and, so far as it remembers to try to achieve it and succeeds, moderately plain speech. As an alternative to plain speech, it distinguishes sharply between obscurity and technicality. It always rejects the first, but the second it sometimes finds a necessity. This feature peculiarly enrages some of its enemies. Wanting philosophy to be at once profound and accessible, they resent technicality but are comforted by obscurity.

The aim of analytical philosophy, as it always says, is to be clear. I am not altogether sure of its title to that claim, still less of its unique title to it. I do not want to discuss that here, partly because if one discusses such issues, one discusses nothing else, and also because I do not care very much whether this work is regarded as analytical philosophy—I merely recognize that it will be. However, I do care that it should be what I call "clear." I suggest in the course of the book that certain interpretations of reason and clear understanding as discursive rationality have damaged ethical thought itself and distorted our conceptions of it. But if claims of that sort are to carry conviction in coming from a philosophical writer, they are themselves best set out with some degree of discursive rationality and argumentative order, and that is what I have tried to give them. I have no doubt often failed, and there are many things that are obscure though I have tried to make them clear. I can acknowledge this with more assurance than I can that some things are obscure because I have tried to make them clear in this way, but that is no doubt true as well.

I am indebted to many people for their help, but none is to blame for the results. I was able to try out various early versions of my criticisms of ethical theory in certain lectures that I was honored to be asked to give: the Tanner Lectures at Brasenose College, Oxford, the Thalheimer Lectures at Johns Hopkins University, and the Gregynog Lectures at the University of Wales at Aberystwyth. On all these occasions I was grateful to those present for comments and criticisms. I had the opportunity to give a seminar on moral philosophy at Princeton University in 1978, as Senior Visiting Fellow in the Humanities, and benefited from discussion with many people, in particular with Thomas Nagel and Tim Scanlon. Ronald Dworkin has for a long time been a friendly, searching, and always unsatisfied critic. Drafts of this book, in whole or part, have been read by Geoffrey Hawthorn, Derek Parfit, Jonathan Lear, and Amartya Sen, to all of whom I am indebted for their comments. I am grateful to Mark Sacks for research assistance and to Peter Burbidge for help with the index.

The quotation from Wallace Stevens on page x is from *The Collected Poems,* copyright 1954 by Wallace Stevens, reprinted by permission of the publishers, Alfred A. Knopf, Inc. (New York), and Faber and Faber (London).

Cambridge, England

Contents

How cold the vacancy
When the phantoms are gone and the shaken realist
First sees reality. The mortal no
Has its emptiness and tragic expirations.
The tragedy, however, may have begun,
Again, in the imagination's new beginning,
In the yes of the realist spoken because he must
Say yes, spoken because under every no
Lay a passion for yes that had never been broken.

WALLACE STEVENS, "Esthétique du Mal"

Quand on n'a pas de caractère, il faut bien se
donner une méthode.

ALBERT CAMUS, *La Chute*

CHAPTER 1

Socrates' Question

I T I S N O T a trivial question, Socrates said: what we are talking about is how one should live. Or so Plato reports him, in one of the first books written about this subject.[1] Plato thought that philosophy could answer the question. Like Socrates, he hoped that one could direct one's life, if necessary redirect it, through an understanding that was distinctively philosophical — that is to say, general and abstract, rationally reflective, and concerned with what can be known through different kinds of inquiry.

The aims of moral philosophy, and any hopes it may have of being worth serious attention, are bound up with the fate of Socrates' question, even if it is not true that philosophy, itself, can reasonably hope to answer it. With regard to that hope, there are two things to be mentioned here at the outset. One is particularly to be remembered by the writer — how large a claim he is making if he says that a particular kind of abstract, argumentative writing should be worth serious attention when these large questions are at issue. There are other books that bear on the question — almost all books, come to that, which are any good and which are concerned with human life at all. That is a point for the philosophical writer even if he does not think his relation to Socrates' question lies in trying to answer it.

The other initial point is one for the reader. It would be a serious thing if philosophy could answer the question. How could it be that a *subject*, something studied in universities (but not only there), something for which there is a large technical literature, could deliver what one might recognize as an answer to the basic questions of life? It is hard to see how this could be so, unless, as Socrates believed, the answer were one that the reader would recognize as one he might have given himself. But how could this be? And how would this be related to the existence of the subject? For Socrates, there was no such subject; he just talked with his friends in a plain way, and the writers he referred to (at least with any respect) were the poets. But within one generation Plato had linked the study of moral philosophy to difficult mathematical disciplines, and after two generations there were treatises on the subject — in particular, Aristotle's *Ethics,* still one of the most illuminating.[2]

Some philosophers would like to be able to go back now to Socrates' position and to start again, reflectively questioning common sense and our moral or ethical concerns, without the weight of texts and a tradition of philosophical study. There is something to be said for this, and in this book I shall try to follow it to the extent of pursuing an inquiry and hoping to involve the reader in it. At another level, however, it is baseless to suppose that one can or should try to get away from the practices of the subject. What makes an inquiry a philosophical one is reflective generality and a style of argument that claims to be rationally persuasive. It would be silly to forget that many acute and reflective people have already labored at formulating and discussing these questions. Moral philosophy has the problems it has because of its history and its present practices. Moreover, it is important that there is a tradition of activity, some of it technical, in other parts of philosophy, such as logic, the theory of meaning, and the philosophy of mind. While few of them outside mathematical logic provide "results," there is certainly a lot to be known about the state of the subject, and some of it bears significantly on moral philosophy.

There is another reason for not forgetting that we exist now and not in Socrates' condition. For him and for Plato it was a special feature of philosophy that it was reflective and stood back from ordinary practice and argument to define and criticize the attitudes involved in them. But modern life is so pervasively reflective, and a high degree of self-consciousness is so basic to its institutions, that these qualities cannot be what mainly distinguishes philosophy from other activities — from law, for instance, which is increasingly conscious of itself as a social creation; or medicine, forced to understand itself as at once care, business, and applied science; to say nothing of fiction, which even in its more popular forms needs to be conscious of its fictionality. Philosophy in the modern world cannot make any special claim to reflectiveness, though it may be able to make a special use of it.

This book will try to give some idea of the most important developments in moral philosophy, but it will proceed by way of an inquiry into its problems, in those directions that seem to me most interesting. I hope that the accounts of other people's work will be accurate, but they will assuredly be selective. It is not merely that my account of the subject will be different from one given by someone else (that must presumably be so if the book is worth reading at all), nor is it a question of how representative it will be, but rather that I shall not be concerned all the time to say how representative it is. There is one respect, at least, in which this book is not representative of ways in which the subject is for the most part now conducted, at least in the English-speaking world. It is more skeptical than much of that philosophy about what the powers of philosophy are, and it is also more skeptical about morality.

What the aims of moral philosophy should be depends on its own results. Because its inquiries are indeed reflective and general, and concerned with what can be known, they must try to give an account of what would have to go into answering Socrates' question: what part might be played by knowledge of the sciences; how far purely rational inquiry can take us; how far the answer to the question might be expected to be different if it is asked in one society rather than another; how much, at the end of all that, must be left to personal decision. Philosophical reflection thus has to consider what is involved in answering this, or any other less general, practical question, and to ask what powers of the mind and what forms of knowledge might be called upon by it. One thing that has to be considered in this process is the place of philosophy itself.

There might seem to be a circle in this: philosophy, in asking how Socrates' question might be answered, determines its own place in answering it. It is not a circle but a progression. Philosophy starts from questions that, on any view of it, it can and should ask, about the chances we have of finding out how best to live; in the course of that, it comes to see how much it itself may help, with discursive methods of analysis and argument, critical discontent, and an imaginative comparison of possibilities, which are what it most characteristically tries to add to our ordinary resources of historical and personal knowledge.

Socrates' question is the best place for moral philosophy to start. It is better than "what is our duty?" or "how may we be good?" or even "how can we be happy?" Each of these questions takes too much for granted, although not everyone will agree about what that is. In the case of the last question, some people, such as those who want to start with the first question, will think that it starts in the wrong place, by ignoring the distinctive issues of morality; others may simply find it rather optimistic. Socrates' question is neutral on those issues, and on many others. It would be wrong, however, to think that it takes nothing for granted. The first thing we should do is to ask what is involved in Socrates' question, and how much we are presupposing if we assume that it can be usefully asked at all.

"How should one live?" — the generality of *one* already stakes a claim. The Greek language does not even give us *one:* the formula is impersonal. The implication is that something relevant or useful can be said to anyone, in general, and this implies that something general can be said, something that embraces or shapes the individual ambitions each person may bring to the question "how should I live?" (A larger implication can easily be found in this generality: that the question naturally leads us out of the concerns of the ego altogether. We shall come back to this later.) This is one way in which Socrates' question goes beyond the everyday "what shall I do?" Another is that it is not immediate; it is not about what I should do now, or next. It is about a manner of life. The Greeks themselves were much impressed by the idea that such a question must, consequently, be about a whole life and that a good way of living had to issue in what, at its end, would be seen to have been a good life. Impressed by the power of fortune to wreck what looked like the best-shaped life, some of them, Socrates one of the first, sought a rational design of life which would reduce the power of fortune and would be to the greatest possible extent luck-free.[3] This has been, in different forms, an aim of later thought as well. The idea that one must think, at this very general level, about *a whole life* may seem less compelling to some of us than it did to Socrates. But his question still does press a demand for reflection on one's life *as a whole*, from every aspect and all the way down, even if we do not place as much weight as the Greeks did on how it may end.

The impersonal Greek phrase translated as *one should* is not only silent about the person whose life is in question. It is also entirely noncommittal, and very fruitfully so, about the kinds of consideration to be applied to the question. "How should I live?" does not mean "what life morally ought I to live?"; this is why Socrates' question is a starting point different from those other questions I mentioned, about duty or about a life in which one would be good. It may be the same as a question about the good life, a life worth living, but that notion in itself does not bring in any distinctively moral claims. It may turn out, as Socrates believed and most of us still hope, that a good life is also the life of a good person (*must be* is what Socrates believed; *can be* is what most of us hope). But, if so, that will come out later. *Should* is simply *should* and, in itself, is no different in this very general question from what it is in any casual question, "what should I do now?"

Some philosophers have supposed that we cannot start from this general or indeterminate kind of practical question, because questions such as "what should I do?", "what is the best way for me to live?", and so on, are *ambiguous* and sustain both a moral and a nonmoral sense. On this view, the first thing one would have to do with the question is to decide which of these two different kinds of thing it meant, and until then one could not even start to answer it. That is a mistake. The analysis of meanings does not require "moral" and "nonmoral" as categories of meaning. Of course, if someone says of another "he is a good man," we can ask whether the speaker means that he is morally good, as contrasted, for instance, with meaning that he is a good man to take on a military sortie — but the fact that one can give these various interpretations no more yields a moral sense of "good" or of "good man" than it does a military sense (or a football sense, etc.).

One can of course ask, on a given occasion, "what should I do from an ethical point of view?" or "what should I do from a self-interested point of view?" These ask for the results of subdeliberations, and invite one to review a particular type of consideration among those that bear on the question and to think what the considerations of that type, taken by themselves, support. In the same way, I can ask what I should do taking only economic or political or family considerations into account. At the end of all that, there is the question "what should I do, all things considered?" There is only one kind of question to be asked about what to do, of which Socrates' is a very general example, and moral considerations are one kind of consideration that bear on answering it.[4]

Here and earlier I have mentioned "moral" considerations, using that word in a general way, which corresponds to what is, irremovably, one name for the subject: moral philosophy. But there is another name for the subject, "ethics," and corresponding to that is the notion of an ethical consideration. By origin, the difference between the two terms is that between Latin and Greek, each relating to a word meaning *disposition* or *custom*. One difference is that the Latin term from which "moral" comes emphasizes rather more the sense of social expectation, while the Greek favors that of individual character. But the word "morality" has by now taken on a more distinctive content, and I am going to suggest that morality should be understood as a particular development of the ethical, one that has a special significance in modern Western culture. It peculiarly emphasizes certain ethical notions rather than others, developing in particular a special notion of obligation, and it has some peculiar presuppositions. In view of these features it is also, I believe, something we should treat with a special skepticism. From now on, therefore, I shall for the most part use "ethical" as the broad term to stand for what this subject is certainly about, and "moral" and "morality" for the narrower system, the peculiarities of which will concern us later on.

I shall not try to define what exactly counts as an ethical consideration, but I shall say something about what goes into the notion of the ethical. It does no harm that the notion is vague. It is in fact *morality,* the special system, that demands a sharp boundary for itself (in demanding "moral" and "nonmoral" senses for words, for instance). This is a function of its special presuppositions. Without them, we can admit that there is a range of considerations that falls under the notion of the ethical, and we can also see why the range is not clearly delimited.

One thing that falls within its range is the notion of an obligation. A rather varied set of considerations is ordinarily counted as obligations, and I shall take up later (in Chapter 10) the question of why this should be so. One familiar kind is the obligation that one can put oneself under, in particular by making a promise. There is also the idea of a duty. The most familiar use of that word nowadays may be in narrow institutional connections, as when there is a list or roster of duties. Going beyond that, duties have characteristically been connected with a role, position, or relationship, such as those that follow from one's "station," as Bradley called it in the title of a famous essay.[5] In a case such as the duties of a job, the job may have been acquired voluntarily, but in general duties, and most obligations other than those of promises, are not acquired voluntarily.

In the thought of Kant and of others influenced by him, all genuinely moral considerations rest, ultimately and at a deep level, in the agent's will. I cannot simply be *required* by my position in a social structure — by the fact that I am a particular person's child, for instance — to act in a certain way, if that *required* is to be of the moral kind, and does not simply reflect a psychological compulsion or social and legal sanctions. To act morally is to act autonomously, not as the result of social pressure. This mirrors some of the characteristic concerns of the subsystem morality. As against that, it has been in every society a recognizable ethical thought, and remains so in ours, that one can be under a requirement of this kind simply because of who one is and of one's social situation. It may be a kind of consideration that some people in Western societies now would not want to accept, but it has been accepted by almost everyone in the past, and there is no necessity in the demand that every requirement of this kind must, under rational scrutiny, be either abandoned or converted into a voluntary commitment. Such a demand is, like other distinctive features of morality, closely related to processes of modernization: it represents an understanding in ethical terms of the process that in the world of legal relations Maitland called the change from status to contract. It corresponds also to a changing conception of the self that enters into ethical relations.[6]

Obligation and duty look backwards, or at least sideways. The acts they require, supposing that one is deliberating about what to do, lie in the future, but the reasons for those acts lie in the fact that I have already promised, the job I have undertaken, the position I am already in. Another kind of ethical consideration looks forward, to the outcomes of the acts open to me. "It will be for the best" may be taken as the general form of this kind of consideration. In one way of taking this, specially important in philosophical theory, *the best* is measured by the degree to which people get what they want, are made happy, or some similar consideration. This is the area of welfarism or utilitarianism (I shall discuss such theories in Chapters 5 and 6). But that is only one version. G. E. Moore also thought that the forward-looking type of consideration was fundamental, but he allowed things other than satisfaction — such as friendship and the awareness of beauty — to count among the good consequences. It was because of this that his theory was so attractive to the Bloomsbury group: it managed to reject at once the stuffiness of duty and the vulgarity of utilitarianism.

There is another kind of ethical consideration, which presents an action as being of some ethically relevant kind. There is a wide range of ethical characteristics of actions under which they may be chosen or, again, refused. A particular action may be refused because it would be theft or murder, for instance, or deceitful or dishonorable, or, less dramatically, because it would let someone down. These descriptions — and there are many of them — operate at different levels; thus an action can be dishonorable because it is deceitful.

Closely connected with these descriptions, under which actions may be chosen or rejected, are various virtues, a virtue being a disposition of character to choose or reject actions because they are of a certain ethically relevant kind. The word "virtue" has for the most part acquired comic or otherwise undesirable associations, and few now use it except philosophers, but there is no other word that serves as well, and it has to be used in moral philosophy. One might hope that, with its proper meaning reestablished, it will come back into respectable use. In that proper use, meaning an ethically admirable disposition of character, it covers a broad class of characteristics, and, as so often in these subjects, the boundary of that class is not sharp and does not need to be made sharp. Some desirable personal characteristics certainly do not count as virtues, such as being sexually attractive. That can be a matter of character (some people have a sexually attractive character), but it does not have to be and it does not rate as a virtue, any more than having perfect pitch does. Again, virtues are always more than mere skills, since they involve characteristic patterns of desire and motivation. One can be a good pianist and have no desire to play, but if one is generous or fair-minded, those qualities themselves help to determine, in the right contexts, what one will want to do.

This is not to say that virtues can never be misused. One kind of virtue that can evidently be misused is the so-called executive virtues, which do not so much involve objectives of their own as assist in realizing other objectives — courage, for instance, or self-control. These are nevertheless virtues, being traits of character, and they are not related to pursuing other objectives as the mere possession of a skill is. According to Socrates, the virtues cannot be misused, and indeed he held something even stronger, that it is impossible for people, because they have a certain virtue, to act worse than if they did not have it. This led him, consistently, to believe that there is basically only one virtue, the power of right judgment. We need not follow him in that. More important, we should not follow him in what motivates those ideas, which is the search for something in an individual's life that can be *unqualifiedly* good, good under all possible circumstances. That search has its modern expressions as well, and we shall encounter one of them in the special preoccupations of morality.

The notion of a virtue is a traditional one in moral philosophy, but it fell out of discussion for some time. In recent work, several writers have rightly emphasised its importance.[7] If one has a certain virtue, then that affects how one deliberates. We need to be clear, however, about the ways in which it can affect the deliberation. An important point is that the virtue-term itself usually does not occur in the content of the deliberation. Someone who has a particular virtue does actions because they fall under certain descriptions and avoids others because they fall under other descriptions. That person is described in terms of the virtue, and so are his or her actions: thus he or she is a just or courageous person who does just or courageous things. But — and this is the point — it is rarely the case that the description that applies to the agent and to the action is the same as that in terms of which the agent chooses the action. "Just" is indeed such a case, one of the few, and a just or fair person is one who chooses actions because they are just and rejects others because they are unjust or unfair. But a courageous person does not typically choose acts as being courageous, and it is a notorious truth that a modest person does not act under the title of modesty. The benevolent or kindhearted person does benevolent things, but does them under other descriptions, such as "she needs it," "it will cheer him up," "it will stop the pain." The description of the virtue is not itself the description that appears in the consideration. Moreover, there is typically no one ethical concept that characterizes the deliberations of a person who has a particular virtue. Rather, if an agent has a particular virtue, then certain ranges of fact become ethical considerations for that agent because he or she has that virtue. The road from the ethical considerations that weigh with a virtuous person to the description of the virtue itself is a tortuous one, and it is both defined and pitted by the impact of self-consciousness.

That same impact, in fact, may have contributed to making the virtues unpopular as an ethical conception. Their discussion used to make much of the *cultivation* of the virtues. In third-personal form, that exercise, if not under that title, is very familiar: it forms a good part of socialization or moral education or, come to that, education. As a first-personal exercise, however, the cultivation of the virtues has something suspect about it, of priggishness or self-deception. It is not simply that to think in this way is to think about oneself rather than about the world and other people. Some ethical thought, particularly if it is self-critical, will of course do that. More than one writer has recently stressed the importance of our capacity to have second-order desires — desires to have certain desires[8] — and its significance for ethical reflection and the practical consciousness. Deliberation toward satisfying those second-order desires must be in a special degree directed toward the self. The trouble with cultivating the virtues, if it is seen as a first-personal and deliberative exercise, is rather that your thought is not self-directed enough. Thinking about your possible states in terms of the virtues is not so much to think about your actions, and it is not distinctively to think about the terms in which you could or should think about your actions: it is rather to think about the way in which others might describe or comment on the way in which you think about your actions, and if that represents the essential content of your deliberations, it really does seem a misdirection of the ethical attention. The lesson of all this, however, is not that the virtues are not an important ethical concept. It is rather that the importance of an ethical concept need not lie in its being itself an element of first-personal deliberation. The deliberations of people who are generous or brave, and also the deliberations of people who are trying to be more generous or braver, are different from the deliberations of those who are not like that, but the difference does not mainly lie in their thinking about themselves in terms of generosity or courage.

These, then, are some kinds of ethical concepts and considerations. What sorts of considerations bear on action but are *not* ethical considerations? There is one very obvious candidate, the considerations of egoism, those that relate merely to the comfort, excitement, self-esteem, power, or other advantage of the agent. The contrast between these considerations and the ethical is a platitude, and is grounded in obviously reasonable ideas about what ethical practices are for, the role they play in human societies. Yet even here distinctions need to be made. One is only a verbal point. We are concerned with Socrates' question "how should one live?" and egoism, in the unvarnished and baldly self-interested sense, is at any rate an intelligible answer to that, even though most of us may be disposed to reject it. It is possible to use the word "ethical" of any scheme for living that would provide an intelligible answer to Socrates' question. In that sense, even the baldest egoism would be an ethical option. I do not think we should follow that use. However vague it may initially be, we have a conception of the ethical that understandably relates to us and our actions the demands, needs, claims, desires, and, generally, the lives of other people, and it is helpful to preserve this conception in what we are prepared to call an ethical consideration.

Egoism can, however, take a step farther than it takes in its baldest form. There is a theory of how we should act which has been called, confusingly enough, *ethical egoism*. This claims that each person ought to pursue his or her own self-interest. This differs from bald egoism because it is a reflective position and takes a general view about people's interests. Whether we call it an ethical system, as it calls itself, does not really matter very much. The important question is how it contributes to the idea of an ethical *consideration*. At first sight it seems to make no contribution to that, since it says that each of us ought to act on nonethical considerations. If it simply says that, it merely seems dogmatic: if people in fact act on considerations other than self-interest, what shows that they are irrational to do so? What this view is more likely to do, in fact, is to *leave open* the role of ethical considerations, and to ask how a life that involves acting on those considerations is related to self-interest.

There is another view, which looks much the same as the last but is different. It also claims something general, saying that *what ought to happen* is that everyone pursue his or her own interest. This view is likely to have an unstable effect on the considerations that one takes into account in acting. It may introduce a consideration that is ethical in the ordinary sense. If I believe that what ought to happen is that people pursue their own interest, then one thing I may have reason to do is to promote that state of affairs, and this may involve my giving a helping hand to others in adopting that policy. Such a line of action may well conflict with my simply pursuing my own self-interest.

In fact, it is quite difficult to sustain the bare belief that what ought to happen is that people pursue their own interest. It is more natural to support this with another consideration, that it is *for the best* if everyone does that. This may take the form of saying such things as that attempts to be kind to others merely confuse the issue. Someone who argues like this (and believes it) actually accepts some other ethical considerations as well, for instance that it is a good thing if people get what they want, and believes in addition that the best way for as many people as possible to get as much as possible of what they want is that each person should pursue what he or she wants. This is, of course, what advocates of laissez-faire capitalism used to claim in the early nineteenth century. Some even claim it in the late twentieth century, in the face of the obvious fact that all economic systems depend on people in society having dispositions that extend beyond self-interest. Perhaps this contradiction helps to explain why some advocates of laissez-faire tend to give moralizing lectures, not only to people who are failing to pursue their own interest but to people who are.

We are contrasting ethical and egoistic considerations. But might not somebody want someone else's happiness? Of course. Then would not egoism, my pursuit of what I want, coincide with what is supposed to be an ethical type of consideration, the concern for someone else's happiness? Again yes, but it is not very interesting unless in some more general and systematic way egoistic and ethical considerations come together. That is a question we shall come to when we consider foundations in Chapter 3.

From all this it will be seen that the idea of the ethical, even though it is vague, has some content to it; it is not a purely formal notion. One illustration of this lies in a different kind of nonethical consideration, which might be called the *counterethical*. Counterethical motivations, a significant human phenomenon, come in various forms, shaped by their positive counterparts in the ethical. Malevolence, the most familiar motive of this kind, is often associated with the agent's pleasure, and that is usually believed to be its natural state; but there exists a pure and selfless malevolence as well, a malice transcending even the agent's need to be around to enjoy the harm that it wills. It differs from counterjustice, a whimsical delight in unfairness. That is heavily parasitic on its ethical counterpart, in the sense that a careful determination of the just is needed first, to give it direction. With malevolence it is not quite like that. It is not that benevolence has to do its work before malevolence has anything to go on, but rather that each uses the same perceptions and moves from them in different directions. (This is why, as Nietzsche remarked, cruelty needs to share the sensibility of the sympathetic, while brutality needs not to.) Other counterethical motivations, again, are parasitic on the reputation or emotional self-image of the ethical rather than on its conclusions. This, as one would expect, can particularly involve the virtues. That an action would be cowardly is not often found by an agent to be a consideration in its favor, but it could be, and in a counterethical way, ministering to a masochism of shame.

I have touched on considerations of egoism and on considerations that go outside the self—of benevolence, for instance, or fairness. But there is a question that has proved very important to ethics of how far outside the self such considerations should range. Will it count as an ethical consideration if you consider the interests and needs only of your family or of your community or of the nation? Certainly such local loyalties have provided the fabric of people's lives and the forum, it seems right to say, of ethical life. However, there are some ethical demands that seem to be satisfied only by a universal concern, one that extends to all human beings and perhaps beyond the human race. This concern is particularly cultivated by the subsystem morality, to the extent that it is often thought that no concern is truly moral unless it is marked by this universality.

For morality, the ethical constituency is always the same: the universal constituency. An allegiance to a smaller group, the loyalties to family or country, would have to be justified from the outside inward, by an argument that explained how it was a good thing that people should have allegiances that were less than universal. (I shall consider in Chapters 5 and 6 the motives and perils of this kind of approach; and also different accounts that have been given of what the universal constituency is.) At a more everyday level (a less reflective one, the moral critic would say), the location of the ethical can move from one side to another of a given contrast.

Relative to my personal interest, the interests of the town or the nation can represent an ethical demand, but the interests of the town can count as self-interested if the demand comes from some larger identification. This is simply because the requirements of benevolence or fairness may always stake a claim against self-interest; *we* can represent a self-interest as much as *I*; and who *we* are depends on the extent of identification in a particular case, and on the boundaries of contrast.

I have mentioned several sorts of ethical consideration, and more than one kind of nonethical. Philosophy has traditionally shown a desire to reduce this diversity, on both sides of the divide. It has tended, first of all, to see all nonethical considerations as reducible to egoism, the narrowest form of self-interest. Indeed some philosophers have wanted to reduce that to one special kind of egoistic concern, the pursuit of pleasure. Kant, in particular, believed that every action not done from moral principle was done for the agent's pleasure. This needs to be distinguished from another idea, that all actions, including those done for ethical reasons, are equally motivated by the pursuit of pleasure. This theory, psychological hedonism, finds it hard to avoid being either obviously false or else trivially vacuous, as it becomes if it simply identifies with the agent's expected pleasure anything that the agent intentionally does. But in any case this theory makes no special contribution to a distinction between the ethical and the nonethical. If there were any true and interesting version of psychological hedonism, those actions that had nonethical motivations would not necessarily form any special class of pleasure-seeking activity. Kant's view, on the other hand, does contribute to the question, by holding that moral action is uniquely exempted from psychological hedonism; that view is certainly wrong.[9] If we are not influenced by such a theory, we can accept the obvious truth that there are different sorts of nonethical motivation — and, moreover, that there is more than one kind of motivation acting against ethical considerations.[10]

The desire to reduce all nonethical considerations to one type is less strong in philosophy now than it was when moral philosophy chiefly concentrated not so much on questions of what is the right thing to do and what is the good life (the answers to such questions were thought to be obvious), but rather on how one was to be motivated to pursue those things, against the motivations of selfishness and pleasure. The desire to reduce all *ethical* considerations to one pattern is, on the other hand, as strong as ever, and various theories try to show that one or another type of ethical consideration is basic, with other types to be explained in terms of it. Some take as basic a notion of obligation or duty, and the fact that we count it as an ethical consideration, for instance, that a certain act will probably lead to the best consequences is explained in terms of our having one duty, among others, to bring about the best consequences. Theories of this kind are called "deontological." (This term is sometimes said to come from the ancient Greek word for duty. There is no ancient Greek word for duty: it comes from the Greek for what one *must* do.)

Contrasted with these are theories that take as primary the idea of producing the best possible state of affairs. Theories of this kind are often called "teleological." The most important example is that which identifies the goodness of outcomes in terms of people's happiness or their getting what they want or prefer. This, as I have already said, is called utilitarianism, though that term has also been used, for instance by Moore, for the more general notion of a teleological system.[11] Some of these reductive theories merely tell us what is rational, or again most true to our ethical experience, to treat as the fundamental notion. Others are bolder and claim that these relations are to be discovered in the meanings of what we say. Thus Moore claimed that "right" simply meant "productive of the greatest good."[12] Moore's philosophy is marked by an affectation of modest caution, which clogged his prose with qualifications but rarely restrained him from wild error, and this, as a claim about what the words mean, is simply untrue. More generally, if theories of this kind are offered descriptively, as accounts of what we actually take to be equivalent, they are all equally misguided. We use a variety of different ethical considerations, which are genuinely different from one another, and this is what one would expect to find, if only because we are heirs to a long and complex ethical tradition, with many different religious and other social strands.

As an enterprise that intends to be descriptive, like anthropology, the reductive undertaking is merely wrongheaded. It may have other aims, however. It may, at some deeper level, seek to give us a theory of the subject matter of ethics. But it is not clear why that aim, either, must encourage us to reduce our basic ethical conceptions. If there is such a thing as the truth about the subject matter of ethics — the truth, we might say, about the ethical — why is there any expectation that it should be simple? In particular, why should it be conceptually simple, using only one or two ethical concepts, such as *duty* or *good state of affairs,* rather than many? Perhaps we need as many concepts to describe it as we find we need, and no fewer.

The point of trying to reduce our ethical concepts must be found in a different aim of ethical theory, which is not just to describe how we think about the ethical but to tell us how we should think about it. Later I shall argue that philosophy should not try to produce ethical theory, though this does not mean that philosophy cannot offer any critique of ethical beliefs and ideas. I shall claim that in ethics the reductive enterprise has no justification and should disappear. My point here, however, is merely to stress that the enterprise needs justifying. A good deal of moral philosophy engages unblinkingly in this activity, for no obvious reason except that it has been going on for a long time.

There is one motive for reductivism that does not operate simply on the ethical, or on the nonethical, but tends to reduce every consideration to one basic kind. This rests on an assumption about rationality, to the effect that two considerations cannot be rationally weighed against each other unless there is a common consideration in terms of which they can be compared. This assumption is at once very powerful and utterly baseless. Quite apart from the ethical, aesthetic considerations can be weighed against economic ones (for instance) without being an application of them, and without their both being an example of a third kind of consideration. Politicians know that political considerations are not all made out of the same material as considerations against which they are weighed; even different political considerations can be made out of different material. If one compares one job, holiday, or companion with another, judgment does not need a particular set of weights.

This is not merely a matter of intellectual error. If it were that, it could not survive the fact that people's experience contradicts it, that they regularly arrive at conclusions they regard as rational, or at least as reasonable, without using one currency of comparison. The drive toward a *rationalistic conception of rationality* comes instead from social features of the modern world, which impose on personal deliberation and on the idea of practical reason itself a model drawn from a particular understanding of public rationality. This understanding requires in principle every decision to be based on grounds that can be discursively explained. The requirement is not in fact met, and it probably does little for the aim that authority should be genuinely answerable. But it is an influential ideal and, by a reversal of the order of causes, it can look as if it were the result of applying to the public world an independent ideal of rationality. As an ideal, we shall see more of it later.[13]

Let us go back to Socrates' question. It is a particularly ambitious example of a personal practical question. The most immediate and uncomplicated question of that sort, by contrast, is "what am I to do?" or "what shall I do?" The various ethical and nonethical considerations we have been discussing contribute to answering such a question. Its answer, the conclusion of the deliberation, is of the form "I shall do . . ." or "what I am going to do is . . ." — and that is an expression of intention, an intention I have formed as a result of my deliberation. When it comes to the moment of action, it may be that I shall fail to carry it out, but then that will have to be because I have forgotten it, or been prevented, or have changed my mind, or because (as I may come to see) I never really meant it — it was not the real conclusion of my deliberation, or it was not a real deliberation. When the time for action is immediate, there is less room for these alternatives, so it is paradoxical if I come out with an answer of this kind and immediately fail to do what I said I was immediately going to do.

The question "what should I do?" allows rather more space between thought and action. Here the appropriate conclusion is "I should do . . ." and there are several intelligible ways of adding here ". . . but I am not going to." *Should* draws attention to the reasons I have for acting in one way rather than another. The usual function of "I should . . . but I am not going to" is to draw attention to some special class of reasons, such as ethical or prudential reasons, which are particularly good as reasons to declare to others — because they serve to justify my conduct, for instance by fitting it into someone's plan of action — but which are not, as it turns out, the strongest reasons for me, now; the strongest reason is that I desire very much to do something else. Desiring to do something is of course a reason for doing it.[14] (It can even be a reason that justifies my conduct to others, though there are some tasks of justification, those particularly connected with justice, which by itself it cannot do.) So, in this sort of case, what I think I have most reason to do, taking all things together, is the thing I very much desire to do, and if *I should* is taken to refer to what I have most reason to do, this is what I should do. There is a further and deeper question, whether I can intentionally and without compulsion fail to do even what I think I have most reason to do; this, from Aristotle's name for the phenomenon, is known as the problem of *akrasia.* [15]

Socrates' question, then, means "how has one most reason to live?" In saying earlier that the force of *should* in the question was just *should,* I meant that no prior advantage is built into the question for one kind of reason over another. In particular, there is no special consideration for respectable justifying reasons. If ethical reasons, for instance, emerge importantly in the answer, that will not be because they have simply been selected for by the question.

Nevertheless, there is a peculiar emphasis given to Socrates' question in that it stands at a distance from any actual and particular occasion of considering what to do. It is a general question about what to do, because it asks how to live, and it is also in a sense a timeless question, since it invites me to think about my life from no particular point in it. These two facts make it a reflective question. That does not determine the answer, but it does affect it. Answering a practical question at a particular time, in a particular situation, I shall be particularly concerned with what I want *then.* Socrates' question I ask at no particular time — or, rather, the time when I no doubt ask it has no particular relation to the question. So I am bound by the question itself to take a more general, indeed a longer-term, perspective on life. This does not determine that I give the answers of long-term prudence. The answer to the question might be: the best way for me to live is to do at any given time what I most want to do at that time. But if I have a weakness for prudence, the nature of Socrates' question is likely to bring it out.

It is, moreover, *anybody's* question. This does not mean, of course, that when asked by some particular person, it is a question about anybody: it is a question about that particular person. But when the question is put before me in the Socratic way, to invite reflection, it is going to be part of the reflection, because it is part of the knowledge constituting it, that the question can be put to anybody. Once constituted in that way, it very naturally moves from the question, asked by anybody, "how should I live?" to the question "how should anybody live?" That seems to ask for the reasons we all share for living in one way rather than another. It seems to ask for the conditions of *the good life* — the right life, perhaps, for human beings as such.

How far must the very business of Socratic reflection carry the question in that direction, and with what effects on the answer? The timelessness of the reflection does not determine that the answer should favor prudence. Similarly, the fact that the reflective question can be asked by anyone should allow its answer to be egoistic. But if it is egoistic, it will be egoism of one kind rather than another — the general egoism, distinguished earlier, which says that all people should favor their own interests. This naturally invites the thought that, if so, then it must be a better human life that is lived in such a way. But if so (it is tempting to go on), then it must be better, in some impersonal or interpersonal sense, that people should live in such a way. Having been led to this impersonal standpoint, perhaps we can be required to look back from it, make our journey in the reverse direction, and even revise our starting point. For if it is not better from an impersonal standpoint that each person should live in an egoistic way, perhaps we have a reason for saying that each of us should not live in such a way, and we must, after all, give a nonegoistic answer to Socrates' question. If all that does indeed follow, then the mere asking of Socrates' reflective question will take us a very long way into the ethical world. But does it follow?

Practical thought is radically first-personal. It must ask and answer the question "what shall *I* do?"[16] Yet under Socratic reflection we seem to be driven to generalize the *I* and even to adopt, from the force of reflection alone, an ethical perspective. In Chapter 4, we shall see whether reflection can take us that far. But even if it cannot, Socratic reflection certainly takes us somewhere. Reflection involves some commitment, it seems, and certainly philosophy is committed to reflection. So the very existence of this book must raise the double question of how far reflection commits us and why we should be committed to reflection. Socrates thought that his reflection was inescapable. What he meant was not that everyone would engage in it, for he knew that not everyone would; nor that anyone who started reflecting on his life would, even against his will, be forced by inner compulsion to continue. His thought was rather that the good life must have reflection as part of its goodness: *the unexamined life,* as he put it, *is not worth living.*

This requires a very special answer to his question, which, for him, gives the final justification for raising it in the first place. If my book is committed to raising the question, is it committed to answering it in such a way? Must any philosophical inquiry into the ethical and into the good life require the value of philosophy itself and of a reflective intellectual stance to be part of the answer?

CHAPTER 2

The Archimedean Point

A NOTE of urgency can sometimes be heard, even in otherwise unhurried writers, when they ask for a justification of morality. Unless the ethical life, or (more narrowly) morality, can be justified by philosophy, we shall be open to relativism, amoralism, and disorder. As they often put it: when an amoralist calls ethical considerations in doubt, and suggests that there is no reason to follow the requirements of morality, *what can we say to him?*

But what can we say to him if there is a justification of morality? Well, we can put the justification before him. But why should he be expected to stay where we have put it? Why should he listen? The amoralist, or even his more theoretical associate the relativist, is represented in these writings as an alarming figure, a threat. Why should it make any difference to such a person whether there is a philosophical justification of the ethical life?

Once at least in the history of philosophy the amoralist has been concretely represented as an alarming figure, in the character of Callicles who appears in Plato's dialogue the *Gorgias*. Callicles, indeed, under the conventions of Platonic dialogue, engages in rational conversation and stays to be humbled by Socrates' argument (an argument so unconvincing, in fact, that Plato later had to write the *Republic* to improve on it). What is unnerving about him, however, is something that Plato displays and that is also the subject of the dialogue: he has a glistening contempt for philosophy itself, and it is only by condescension or to amuse himself that he stays to listen to its arguments at all.

—That is not the point. The question is not whether he will be convinced, but whether he ought to be convinced.

—But is it? The writers' note of urgency suggests something else, that what will happen could turn on the outcome of these arguments, that the justification of the ethical life could be a *force*. If we are to take this seriously, then it is a real question, who is supposed to be listening. Why are they supposed to be listening? What will the professor's justification do, when they break down the door, smash his spectacles, take him away?

In any case, even if there is something that the rest of us would count as a justification of morality or the ethical life, is it true that the amoralist, call him Callicles, *ought* to be convinced? Is it meant only that it would be a good thing if he were convinced? It would no doubt be a good thing for us, but that is hardly the point. Is it meant to be a good thing for him? Is he being imprudent, for instance, acting against his own best interests? Or is he irrational in a more abstract sense, contradicting himself or going against the rules of logic? And if he is, why must he worry about that? Robert Nozick has well raised the question of what force the charge of inconsistency has against the "immoral man":

Suppose that we show that some X he holds or accepts or does commits him to behaving morally. He now must give up at least one of the following: (a) behaving immorally, (b) maintaining X, (c) being consistent about this matter in this respect. The immoral man tells us, "To tell you the truth, if I had to make the choice, I would give up being consistent."[1]

It is not obvious what a justification of the ethical life should try to do, or why we should need such a thing. We should ask a pretended justification three questions: To whom is it addressed? From where? Against what? Against what, first of all, since we must ask what is being proposed as an alternative to the ethical life. It is important that there are alternatives to it. "The amoralist" is the name of somebody. This helps to define these questions in relation to a recurrent philosophical concern, skepticism. Skepticism can touch every kind of thing people claim to know: that there is an "external" world; that other people have experiences (that there are other people, one may also say); that scientific inquiry can yield knowledge; that ethical considerations have force. Philosophical skepticism touches all these things, but in very different ways and with very different effects. In the case of the external world, the real question raised by skepticism, for any sane person, is not whether any of what we say about the world is true, or even whether we know any of it to be true, but how we know any of it to be true, and how much. There is no alternative within life to such beliefs: any alternative would have to be an alternative to life. In the case of "other minds," as that problem is often called, much the same is true, within the limits of sanity, but the problem shifts disquietingly toward *how much?* Certainly we know that other people have feelings, but how much do we know about those feelings? This is, in part, a philosophical question, one that has more practical effect than the mere question "how do I know?"

Ethical skepticism, in these respects, is at the opposite end of a line from skepticism about the external world. It is not, on the other hand, like skepticism about psychical research or psychoanalysis, where a real doubt is raised that might come eventually to be accepted, with the result that these activities would meet the same fate as phrenology: we would come to reject them altogether, finding that their claims to knowledge or even reasoned belief were baseless. It is not possible for ethical considerations to meet a collective rejection of that sort. For the individual, however, there does seem to be an alternative to accepting ethical considerations. It lies in a life that is not an ethical life.

Ethical skepticism of this sort differs so much from skepticism about the external world that it cannot be treated by the same methods. Moore famously disconcerted the skeptic about material objects by confronting him with one, Moore's hand (at any rate, it would have been a confrontation if such a skeptic had been there).[2] There has been much discussion about the effect of Moore's gesture — as, for instance, whether it begged the question — but it undoubtedly has some effect, in reminding us that to take such a skeptic seriously might be to take him literally, and that there is some problem about what counts as doing that. There is no analogy here to the ethical. It may possibly be that if there are any ethical truths, some of them can be displayed as certain: given the choice, say, one should not surgically operate on a child without an anaesthetic;[3] but the production of such as example does not have the same disquieting effect on the ethical skeptic as the display of Moore's hand on the other kind. For one thing, one detached proposition known to be true about a material object will finish that first kind of skeptic: Moore's hand is an example of a material object, and, as *one* refutes *none,* so *certainly one* refutes *possibly none.* But the example of the child, or any other detached case of a striking sort, will count as an example of the ethical only to one who recognizes the ethical. The amoralist, Callicles himself if it took him that way, could help or spare a child. A limited benevolent or altruistic sentiment may move almost anyone to think that he should act in a certain way on a given occasion, but that fact does not present him with the ethical, as Moore's hand presented the skeptic with something material. The ethical involves more, a whole network of considerations, and the ethical skeptic could have a life that ignored such considerations altogether.

The traditional skeptic was basically a skeptic about *knowledge,* but an ethical skeptic is not necessarily the same as someone who doubts whether there is any ethical knowledge. In my sense, to be skeptical about ethics is to be skeptical about the force of ethical considerations; someone may grant them force, and so not be a skeptic, but still not think that they constitute knowledge because he does not think that the point lies in their being knowledge. (For the question whether there is ethical knowledge, see Chapter 8.) But, even when ethical skepticism is taken in this way, we should not assume that the skeptic must be someone who leads a life that goes against ethical considerations. Perhaps we should rather say that he leaves room for such a life. A skeptic, after all, is merely skeptical. As far as possible, he neither asserts nor denies, and the total skeptic, the Pyrrhonian of antiquity, was supposed neither to assert nor to deny anything. He could not bring it off,[4] and it is doubtful that the ethical skeptic could bring *that* off—engage himself to use the ethical vocabulary, but with regard to every ethical question, suspend judgment. There are difficulties in the very idea of doing that. It is hard, for instance, to use the vocabulary of promising and at the same time to sustain the position that there is nothing decisive to be said, for or against, on the question whether one ought to keep promises. Moreover, the skeptic has to act, and if he includes himself in the world of ethical discourse at all, then what he does must be taken as expressing thoughts he has within that world. If he speaks in terms of actions being ethically all right or not, and he cheerfully does a certain action, then we must take him to regard it as all right. So this is not an option for ethical skepticism. But there is another, which is to opt out of using ethical discourse altogether, except perhaps to deceive. While it is not an easy thing to do, the skeptic might be able to establish himself as one who is not at all concerned with ethical considerations. One can then see the force of the point that there are alternatives. He is not left with nothing to do.

The motivations the amoralist could be left with constitute one thing that the ethical claims might seek a justification *against*. Yet it is a mistake (as we shall see in the next chapter) to think that there is some objective presumption in favor of the nonethical life, that ethical skepticism is the natural state, and that the person we have been imagining is what we all would want to be if there were no justification for the ethical life and we had discovered that there was none. The moral philosopher in search of justifications sometimes pretends that this is so, overestimating in this respect the need for a justification just as he had overestimated its effect — its effect, at least, on the practicing skeptic.

This returns us to the question of "to whom?" When the philosopher raised the question of what we shall have to say to the skeptic or amoralist, he should rather have asked what we shall have to say about him. The justification he is looking for is in fact designed for the people who are largely within the ethical world, and the aim of the discourse is not to deal with someone who probably will not listen to it, but to reassure, strengthen, and give insight to those who will. This puts into a different perspective the idea we saw rather optimistically deployed in the case of the amoralist, that a justification of the ethical would be a force. Plato, who saw more deeply than any other philosopher into the questions raised by the possibility of a life outside the ethical, did not himself take it for granted that a justification of the ethical life would be a force. He thought that the power of the ethical was the power of reason, and that it had to be *made* into a force. He saw it as a problem of politics, and so it is. But he believed that the justification was intellectual and very difficult and, further, that everyone had some natural inclination to break out of the ethical order and destroy it. This inclination was a constant presence in most people, who lacked the capacity to master the justification and hence themselves.[5] For Plato, the political problem of making the ethical into a force was the problem of making society embody the rational justification, and that problem could only have an authoritarian solution. If, by contrast, the justification is addressed to a community that is already an ethical one, then the politics of ethical discourse, including moral philosophy, are significantly different. The aim is not to control the enemies of the community or its shirkers but, by giving reason to people already disposed to hear it, to help in continually creating a community held together by that same disposition.

So far I have assumed for the most part that if we can engage in rational argument with someone, then we and that person are both within some ethical life (though not necessarily the same one): people outside any ethical life are unlikely to argue with us, and we have no great reason to trust them if they do. But that is not necessarily so. Leaving aside the desultory or, indeed, artificial motives that Callicles had for his conversation with Socrates, there is the important fact that people may be driven by a common need — at the limit, by a common fear of disaster — to negotiate understandings of limited cooperation or at least of nonaggression. There are inherent reasons why such agreements, without some external sanction, are bound to be unstable.[6] In any case, they do not in themselves issue in any shared ethical understanding. This is enough to show that people can have a rational discussion without sharing an ethical system. Perhaps, for a limited purpose, they could rationally discuss without any of them having an ethical system. Yet for the most part this is not possible, because rational conversation between two parties, as an actual event, needs something to hold it together. This may, of course, be some particular relationship that does not extend more generally to the ethical, but if it is not that, and not the condescension of Callicles or the needs shared by those in a common emergency, then it must involve some minimal trace of an ethical consciousness.

This brings out once more the platitude that not all members of a community can live outside ethical life. But one person may be able to live outside it. This leads us to a first-personal form of the question whether it is possible to justify ethical considerations from the ground up. An agent who is asking Socrates' question may wonder whether he could come to have reason for the ethical life, granted only some minimal structure of action, desire, or belief. This agent does not have to be someone who actually possesses only the minimum: he does not have to be outside the ethical world trying to see whether there is a way into it. He may as well, indeed better, be someone in it, who is considering what kinds of reasons he has for being there. (Again, how he might understand his reflection will itself be affected by its results.) Here we have no problem with the question "to whom?" The important question now is the last of our original three, "from what?" What is the minimum this person is assumed to have? If he is trying to justify the ethical life from the ground up, what is the ground?

In another well-worn image, where is there an Archimedean point? That question is not only worn, but profoundly discouraging for any inquiry it is taken to represent. In the case of some inquiries, we are so familiar with the discouragement that we find it hard to imagine what could count as success. If we were now set the task of finding some position outside all our knowledge and belief from which we could validate them, we might not understand the idea enough even to recognize it as a task. In the ethical case, however, we do have a better idea of what the task would look like. We would need to find a point of leverage in the idea of rational action. That idea in itself, as we have seen, does not immediately display a commitment to the ethical. That is why Socrates' question is not already an ethical one, and also why the amoralist or skeptic seems to hold out the possibility of a rational life outside ethical considerations. Still, perhaps that is merely how it seems before one has reflected enough. The question itself did not use any specifically ethical terms, and that remains a fact. Nonetheless, it might turn out that when we properly think about it, we shall find that we are committed to an ethical life, merely because we are rational agents. Some philosophers believe that this is true. If they are right, then there is what I have called an Archimedean point: something to which even the amoralist or the skeptic is committed but which, properly thought through, will show us that he is irrational, or unreasonable, or at any rate mistaken.

There are two basic types of philosophical venture that fit this pattern. One of them works from the minimal and most abstract possible conception of rational agency. This will concern us in Chapter 4. The other, which we shall turn to immediately, assumes a richer and more determinate view of what rational agency is, taking it to be expressed in living a specifically human life. Both sets of ideas are rooted in past philosophies, the richer and more determinate conception in Aristotle, the more abstract in Kant. Neither of those philosophers, however, thinks that Socrates' question can be taken simply as it stands, as a question, so to speak, waiting to be answered. Each of them redefines the search for an Archimedean point. They do so in different ways — but they have something important in common, which connects them with Socrates' original questioning, as contrasted with other and less fruitful lines in the history of moral philosophy. Each of them yields an argument in practical reason. Neither aims in the first instance to prove the truth of some ethical proposition, which we are then asked to accept in virtue of our interest in believing the truth. Each of them rather commends certain action to us because of our interest in acting rationally or leading a satisfying human life. For both Aristotle and Kant, the justification of ethical propositons will come only from this, that they will be propositions accepted by one who acts rationally or leads such a life.

CHAPTER 3

Foundations: Well-Being

S OCRATES asks his question, in Plato's *Republic*, in the course of a discussion with Thrasymachus, a fictional figure, it appears, created to embody some of the rougher assumptions of contemporary sophists. Thrasymachus concedes that one often does have a reason for being concerned with others' interests as well as one's own, but holds that this is only because one's power is limited — typically, by the greater power of others. Naturally, according to Thrasymachus, human beings pursue power and pleasure. They may, rationally, have to curtail that pursuit because of other people's power. They may also, irrationally, come to think that it is right or noble to respect others' interests; but in that case they are being misled by conventions, social rules that inculcate these respectable but baseless assumptions. When they come to think like this, it is usually because, once more, someone else has greater power; their error is a deceit, and the conventions that deceive them are an instrument of coercion.

Thrasymachus says that the conventions that enjoin respect for others' interests — "justice," as it may be called[1] — are an instrument of the strong to exploit the weak. This immediately raises the question, what makes these people strong? Thrasymachus speaks as if political or social power were not itself a matter of convention, and that is a view barely adequate to the school playground. His position is rapidly followed in the *Republic* by another, which takes this point. According to this, justice is the product of a convention adopted by a group of people to protect themselves. It is a contractual device of the weak to make themselves strong. This formulation is on the surface the opposite of the first one, and it is certainly more sophisticated, but the two have a good deal in common. By both views, justice is represented as an instrument for the satisfaction of selfish desires that exist naturally, independent of any ethical outlook. Both see justice as something one would not want to follow if one did not need to.

For Plato, this was a basic weakness. He thought that an account of the ethical life could answer Socrates' question, and combat skepticism, only if it showed that it was rational for people to be just, whoever they were and whatever their circumstances. The second, contractual, account did no better in this respect than the original brutal view. If a man were powerful and intelligent and luckily enough placed, it would not be rational for him to conform to the conventional requirements of justice. The contractual theory was particularly weak in this respect because it was unstable with respect to a superior agent, one more intelligent and resourceful and persuasive than the rest. It was above all for this sort of agent that Plato thought skepticism had to be met, and justice and the ethical life shown to be rational.

In this respect, for Plato, the contractual theory failed. It failed, moreover, because of a certain structural feature: it represented as ethically basic a desirable or useful *practice,* the conventions of justice. But for Plato and for Socrates, what was first ethically desirable would have to be something that lay in the agent. If anything outside the soul, as they put it, is ethically primary — some rule, for instance, or institution — then we are left with the possibility that there could be a person whose deepest needs and the state of whose soul were such that it was not rational for him to act in accordance with that rule or institution and, so long as that was possible, the task of answering Socrates' question in a way favorable to the ethical life would not be carried out. The demand to show to *each* person that justice was rational *for that person* meant that the answer had to be grounded first in an account of what sort of person it was rational to be.

It is sometimes said by modern critics that Platonic ethics —

and the same point arises with Aristotle's outlook as well — is egoistic, in a way that conflicts with the fundamental character of morality.[2] The Greeks, it is suggested, had not arrived at a mature understanding of the moral consciousness. They had certainly not arrived at the distinctive preoccupations of the system *morality,* with its emphasis on a very special notion of obligation. (In this, as we shall see later, they were very fortunate.) But neither Plato nor Aristotle thought of the ethical life as a device that increased selfish satisfactions. Their outlook is formally egoistic, in the sense that they suppose that they have to show to each person[3] that he has good reason to live ethically; and the reason has to appeal to that person in terms of something about himself, how and what he will be if he is a person with that sort of character. But their outlook is not egoistic in the sense that they try to show that the ethical life serves some set of individual satisfactions which is well defined before ethical considerations appear. Their aim is not, given an account of the self and its satisfactions, to show how the ethical life (luckily) fits them. It is to give an account of the self into which that life fits.

This is, already, a much more sophisticated objective than that of the crudest religious accounts, which represent ethical considerations as a set of laws or commands sanctioned by the promised punishments or rewards of God. This, crudest, level of religious morality is more egoistic. Even this kind of account, however, should not be dismissed on the ground that the egoistic motive it invokes could not possibly count, nor because we supposedly could not derive an *ought* from the fact of God's power but only from his goodness.[4] There is nothing wrong with the general shape of this account: it explains why one would have good reason to live the kind of life that respected others' interests. It is rather that we know that it could not be true — *could* not be true, since if we understand anything about the world at all, we understand that it is not run like that. Indeed many, including many Christians, would now say we know that it is not run at all.

It is a natural thing to say that this religious account is crude, meaning not that it is crude because it is religious, but that it is a crude piece of religion. A less crude religious ethics will not add the religious element merely as an external sanction, but will give an account of human nature that provides equally for ethical objectives and for a relation to God. However, the criticism in terms of crude religion does raise a significant question. If religion is ultimately a matter of what the world is like, why should the world *not* be that crude? Why should religion be judged in terms of ethical understandings that are ranked as more or less sophisticated or mature in secular terms? The answer must be, presumably, that the original crude idea of God as an omnipotent law enforcer was itself gained through our (crude) ethical understanding. But then, if ethical understanding is going to develop, and if religion is going to understand its own development in relation to that, it seems inevitable that it must come to understand itself as a human construction; if it does, it must in the end collapse.

It is true that the development of the ethical consciousness means the collapse of religion, but not because a religious ethics, even a crude one, is logically debarred from being ethical. It is rather for a dialectical reason, that if the self-understanding of religion is not to be left behind by the ethical consciousness, it has to move in a direction that will destroy religion. The center of the matter does not lie in purely logical questions. In fact, the logical or structural questions about religious ethics, like many questions about God, are interesting only if you believe in God. If God exists, then arguments about him are arguments about the cosmos and of cosmic importance, but if he does not, they are not about anything. In that case, the important questions must be about human beings, and why, for instance, they ever believed that God existed. The issues about religious ethics are issues about the human impulses that expressed themselves in it, and they should be faced in those terms. For those who do not believe in a religious ethics, there is some evasion in continuing to argue about its structure: it distracts attention from the significant question of what such outlooks tell us about humanity. Nietzsche's saying, God is dead, can be taken to mean that we should now treat God as a dead person: we should allocate his legacies and try to write an honest biography of him.

Plato's aim, to return to that, was to give a picture of the self of such a kind that if people properly understood what they were, they would see that a life of justice was a good not external to the self but, rather, an objective that it must be rational to pursue. For him, as for Aristotle, if it was rational to pursue a certain kind of life or to be a certain sort of person, then those things had to make for a satisfactory state called *eudaimonia*. That term is usually translated "happiness," but what it refers to in the hands of these philosophers is not the same as modern conceptions of happiness. For one thing, it makes sense now to say that you are happy one day, unhappy another, but eudaimonia was a matter of the shape of one's whole life. I shall use the expression *well-being* for such a state.

Socrates gave an account of it in terms of knowledge and the powers of discursive reason, and he could give this account because of the drastically dualistic terms in which he conceived of soul and body. Well-being was the desirable state of one's soul — and that meant of oneself as a soul, since an indestructible and immaterial soul was what one really was.[5] Such a conception underlay Socrates' conception of our deepest interests and made it easier for him to believe that, in a famous phrase, *the good man cannot be harmed,* since the only thing that could touch him would be something that could touch the good state of his soul, and that was inviolable. It is a problem for this view that, in describing ethical motivations, it takes a very spiritual view of one's own interests, but the subject matter of ethics requires it to give a less spiritual view of other people's interests. If bodily hurt is no real harm, why does virtue require us so strongly not to hurt other people's bodies?

There is another special consequence of Socrates' picture, which relates to the hopes he had for the regenerative powers of philosophy. He, and to some extent Plato, believed that the discipline of philosophy could uniquely lead to well-being, through its power to develop the virtues. Rational philosophy was to provide the insight that led to well-being. This meant that philosophy either taught means to satisfy needs that were innate, or else it enabled us rationally to form a new conception of our needs. Aristotle's outlook is less ambitious, and this is one reason, along with its much greater psychological and social elaboration, why Aristotle's *Ethics*[6] still serves as the paradigm of an approach that tries to base ethics on considerations of well-being and of a life worth living. For him, a human being is not an immaterial soul, but is essentially embodied and essentially lives a social life. Aristotle makes a basic distinction among the powers of reason, so that the intellectual faculty central to the ethical life, practical reason, is very different in its functions and objects from theoretical reason, which is what is deployed in philosophy and the sciences. He did indeed think that the cultivation of philosophy and sciences was the highest form of human activity, but he supposed that the exercise of practical reason in a personal and civic life was necessary to this, not only in the (Platonic) sense that such activities were necessary in society, but also in the sense that each individual needed such a life. The emphasis wobbles in Aristotle, though, between the civic life as a necessity the sage cannot escape and (what is certainly the more consistent and convincing consequence of his philosophical anthropology) as a necessity for each man if he is fully to express his powers.

Central to the life of practical reason are certain excellences of character or virtues, which are internalized dispositions of action, desire, and feeling. In some part, Aristotle's account of the virtues, with regard to courage, for instance, or self-control, seems very recognizable; in other respects it belongs to another world. What matters for moral philosophy is whether the elements that are culturally more specific can be separated from the main structure. Some of them can be, and these include serious matters: an Aristotelian outlook is not committed to Aristotelian views on slavery or on the position of women. A center of doubt gathers, however, on the point that when Aristotle seems most removed from modern ethical perceptions, it is often because the admired agent is disquietingly concerned with himself. Aristotle does allow that the good man needs friends, and indeed that friendship is part of the good life; but he finds it necessary to argue for this in order to reconcile friendship with the ideal of self-sufficiency.[7] Even his account of truthfulness has the oddly self-obsessed feature that the vices or faults contrasted with this virtue are not, as one would expect, untruthfulness (unreliability with regard to truth), but boasting and false modesty. We shall have to consider later whether the more self-centered aspects of Aristotle's ethics stem from the structure itself.

I said that for Aristotle a virtue was an internalized disposition of action, desire, and feeling. It is an intelligent disposition. It involves the agent's exercise of judgment, that same quality of practical reason, and so it is not simply a habit. It also involves favorable and unfavorable reactions to other people, their characters and actions. Aristotle's own views on this subject are bound up with one of the most celebrated and least useful parts of his system, the doctrine of the Mean, according to which every virtue of character lies between two correlative faults or vices (illustrated in the example of truthtelling), which consist respectively of the excess and the deficiency of something of which the virtue represents the right amount. The theory oscillates between an unhelpful analytical model (which Aristotle himself does not consistently follow) and a substantively depressing doctrine in favor of moderation. The doctrine of the Mean is better forgotten, but it does correctly imply that, since virtuous people are supposed to know what they are doing, they will see others' failings or vices as such and will see those who have them, or at least those people's actions, as variously bad or unpleasant or unhelpful or base.

Some of us are resistant to the idea that having a virtue or admirable disposition of character should also involve a disposition to assess others. The resistance has various roots, some of them very distant from any concern of Aristotle's. One is a conception of innocence, the image of a virtue that is entirely unselfconscious and lacking the contrast with self that is implied by judgment of others. Another root is skepticism, a suspicion that no one ever knows enough about anyone (including, in its more insidious versions, oneself) to make judgments. Still another is the fact that we accept, indeed regard as a platitude, an idea that Aristotle rejected, that someone can have one virtue while lacking others. For Aristotle, as for Socrates, practical reason required the dispositions of action and feeling to be harmonized; if any disposition was properly to count as a virtue, it had to be part of a rational structure that included all the virtues. This is quite different from our assumption that these kinds of disposition are enough like other psychological characteristics to explain how one person can, so to speak, do better in one area than another. This assumption, too, does something to inhibit reactions to other people.

Despite these considerations, there is still a connection between the ethical dispositions and reactions to others. The exact nature or depth of those reactions, and the degree of their self-confidence, will vary between individuals and in different cultural climates — but, as Aristotle claimed, an ethical disposition is not simply a personal pattern of behavior to which there may be contingently added a tendency to deplore or regret its absence in others. It is a kind of disposition that itself structures one's reactions to others. Because we do not believe in the unity of the virtues, we may accept the idea that it is simply a peculiarity of some people to lack certain ethical dispositions. It may even be that every ethical disposition can be seen in this way by someone, and none is so basic as to be exempt from being made, as one might put it, a subject of anecdote. But someone who sees every ethical disposition (or rather their subject matter, since he may not use those concepts himself) as a subject of anecdote surely lacks some basic ethical disposition. (Needless to say, it may be hard to find out whether someone does see them in that way.)

I have referred for the most part to the "reactions" to others that are involved in having ethical dispositions.[8] It is a conveniently broad and unrevealing term, and there is much to be said about the range of attitudes, both positive and negative, that may fall under this heading. It is surprising how little of it has been said by moral philosophy, at least in the English-speaking tradition. By far the most important reason for this is the domination of morality, which is disposed to class all the relevant — that is to say, "moral" — reactions under headings such as *judgment, assessment,* and *approval* or *disapproval.* This is misleading in several ways. First, all these notions suggest a position of at least temporary superiority, the position of a judge, and this is so even if they occur within a moral theory that does not encourage superiority. Further, they suggest some binary judgment, as it might be of guilt or innocence. Moreover, they are supposedly directed only toward the voluntary: no one can properly attract moral judgment for what is not his fault. Because in this way it tries to cleave to an ultimate justice, morality does not merely provide a typology of reactions. It is not concerned simply with the question of what reactions are to be called moral.

The justice that is the aim of morality reaches further than the question of what your reactions should be called, to the issue of what reactions you may justly have, so that it comes to demand first a voice, then supremacy, and at last ubiquity. The "nonmoral" reactions such as dislike, or resentment or contempt, or such minor revelations of the ethical life as the sense that someone is creepy, are driven by a well-schooled moral conscience into a grumbling retreat, planning impersonation and revenge.

These various features of the moral judgment system support one another, and collectively they are modeled on the prerogatives of a Pelagian God. The strictness of the criteria for judgment responds to the supposed immensity of what is handed out, the finality of the only final justice there is. For the same reason, they collectively invite the skepticism I have mentioned. They face a problem of how people's character or dispositions could ever be the object of such a judgment. They are unlikely to be fully responsible for them, and it is even less likely that we can know to what extent they are responsible for them — even supposing we understand what we should know if we did know that. Yet does morality require us to judge people's actions in isolation from their characters?

These are not Aristotelian worries. Aristotle did in fact think that human beings were in some absolute sense free, and that they brought forth their actions "like children."[9] He also thought that there were reactions of praise and blame directed to actions, and to people through those actions, which required the actions to be voluntary. But he would not have understood the suggestion that this was the limit to the reactions appropriate to others because of their ethical dispositions. In accepting, as we should, the idea that ethical dispositions are also dispositions to react, we must remember how much wider this range of reactions may be than is suggested by the conceptions of morality.

Aristotle should not have believed that in the most basic respects, at least, people were responsible for their characters.[10] He gives an account of moral development in terms of habituation and internalization that leaves little room for practical reason to alter radically the objectives that a grown-up person has acquired.

Granted this conclusion, there is a problem about the way in which Aristotle presents his inquiry. Indeed, there is a problem about what he can take ethical philosophy to be. He presents it as a practical inquiry, one that is directed, in effect, to answering Socrates' question. He makes it seem as though you might review the whole of your life and consider whether it was aimed in the most worthwhile direction, but, on his own account, this cannot be a sensible picture. He shares with Plato the idea that, if virtue is part of human good, then it cannot be external to the ultimately desirable state of well-being: that state must be constituted in part by the virtuous life. But this is not a consideration that one could use to any radical effect in practical reasoning, as he seems to suggest. One becomes virtuous or fails to do so only through habituation. One should not study moral philosophy until middle age, Aristotle believes, for a reason that is itself an expression of the present difficulties — only by then is a person good at practical deliberation. But by then it will be a long time since one became, in relation to this deliberation, preemptively good or irrecoverably bad. (Only the powers of practical reason are in question here; it is consistent with everything Aristotle says that someone's life might be radically changed by other means, such as conversion.)

Some of Aristotle's reasonings might have an actual deliberative effect. He has an excellent argument about people who make the aim of their life political honor, that they tend to defeat themselves by making themselves dependent on those to whom they aim to be superior, and this discovery of *Coriolanus' paradox,* as it might be called, could surely serve some experienced person as a discovery or a diagnosis. But, in general, Aristotle cannot reasonably believe that his reflections on the virtuous life and its role in helping to constitute well-being could play a formative part in some general deliberation that a given person might conduct. In the light of this, the definition of ethical philosophy, and its aspirations, has to be revised. It no longer addresses its considerations to each person, so that each may answer the Socratic question. We come back to a point foreseen earlier, that the answer to the skeptic would be primarily for the benefit of the rest of us. Aristotle is in fact not interested in skepticism about the ethical life, and this is one of many differences in urgency between his world and that of Socrates and Plato. He is concerned simply with men who have the wrong values or a bad character. But the point is the same, that the answer to Socrates' question cannot be used by those who (from the perspective of the rest) most need it.

Still, this does not cast us to the opposite extreme, that the answer is simply meant to keep up the spirits of those within the system, give them more insight, and help them to bring up their children. The answer does that, but not only that. On Aristotle's account a virtuous life would indeed conduce to the well-being of the man who has had a bad upbringing, even if he cannot see it. The fact that he is incurable, and cannot properly understand the diagnosis, does not mean that he is not ill. The answer Aristotle gives to Socrates' question cannot be given to each person, as we have seen, but it is an answer *for* each person. Where exactly should we locate that thought? What exactly is being said about the bad man? We are not simply saying that we find him a dangerous nuisance (if we do), or that he is statistically unusual (if he is). We are saying that he lacks certain qualities characteristic of human beings which are necessary for creatures to live a life typical of human beings. But we have to say more, if we are to make the point essential to Aristotle's philosophy and to any like it, that it is *this man's* well-being and interests that are in question. We have to say that this man misconceives his interests and, indeed, that his doing so is a main symptom of what is wrong with him.

The notion that people may have "real interests" different from the interests they think they have is one that has generated a vast literature, and an almost equal amount of suspicion. The literature stems for the most part from the use of this notion made by Hegelian and, following Hegel, Marxist writers; the applications of the notion have been largely political; and in the light of those applications, the suspicions are largely well founded, since an appeal to people's real interests is often deployed as a reason for coercing them contrary to their "apparent" (that is to say, perceived) interests. Some of these suspicions and criticisms, however, are wrongly directed at the notion of real interests itself. Even if a course of action were in someone's real interests, the fact that it is not in his perceived interests does mean that, granted he cannot be persuaded, he will need to be coerced if his real interest is to be pursued. But in those circumstances, some further justification will be needed for our pursuing his real interests. It may be in Robinson's real interests to stop drinking, but that does not instantly give anyone the right to stop him. (Who? — you? the doctor? the state?) The mere fact that real interests do not coincide with perceived interests *already* raises political and ethical issues.

The question of real interests in political thought raises further issues, in particular about class interests, which cannot be taken further here. The most general outlines of the problem, however, are clear. First, no controversial idea of real interests is involved if an agent merely lacks information which in the light of his other existing preferences and attitudes would alter his desires. He thinks that it is in his interest to drink this stuff because he believes it to be medicine prepared by his friendly pharmacist, but if it is actually cyanide, then he is certainly mistaken about his interests. The same applies to confusions of deliberative reasoning — though here there are pressing questions of what counts as a purely rational constraint on deliberative reasoning. Thus many philosophers[11] think it irrational to prefer an earlier satisfaction to a later one just because it is earlier. (They admit that differences in certainty affect the issue in practice.) Others take it as obvious that the "proximity" of satisfactions, in Bentham's phrase, is itself a dimension of practical reasoning. A conclusion on this point is certainly relevant to the question of what counts as a mistake in self-interested rationality.

The most significant questions about real interests arise when what is wrong with the agent goes beyond lack of information or mere rationality (whatever the boundaries of that may be) and affects the desires and motivations from which he deliberates; or, again, when what is wrong with the agent is that he will not believe something that he rationally should believe. A paradigm is the case of the despairing adolescent who attempts suicide (I mean that suicide is what he or she attempts, not that other thing, an attempted suicide). Susan, who has just attempted suicide, does not believe that things will look different in three months' time, or if she does believe that, she does not care — she does not want to be there for things to be better in three months' time. If we believe that it will all be different in three months' time, and we take steps to keep Susan alive, then it seems that we act in her real interest, an interest that, if we are right, she may well acknowledge in (say) six months' time. That interest fails to be represented in her present motivations in a way that goes deeper than what has been discussed before. Susan's lack of a desire to live, her disbelief in a better future, is itself part of the condition that will be cured in three months' time. The inability to see what is in her interest is itself a symptom.

But we cannot simply say that a change is in someone's real interest if, as a result of that change's being made, she would acknowledge that it was in her interest. Perhaps, if you were to be brainwashed by a certain religious group, you would strongly identify your interests with those of the group. As a brainwashed believer, you might have much to say about an increase in enlightenment and the understanding you have now reached of your previous blindness — but that would not establish the value of brainwashing. Such difficulties arise with any psychological process that tends to generate belief in itself. One reaction to these difficulties is to give up and to regard the notion of real interests as incurably subjective or, perhaps, ideological. But a real problem remains, merely because there are some restrictions on what we can decently count as a certain person's being better off as the result of a change, as opposed to things in general being better, or our being better off ourselves. "He would be better off dead" can be said for many dubious reasons: the most dubious is that we would be better off if he were dead.

If there is firmer footing to be found for the notion (and it seems that even the most skeptical treatment requires some further constraints), it will have to lie in the direction of excluding the self-validating changes, of the brainwashing type. A natural suggestion is the following. If an agent does not now acknowledge that a certain change would be in his interest and if, as a result of the change, he comes to acknowledge that it was in his interest, this will show that the change was really in his interest only on condition that the alteration in his outlook is explained in terms of some *general incapacity* from which he suffered in his original state, and which has been removed or alleviated by the change. "General incapacity" is a vague phrase, but it carries two relevant ideas. One is that the agent's alleged inability before the change to recognize his real interests is not simply tailor-made to the content of the recommended change, but has some more general implications, as the supposed inability to recognize the merits of the religious group did not. The second idea is that what is in question is indeed an *incapacity*. It is not simply that he does not acknowledge some things that he will acknowledge after the change, but that a capacity to acknowledge such things in cultural circumstances of that kind is to be expected in human beings, as part of their effective functioning. It is this last element, the normative conception of human functioning, that invited the terms "cure" and "symptom" in the description of the attempted suicide.

If we are going to bring in these notions eventually, why not do so earlier? Why not just say that a change is in someone's real interest if the result of that change would be to bring him closer to normal human functioning? The answer is that not everything in someone's interests is necessary to his human functioning, or is something that he *needs*. What he does need are the capacities, including the basic patterns of motivation, to pursue some of the things that are in his interests. If it is not to be purely ideological, the idea of real interests needs to be provided with a theory of error, a substantive account of how people may fail to recognize their real interests.[12]

Aristotle himself held a very strong theory of general teleology: each kind of thing had an ideal form of functioning, which fitted together with that of other things. He believed that all the excellences of character had to fit together into a harmonious self. Moreover, he was committed to thinking that the highest developments of human nature, which he identified with intellectual inquiry, would fit together with the more ordinary life of civic virtue, even though they represented the flowering of rather different powers, theoretical rather than practical reason. He was not very successful in showing this. Moreover, despite the rich teleological resources of his general account, he did not in fact do much to provide the theory of error that the notion of real interests requires. He does describe various kinds of bad people, and his descriptions are more realistic than Plato's in the *Republic,* who (there, but not always) gives in to the moralist's temptation to represent the bad person as a compulsive addict, an unenviable wreck. Aristotle sees that someone can be in bad shape from the ethical point of view without being at all like that—in particular, he may be able to use reason effectively to pursue what he supposes is his advantage. Aristotle explains that person's condition by saying that he was poorly brought up, so that he acquired habits of pursuing the wrong kinds of pleasure. But in Aristotle's teleological universe, every human being (or at least every nondefective male who is not a natural slave) has a kind of inner nisus toward a life of at least civic virtue, and Aristotle does not say enough about how this is frustrated by poor upbringing, to make it clear exactly how, after that upbringing, it is still in this man's real interest to be other than he is.

If Aristotle, with his strong assumptions about the nisus of each natural kind of thing toward its perfection, cannot firmly deliver this result, there is not much reason to think that we can. Evolutionary biology, which gives us our best understanding of the facts that Aristotle represented in terms of a metaphysical teleology, cannot do better in trying to show that an ethical life is one of well-being for each person. This is not because it delivers one answer for all individuals, but one hostile to ethical life—for instance, the answer that an entirely "hawkish" strategy would be right for each and every individual. This is not so, since the outcome would not constitute an "evolutionarily stable state," as John Maynard Smith has called it.[13] The important point is that evolutionary biology is not at all directly concerned with the well-being of the individual, but with fitness, which is the likelihood of that individual's leaving offspring. The most that sociobiology might do for ethics lies in a different direction, inasmuch as it might be able to suggest that certain institutions or patterns of behavior are not realistic options for human societies. That would be an important achievement, but first sociobiology will have to be able to read the historical record of human culture much better than it does now.

If any science is going to yield conclusions that are *for* each person, as I put it before, it will be some branch of psychology. There are theories, particularly of a psychoanalytical kind, in which hopes have been placed that they will support some ethical conception as a necessary part of human happiness. In some cases the theories seem like this because they themselves involve what is already ethical thought.[14] They are none the worse for that, as channels of individual help, and probably better, but this does disqualify them from giving an independent account of well-being and so providing a foundation for ethical life. Perhaps it is unrealistic to suppose that there could be any psychological discipline capable of doing this. It would be silly to try to determine *a priori* and in a few pages whether there could be such a theory. It would have to be at once independent of assumed ethical conceptions, closely related to the complex aspects of human personality that are involved in ethical life, determinate in its results, and — of course — favorable to ethical considerations in some form. The last it would "of course" have to be, not just for the boring reason that only then would it count as providing foundations for ethical considerations but because, if it failed to be favorable to ethical considerations, it would have a different relation to practice altogether. We need to live in society — and that is certainly an inner need, not just a technological necessity — and if we are to live in society, some ethical considerations or other must be embodied in the lives of quite a lot of people. So a psychological theory which showed that we could not really be happy in any adequate set of ethical considerations would not tell us how to live: rather, it would predict that we could not live happily.

Any adequate psychology of character will presumably include the truth, in some scientifically presentable form, that many people are horrible because they are unhappy, and conversely: where their unhappiness is not something specially defined in ethical terms, but is simply basic unhappiness — misery, rage, loneliness, despair. That is a well-known and powerful fact; but it is only one in a range of equally everyday facts. Some who are not horrible, and who try hard to be generous and to accommodate others' interests, are miserable, and from their ethical state. They may be victims of a suppressed self-assertion that might once have been acknowledged but now cannot be, still less overcome or redirected. There is also the figure, rarer perhaps than Callicles supposed, but real, who is horrible enough and not miserable at all but, by any ethological standard of the bright eye and the gleaming coat, dangerously flourishing. For those who want to ground the ethical life in psychological health, it is something of a problem that there can be such people at all. But it is a significant question, how far their existence, indeed the thought of their existence, is a cultural phenomenon. They seem sleeker and finer at a distance. Some Renaissance grandee fills such a role with more style than the tawdry fascist bosses, gangsters, or tycoons who seem, even as objects of fantasy, to be their chief contemporary instances. Perhaps we deceive ourselves about the past. Or perhaps it is an achievement of the modern world to have made it impossible to rear that type, because it has made evil, like other things, a collective enterprise, a process that makes it more powerful but less interesting.[15]

Above all, in this table of naive perceptions, there is the matter of other goods. A certain man is horrible and rather miserable, but he is successful and has some pleasures, and if he were less horrible he would not be successful, and would be no less anxious, because he would be frustrated . . . Simply not to accept anything as valuable except the ethical dispositions — to turn, that is to say, the conception of psychological health in the direction of renouncing the other values — would be a reversion to Socratic asceticism and would need a reconstruction of the self to suit it. It would need also a utopian politics of renunciation by everyone; or else it would have to admit that virtue as purity of heart, while it was the only good, could be only a minority accomplishment, and this would need another politics in its turn, in order to construct the relation of that virtue to unregenerate society.

These problems take on a special significance, both for the individual and for the rest of society, when the "other goods" are of a creative and cultural kind. I have already said that it was a strain on Aristotle's account of human nature to see such achievements as harmoniously of a piece with ordinary civic virtue. It is not of course a peculiarly modern thought, that it may not be possible to harmonise them; indeed Plato had taken a much more pessimistic view, and consequently had wished to banish the arts from the virtuous republic, or to domesticate them. But modern conceptions of the arts and the sciences and of the psychology of their creation can only make more intense, from these ethical perspectives, the problems of the wound and the bow, the unhappiness and the unloveliness that may be part of creative activity, which often has much to do with an imbalance, a hypertrophy of certain powers and sensibilities.

It is a problem also for any program that wants to connect the ethical life with psychological health through notions of integration, or reduction of conflict. These psychological aims in themselves cannot carry ethical weight unless they are already defined to do so; the best way of integrating some people would be to make them more ruthless. But apart from that, and also leaving aside those creative conflicts that raise doubts about how far conflict reduction may be psychologically desirable, there is a different sort of question, of how far and in what circumstances eliminating conflict may be *ethically* desirable. Conflict, in particular ethical conflict, may be the appropriate response to some kinds of situation. If these situations are to be eliminated, it will be a matter not only (perhaps not mainly) of reforming the psyche, but of changing society.

When one is considering the difficulties in psychology's making a substantial contribution to the foundation of ethics, it is important to bear in mind how far we can go without it. We can go quite far. The formation of ethical dispositions is a natural process in human beings. This does not mean that it is spontaneous and needs no education or upbringing: in that sense, virtually nothing in human beings is "natural," including the use of language — for while the capacity to learn a language is itself innate, and very probably specific,[16] no child will learn any language unless exposed to a particular language, which is itself, of course, a cultural product. Nor does it mean that the ethical life does not involve convention: it is natural to human beings to live by convention. There is no sense in which it is *more* natural, as Thrasymachus supposed, to live outside ethical considerations. Moreover, we ourselves (most of us) are identified with some ethical considerations and have a conception of human well-being that gives a place to such considerations. We wish, consequently, to bring up children to share some of these ethical, as of other cultural, conceptions, and we see the process as good not just for us but for our children, both because it is part of our conception of their well-being and also because, even by more limited conceptions of happiness or contentment, we have little reason to believe that they will be happier if excluded from the ethical institutions of society. Even if we know that there are some people who are happier, by the minimal criteria, outside those institutions, we also know that they rarely become so by being educated as outlaws. As a result of all that, we have much reason for, and little reason against, bringing up children within the ethical world we inhabit, and if we succeed they themselves will see the world from the same perspective.

If we accept the displacement of Socrates' question implicit in what Aristotle admitted — that one cannot regenerate one's life by answering the question — we can, at one level, answer it with less than Aristotle offered. Displaced, it becomes a question about how *we* should live, and, at one level, we can give an ethical answer to that on the basis of the ethical life we have, even if we cannot claim, as Aristotle did, to have a teleological answer for each person, favoring an ethical life. At this level, the question will simply be whether society should be ethically reproduced, and to that question, merely from within society, we have an answer.

At this level. That argument presents only the choice between some ethical life and none. But ethical life is not a unitary given thing, and there are many different possibilities within it for education, social decision, even perhaps for personal regeneration. Within the kind of ethical life we find ourselves in, there are diversities, incoherences, and instruments of self-criticism. In our modern society there are more of all these, perhaps, than in any society that has ever existed, and this is a fact of the greatest importance, which changes the role of moral philosophy from anything imagined by an ancient writer. After I have considered, in the next chapter, a very different and more modern attempt to find foundations for the whole ethical enterprise, I shall go on to questions raised by these different possibilities for ethical life: some of them possibilities for different cultures, others for our own culture. We shall see what moral philosophy can do to help us understand them, and to ground self-criticism.

First, however, there is a question to be discussed about the extent of the distance we should acknowledge between Aristotle's conceptions and styles of ethical thought we might find acceptable now. In many substantial respects, as I have said, no modern discussion can share the outlook of an ancient writer. But how far does this extend to the logical shape of the whole enterprise? I said that, if the Socratic demand was to be met in its original form and the ethical life was to be justified to each person, then ethical value had to lie in some state of the self. The same would apply if, as I expressed Aristotle's aim, that justification could be given only *for* each person. But if we give up that objective as well, will ethical value still lie in states of the person? It is often thought to be a distinction between the ethics of the Greeks and modern conceptions that they approached ethical thought in this way and we do not. Moreover, that idea is associated with a deeper version of a criticism I mentioned before, that Greek ethical thought is incurably egoistic.

One kind of argument for this conclusion goes as follows. The person of Aristotelian virtue desires, quite often, to do various virtuous things. But anything motivated by desire is directed toward pleasure, and the pursuit of pleasure is egoistic. The only motivation opposed to this is the sense of obligation. Ethical motivation involves a contrast with the egoistic, so the ethical must be concerned with obligation, not with the desires that are involved in living a life of well-being, as Aristotle supposed. (This way of looking at things is a specially concentrated and crude version of the outlook of morality.) Almost all the assumptions of this argument are wrong. It is false, indeed incoherent, to suppose that every desire aims at pleasure, and it would be false even if the satisfaction of each desire issued in pleasure (which is not so either). Moreover, if it were true that every desire aimed at pleasure, one could not rely on the common-sense assumption that there is a contrast between ethical motivations and pleasure seeking. Ethical motivations would then aim at certain sorts of pleasure. Some of them do indeed issue in pleasure, and Hume, in line with Greek thought on this point, agreeably thought that it was the mark of a virtuous person to take pleasure in doing generous or helpful actions.

One obvious reason why my desires do not all have as their object my pleasure is that some of my desires aim at states of affairs that do not involve me at all: I am not mentioned in a full specification of what would satisfy such a desire.[17] There are self-transcending desires. They are not all altruistic or benevolent — they may be malicious or frivolous. Those who make provisions in their wills to mortify their relatives or to promote some absurd object do not usually believe that they will be there to enjoy the outcome; yet it is *the outcome* they want, not merely the pleasure of thinking about it now. For all these reasons, the line between self-concern and other-concern in no way corresponds to a line between desire and obligation. (Indeed, some moralists admit this in their own way by inventing a class of *duties to oneself,* self-regarding obligations. These serve a number of functions in that economy. One is to encourage long-term investment as against consumption; another is merely to launder the currency of desire.)

Even when we have got rid of these misconceptions about desire and pleasure, however, there may still seem to be something left to the charge of egoism. The ethical dispositions are dispositions to want certain things, to react in certain ways to other people and to their actions, to use such notions as that of obligation, to promote certain outcomes as being just, and so on. The agent will probably be a party to the relations involved, and of course it is the agent who asks and decides how he is going to act. None of these conceptions (including his wants) need damagingly involve the agent's self in its content: none of this, in itself, involves any kind of egoism. But the Socratic question brings in another idea. It involves the agent's *thinking about* these dispositions themselves and relating them to a life of well-being. Even if the dispositions are not themselves directed toward the self, it is still his own well-being that the agent in Socratic reflection will be considering. Egoism seems to be back again.

The answer to this problem lies in the vital fact that the Aristotelian account puts the substantive ethical dispositions into the content of the self. I am, at the time of mature reflection, what I have become, and my reflection, even if it is about my dispositions, must at the same time be expressive of them. I think about ethical and other goods *from* an ethical point of view that I have already acquired and that is part of what I am. In thinking about ethical and other goods, the agent thinks from a point of view that already places those goods, in general terms, in relation to one another and gives a special significance to ethical goods. Looked at from the outside, this point of view belongs to someone in whom the ethical dispositions he has acquired lie deeper than other wants and preferences.

The difference between the inside point of view, the view from one's dispositions, and the outside view of those dispositions shows how it is that in the most obvious sense it is not true that all ethical value rests in the dispositions of the self, and yet, in another way, it is true. It is not true from the point of view constituted by the ethical dispositions — the internal perspective — that the only things of value are people's dispositions; still less that only the agent's dispositions have value. Other people's welfare, the requirements of justice, and other things, have value. If we take up the other perspective, however, and look at people's dispositions from the outside, we may ask the question "what has to exist in the world for that ethical point of view to exist?" The answer can only be, "people's dispositions." There is a sense in which they are the ultimate supports of ethical value. That has a practical as well as a metaphysical significance. The preservation of ethical value lies in the reproduction of ethical dispositions.

The outside point of view of his dispositions is available to the agent himself. But if he tries in his reflection to abstract himself totally from those dispositions, and to think about himself and the world as though he did not have them, then he should not be surprised if he cannot get an adequate picture of the value of anything, including his own dispositions. He cannot do so, precisely because those dispositions are part of the content of his actual self. Moreover, if he is to conduct any reflection in which he stands back from his own dispositions, it is important whether there is anything in the view of things he takes from the outside that conflicts with the view of things he takes from the inside.[18] For Aristotle, the virtuous agent would find no such conflict. He could come to understand that the dispositions that gave him his ethical view of the world were a correct or full development of human potentiality. This was so *absolutely,* in the sense at least (Aristotle no doubt meant more) that the best possible theory of humanity and its place in the world would yield this result. Also, this perfection could be displayed harmoniously, so that the development of these ethical capacities would fit with other forms of human excellence. Aristotle's theory means that when the agent reflects, even from the outside, on all his needs and capacities, he will find no conflict with his ethical dispositions.

Here we meet again the many modern doubts that weaken this account. Our present understanding gives us no reason to expect that ethical dispositions can be fully harmonized with other cultural and personal aspirations that have as good a claim to represent human development. Even if we leave the door open to a psychology that might go some way in the Aristotelian direction, it is hard to believe that an account of human nature — if it is not already an ethical theory itself — will adequately determine one kind of ethical life as against others. Aristotle saw a certain kind of ethical, cultural, and indeed political life as a harmonious culmination of human potentialities, recoverable from an absolute understanding of nature. We have no reason to believe in that. Once we lose the belief, however, a potential gap opens between the agent's perspective and the outside view. We understand — and, most important, the agent can come to understand — that the agent's perspective is only one of many that are equally compatible with human nature, all open to various conflicts within themselves and with other cultural aims. With that gap opened, the claim I expressed by saying that agents' dispositions are the "ultimate supports" of ethical value takes on a more skeptical tone. It no longer sounds enough.

I believe that the claim is true, and that in its general outline the description of the ethical self we have recovered from the ancient writers is correct. At the same time, we must admit that the Aristotelian assumptions which fitted together the agent's perspective and the outside view have collapsed. No one has yet found a good way of doing without those assumptions. That is the state of affairs on which the argument of this book will turn, and I shall come back in various connections to the relations between the inside and the outside points of view. My next concern, however, is with a different attempt to start from the ground up, one that tries to find an Archimedean point without using Aristotelian assumptions.

CHAPTER 4

Foundations:
Practical Reason

THE PROJECT of the last chapter, which tried to ground ethical life in well-being, sought determinate conclusions about the shape of a whole life, from substantive beliefs about human nature. We saw that it needed very strong assumptions to hold it together, assumptions we cannot accept.

There is another project that also tries to start from the ground up but claims to deliver less, from less. Instead of giving an account of a fully developed life, it offers certain structural or formal features of ethical relations. Instead of relying on a specific teleology of human nature, it starts from a very abstract conception of rational agency. It still tries to give an answer to Socrates' question, though a minimal one. It gives the answer to each agent, merely because the agent can ask the question. Hence its answers are more abstract and less determinately human than those in the Aristotelian style. This type of argument yields, if anything, general and formal principles to regulate the shape of relations between rational agents. These are the concerns of Kant.

This may seem a surprising thing to say. Kant's name is associated with an approach to morality in which, it is often supposed, there can be no *foundations* for morality at all. He insisted that morality should be "autonomous," and that there could be no reason for being moral. A simple argument shows why, in the Kantian framework, this must be so. Any reason for being moral must be either a moral or a nonmoral reason. If it is moral, then it cannot really be a reason for being moral, since you would have to be already inside morality in order to accept it. A nonmoral reason, on the other hand, cannot be a reason for being *moral;* morality requires a purity of motive, a basically moral intentionality (which Kant took to be obligation), and that is destroyed by any nonmoral inducement. Hence there can be no reason for being moral, and morality presents itself as an unmediated demand, a categorical imperative.

It is specifically *morality* that Kant introduces, and we shall face wider questions about this conception of the ethical life when we come to that subject in Chapter 10. Kant's outlook indeed requires that there be no reason for morality, if that means a motivation or inducement for being moral, but it does not imply that morality has no foundations. Kant thought that we could come to understand why morality should rightly present itself to the rational agent as a categorical demand. It was because rational agency itself involved accepting such a demand, and this is why Kant described morality in terms of laws laid down by practical reason for itself.[1]

In his extraordinary book *The Groundwork of the Metaphysic of Morals,* the most significant work of moral philosophy after Aristotle, and one of the most puzzling, he tries to explain how this can be. I do not want to try to set out the argument, however, by directly expounding Kant. That would involve many special problems of its own. I shall treat his outlook as the destination rather than the route and shall develop in the first place an argument that will be simpler and more concrete than Kant's.[2] The failure of that argument to give morality a foundation will help to show why the Kantian conception needs to be as metaphysically ambitious as it is. I do not believe that Kant's argument succeeds either, but one has to follow it a long way down to find out why not.

Is there anything that rational agents necessarily want? That is to say, is there anything they want (or would want if they thought hard enough about it) merely as part or precondition of being agents?

When they are going to act, people necessarily want, first of all, some outcome: they want the world to be one way rather than another. You can want an outcome without wanting to produce that outcome—you might prefer that the outcome merely materialize. Indeed, there are some cases in which the outcome you want will count only if you do not directly produce it (you want her to fall in love with you). But, in direct contrast to that possibility, in many cases you essentially want not only the outcome, but to produce the outcome. To put it another way (a way that is complicated but still conceals some complications), the outcome you want itself includes the action that your present deliberation will issue in your doing.[3]

We do not merely want the world to contain certain states of affairs (it is a deep error of consequentialism to believe that this is all we want). Among the things we basically want is to act in certain ways. But even when we basically want some state of affairs, and would be happy if it materialized, we know that we do not live in a magical world, where wanting an outcome can make it so. Knowing, therefore, that it will not come about unless we act to produce it, when we want an outcome we usually also want to produce it. (There is an direct analogy to this in the principle that, when we want the truth, we want to know the truth.[4]) Moreover, we do not want it merely to *turn out* that we produced it; we want these thoughts of ours to produce it. The wants involved in our purposive activities thus turn out to be complex. At the very least, what we want is that the outcome should come about because we wanted it, because we believed certain things, and because we acted as we did on the basis of those wants and beliefs.[5] Similar considerations apply to keeping things that we want to keep.

This adds up, then, to the following: on various occasions we want certain outcomes; we usually want to produce those outcomes; we usually want to produce them in a way that expresses our want to produce them. Obviously enough, on those occasions we do not want to be frustrated, for instance by other people. Reflecting on all this, we can see that we have a general, dispositional, want not to be frustrated, in particular by other people. We have a general want, summarily put, for freedom. This is not to deny that sometimes we want to lose freedom, to be frustrated by others, even to be coerced—but then we do not want to be frustrated in obtaining *that*.[6]

It is not enough, though, for this freedom merely that we should not be frustrated in doing whatever it is we want to do. We might be able to do everything we wanted, simply because we wanted too little. We might have unnaturally straitened or impoverished wants. This consideration shows that we have another general want, if an indeterminate one: we want (to put it vaguely) an adequate range of wants.

It does not follow from all this that we want our choices to be as little limited as possible, by anything or anyone. We do not want our freedom to be limitless. It may seem to follow,[7] but to accept it would be to leave out another vital condition of rational agency. Some things, clearly, are accessible to an agent at a given time and others are not. Moreover, what is accessible, and how easily, depends on features both inside and outside the agent. He chooses, makes up plans, and so on, in a world that has a certain practicable shape, in terms of where he is, what he is, and what he may become. The agent not only knows this is so (that is to say, he is sane), but he also knows, on reflection, that it is necessary if he is indeed going to be a rational agent. Moreover, he cannot coherently think that in an ideal world he would not need to be a rational agent. The fact that there are restrictions on what he can do is what requires him to be a rational agent, and it also makes it possible for him to be one; more than that, it is also the condition of his being some particular person, of living *a* life at all. We may think sometimes that we are dismally constrained to be rational agents, and that in a happier world it would not be necessary. But that is a fantasy (indeed it is *the* fantasy).

Similar conditions apply to the agent's knowledge. Acting in a particular situation, he must want his plans not to go wrong through ignorance or error. But even in that particular case, he does not want to know everything, or that his action should have no unintended consequences. Not to know everything is, once more, a condition of having a life — some things are unknown, for instance, because they will form one's future. If you cannot coherently want to know everything, then you also cannot coherently want never to be in error. They are not the same thing (omniscience is not the same as infallibility), but there are many connections between them. For one thing, as Karl Popper has always emphasized, you must make errors, and recognize them, if you are going to extend such knowledge as you have.

These last considerations have concerned things a rational agent does not need to want, indeed needs not to want, as a condition of being such an agent. They assume him or her to be a finite, embodied, historically placed agent: the only kind of agent I take there to be, with the marginal or dubious exception of corporations and similar agencies, and (with the same exceptions) the only ones that could be the concern of ethics. (Even those who believe in God, though they take him to be an agent, should not take him to be the concern of ethics.) I suppose this is what most people would expect. But it has some important consequences, which will concern us later.

As rational agents, then, we want what I have summarily called freedom, though that does not mean limitless freedom. Does this commit us to thinking that our freedom is a good and that it is a good thing for us to be free? One path leading to this conclusion would be to say that when an agent wants various particular outcomes, he must think that those various outcomes are good. Then he would be bound to think that his freedom was a good thing, since it was involved in securing those outcomes.[8]

Is it true that if we want something and purposively pursue it, then we think of our getting that thing as good? This is a traditional doctrine, advanced in Plato's *Meno* and hallowed in a saying of scholastic philosophy, *omne appetitum appetitur sub specie boni*, everything pursued is pursued as being something good. It seems to me not true. In any ordinary understanding of *good*, surely, an extra step is taken if you go from saying that you want something or have decided to pursue it to saying that it is good, or (more to the point) that it is good that you should have it. The idea of something's being good imports an idea, however minimal or hazy, of a perspective in which it can be acknowledged by more than one agent as good. An agent who merely has a certain purpose may of course think that his purpose is good, but he does not have to. The most he would commit himself to merely by having a purpose would presumably be that it would be good *for him* if he succeeded in it, but must even this much be involved? Even this modest claim implies a perspective that goes somewhere beyond the agent's immediate wants, to his longer-term interests or well-being. To value something, even relatively to your own interests, as you do in thinking that it would be better "for me," is always to go beyond merely wanting something. I might indeed come to put all the value in my life into the satisfaction of one desire, but if I did, it would not simply be because I had only one desire. Merely to have one desire might well be to have no value in my life at all; to find all the value in one desire is to have just one desire that *matters* to me.[9]

Even if we give up the traditional doctrine, however, so that I do not have to see everything I want as good, it might still be true that I should see my freedom as good. "Good for me," I suggested, introduces some reference to my interests or well-being that goes beyond my immediate purposes, and my freedom is one of my fundamental interests. So perhaps I must regard my own freedom as a good. But if so, I must not be misled into thinking that my freedom constitutes a good, period. This would be so only if it were a good, period, that I should be a rational agent, and there is no reason why others should assent to that. In fact, it is not even clear that *I* have to assent to it. This begins to touch on some deeper questions about my conception of my own existence.

Everything said so far about the basic conditions and presuppositions of rational action seems to be correct. The argument that tries to provide a foundation for morality attempts to show that, merely because of those conditions, each agent is involved in a moral commitment. Each agent, according to this argument, must think as follows. Since I necessarily want my basic freedom, I must be opposed to courses of action that would remove it. Hence I cannot agree to any arrangement of things by which others would have the right to remove my basic freedom. So when I reflect on what arrangement of things I basically need, I see that I must claim a *right* to my basic freedom. In effect, I must lay it down as a rule for others that they respect my freedom. I claim this right solely because I am a rational agent with purposes. But if this fact alone is the basis of my claim, then a similar fact must equally be the basis of such a claim by others. If, as I suppose, I legitimately and appropriately think that they should respect my freedom, then I must recognize that they legitimately and appropriately think that I should respect their freedom. In moving from my need for freedom to "they ought not to interfere with me," I must equally move from their need to "I ought not to interfere with them."

If this is correct, then each person's basic needs and wants commit him to stepping into morality, a morality of rights and duties, and someone who rejects that step will be in a kind of pragmatic conflict with himself. Committed to being a rational agent, he will be trying to reject the commitments necessarily involved in that. But is the argument correct? Its very last step — that if in my case rational agency alone is the ground of a right to noninterference, then it must be so in the case of other people — is certainly sound. It rests on the weakest and least contestable version of a "principle of universalizability," which is brought into play simply by *because* or *in virtue of.* If a particular consideration is really enough to establish a conclusion in my case, then it is enough to establish it in anyone's case. That must be so if enough is indeed enough. If the conclusion that brings in morality does not follow, it must be because of an earlier step. Granted that the original claims are correct about a rational agent's wants and needs, the argument must go wrong when I first assert my supposed right.

It is useful to consider what the agent might say in thinking out his claims. It could be put like this:

I have certain purposes.
I need freedom to pursue these or any other purposes.
So, I need freedom.
I prescribe: let others not interfere with my freedom.

Call the one who is thinking this, the agent A. Assume for the moment that we know what a "prescription" is, and call this prescription of A's, *Pa*. Then A also thinks

Pa is reasonable,

where what this means is that *Pa* is reasonably related to his, A's, being a rational agent. A can of course recognize that another agent, say B, can have thoughts just like his own. He knows, for instance, that

B prescribes: let A not interfere with my freedom,

and, calling B's prescription *Pb*, the principle of universalizability will require A to agree that

Pb is reasonable.

It may look as if he has now accepted B's prescription as reasonable in the sense of making some claim on himself. This is what the argument to morality requires. But A has not agreed to this. He has agreed only that *Pb* is reasonable in the same sense that *Pa* is, and what this means is only that *Pb* is reasonably related to B's being a rational agent — that is to say, B is as rational in making his prescription as A is rational in making his. It does not mean that B would be rational in accepting *Pa* (or conversely) if in accepting it he would be committing himself not to interfere with A's freedom.

The same point comes out in this: one could never get to the required result, the entry into the ethical world, just from the consideration of the *should* or *ought* of rational agency itself, the *should* of the practical question. The reasons that B has for doing something are not in themselves reasons for another's doing anything. The *should* of practical reason has, like any other, a second and a third person, but these forms merely represent my perspective on your or his interests and rational calculations, the perspective of "if I were you." Considering in those terms what B should do, I may well conclude that he should interfere with my freedom.

But can I "prescribe"[10] this for him? What does it mean? Certainly I do not want him to interfere with my freedom. But does this, in itself, generate any prescription that leads to obligations or rights? The argument suggests that if I do not prescribe that others ought not to interfere with my freedom, I shall be logically required to admit that they *may* interfere with it — which I do not want to do.[11] What the argument claims is that I must either give them the right to interfere with my freedom or withold that right from them. The argument insists, in effect, that if I am to be consistent, I must make a rule to the effect that others should not interfere with my freedom, and nothing less than this rule will do. But the rule, of course, just because it is a general rule, will equally require me not to interfere with their freedom.

But why must I prescribe any rule? If I am in the business of making rules, then clearly I will not make one enjoining others to interfere with my freedom, nor will I make one permitting them to do so. But there is another possibility: I do not regard myself as being in this business, and I make no rule either way. I do not have to be taken as giving permission. If there is a system of rules, then no doubt if the rules are silent on a certain matter (at least if the rules are otherwise wide enough in their scope), that fact can naturally be taken to mean permission. The law, like other sovereign agencies, can say something by remaining silent. But if there is no law, then silence is not meaningful, permissive, silence: it is simply silence. In another sense, of course, people "may" interfere with my freedom, but that means only that there is no law to stop, permit, or enjoin. Whether they "may" means they "can" depends on me and what I can do. As the egoist Max Stirner put it: "The tiger that assails me is in the right, and I who strike him down am also in the right. I defend against him not my *right,* but *myself.*"[12]

I can also ask why, if I am going to prescribe that much, I should not more ambitiously prescribe that no one interfere with whatever particular purposes I may happen to have. I *want* the success of my particular projects, of course, as much as anything else, and I want other people not to interfere with them. Indeed, my need for basic freedom was itself derived from that kind of want. But the argument is certainly not going to allow me to prescribe for all my particular wants.

The argument depends on a particular conception of the business of making rules, a conception that lies at the heart of the Kantian enterprise. If I were in a position to make any rules I liked and to enforce them as an instrument of oppression, then I could make a law that suited my interests and attacked the competing interests of others. No one else would have a reason to obey such a law, except the reason I gave him. But the laws we are considering in these arguments are not that kind of law, have no external sanction, and respond to no inequalities between the parties. They are *notional* laws. The question "what law could I make?" then becomes "what law could I make that I could reasonably expect others to accept?" When we reflect on the fact that everyone asks it from an equal position of powerlessness — since these are laws for a kingdom where power is not an issue — we see that the question could equally be "what law could I accept?" and so, finally, "what laws should there be?"

If this is the question, asked in such a spirit, for such a kingdom, then we can see why its answer should be on the lines of Kant's fundamental principle of action, the Categorical Imperative of morality, which (in its first formulation[13]) requires you to "act only on that maxim through which you can at the same time will that it should become a universal law." But the problem immediately becomes: Why should one adopt such a picture? Why should I think of myself as a legislator and — since there is no distinction — at the same time a citizen of a republic governed by these notional laws? This remains a daunting problem, even if one is already within ethical life and is considering how to think about it. But it is a still more daunting problem when this view of things is being demanded of any rational agent. The argument needs to tell us what it is about rational agents that requires them to form this conception of themselves as, so to speak, abstract citizens.

It might be thought that the question answers itself because, simply as rational agents, there is nothing else for them to be, and there is no difference among them. But to arrive at the model in this way would be utterly unpersuasive. We are concerned with what any given person, however powerful or effective he may be, should reasonably do as a rational agent, and this is not the same thing as what he would reasonably do if he were a rational agent *and no more*. Indeed, that equation is unintelligible, since there is no way of being a rational agent and no more. A more sensible test would be to ask what people should reasonably do if they did not know anything about themselves except that they were rational agents; or, again, what people should do if they knew more than that, but not their own particular powers and position.[14] This is an interesting test for some things; in particular, it is a possible test for justice, and in that role it can be proposed to those with a concern for justice. But it is not a persuasive test for what you should reasonably do if you are not already concerned with justice. Unless you are already disposed to take an impartial or moral point of view, you will see as highly unreasonable the proposal that the way to decide what to do is to ask what rules you would make if you had none of your actual advantages, or did not know what they were.

The Kantian project, if it is to have any hope, has to start farther back. It has to be, in a vital way, more like Kant's own project than the argument I have just outlined. The argument started from what rational agents need, and while what it said about that was true, it was not enough to lead each agent into morality. Kant started from what in his view rational agents essentially *were*. He thought that the moral agent was, in a sense, a rational agent and no more, and he presented as essential to his account of morality a particular metaphysical conception of the agent, according to which the self of moral agency is what he called a "noumenal" self, outside time and causality, and thus distinct from the concrete, empirically determined person that one usually takes oneself to be. This transcendental idea of the self, Kant believed, will be uncovered if we reflect on the requirements of freedom, requirements lying deeper than any that have been uncovered at the level of inquiry we have been pursuing up to now. He did not believe that we could fully understand this conception, but we could see that it was possible and could know that it was involved in both morality and rational action.

Kant's account presents great difficulties and obscurities. First, he believed that all actions except those of moral principle were to be explained not only deterministically but in terms of egoistic hedonism.[15] Only in acting from moral principle could we escape from being causally determined by the drive for pleasure, like animals; and sometimes he marked this by saying that only actions of principle counted as exercises of the will (which he equated with practical reason) and hence were truly free. Our other actions, according to this way of putting it, are the product merely of causality — of "blind" causality, as people tend to say, unhappily, since, as Kant himself recognized, such a causality can often enable agents, and certainly animals, to see very well where they are going.

I shall not go into the question of how far Kant's own theory can be rescued from these difficulties. Any theory that is going to provide foundations will certainly need to avoid them. We are interested in the idea that ethical considerations are presupposed by rational freedom, and this will have to mean a freedom to which the moral skeptic, among others, is *already* committed. It is open to Kant or another arguing like him to say that the moral skeptic is committed, in his desire for individual autonomy and rationality, to conceptions that are *fully* realized only in the moral law, but it will be useless to say that the moral skeptic must aspire to a kind of rational freedom quite different from anything manifested in non-moral practical intelligence or deliberation. The skeptic's commitment to freedom and rationality cannot be so detached from things he already experiences, such as the difference between deciding clear-headedly and finding himself doing things he did not intend. Moreover, this is not simply a dialectical point, about the hold one can hope to get on the skeptic. It is also a question of what conception of rational freedom it is reasonable to hold.

What we are looking for, then, is an argument that will travel far enough into Kant's territory to bring back the essential conclusion that a rational agent's most basic interests must coincide with those given in a conception of himself as a citizen legislator of a notional republic; but does not bring back the more extravagant metaphysical luggage of the noumenal self. The argument might go something like this. We have already agreed that the rational agent is committed to being free, and we have said something about what is required for that freedom. But we have not yet reached a deep enough understanding of what that freedom must be. The idea of a rational agent is not simply the third-personal idea of a creature whose behavior is to be explained in terms of beliefs and desires. A rational agent acts *on* reasons, and this goes beyond his acting in accordance with some regularity or law, even one that refers to beliefs and desires. If he acts *on* reasons, then he must not only be an agent but reflect on himself as an agent, and this involves his seeing himself as one agent among others. So he stands back from his own desires and interests, and sees them from a standpoint that is not that *of* his desires and interests. Nor is it the standpoint of anyone else's desires and interests. That is the standpoint of impartiality. So it is appropriate for the rational agent, with his aspiration to be genuinely free and rational, to see himself as making rules that will harmonize the interests of all rational agents.

In assessing this line of argument, it is important to bear in mind that the kind of rational freedom introduced by it is manifested, according to Kant, not only in decisions to act but also in theoretical deliberation, thought about what is true. It is not merely freedom as an agent — the fact (roughly speaking) that what I do depends on what I decide — that leads to the impartial position, but my reflective freedom as a thinker, and this applies also to the case of factual thought.[16] In both cases, Kant supposed, I am not merely caused to arrive at a conclusion: I can stand back from my thoughts and experiences, and what otherwise would merely have been a cause becomes *a consideration for me.* In the case of arriving by reflection at a belief, the sort of item that will be transmuted in this way will be a piece of evidence, or what I take to be evidence: it might for instance be a perception. In the case of practical deliberation, the item is likely to be a desire, a desire which I take into consideration in deciding what to do. In standing back from evidence, or from my desires, so that they become considerations in the light of which I arrive at a conclusion, I exercise in both cases my rational freedom. When, in the practical case, I adopt the standpoint outside my desires and projects, I may endorse my original desires, as in the factual case I may endorse my original disposition to believe. If I do this my original desire may in the outcome be my motive for action (though someone who uses this picture would naturally say that on some occasions what I eventually do will be motivated by none of the desires I originally had, but is radically produced by my reflection.)[17]

The fact that Kant's account of rational freedom is meant to apply to factual deliberation as much as to practical brings out what is wrong with the Kantian argument. What it says about reflection does indeed apply to factual deliberation, but it does so because factual deliberation is not essentially first-personal. It fails to apply to practical deliberation, and to impose a necessary impartiality on it, because practical deliberation is first-personal, radically so, and involves an *I* that must be more intimately the *I* of my desires than this account allows.

When I think about the world and try to decide the truth about it, I think *about the world,* and I make statements, or ask questions, which are about it and not about me. I ask, for instance,

Is strontium a metal?

or confidently say to myself

Wagner never met Verdi.

Those questions and assertions have first-personal shadows, such as

I wonder whether strontium is a metal,

or

I believe that Wagner never met Verdi.

But these are derivative, merely reflexive counterparts to the thoughts that do not mention me. I occur in them, so to speak, only in the role of one who has this thought.[18]

Of course, I can occur in my own thoughts in a more substantive and individual way. My thoughts may be specifically about myself, as in

Am I ill?

Thoughts of that kind are about myself in a sense in which other thoughts I have are not about myself, but about someone or something else. More interestingly, I may occur in my thought as a locus of evidence, as in

It looks blue to me.

In such a case I occur as specifically myself, and my actual psychological properties are relevant (thus, given my eyesight, the thing's looking blue to me may be a reliable indicator of its being green). If I ask

What do I think about this question?

in one sense it also involves a specific reference to myself, with my actual psychological properties; it can be an invitation to me to find out about my beliefs, as I might find out about someone else's (if not in exactly the same ways). But

What should I think about this question?

where that has the same effect as

What is the truth about this question?

is again a case in which *I* occurs only derivatively: the last question is the primary one.

Because of this, the *I* of this kind is also impersonal. The question,

What should I think about this question?

could as well be

What should anyone think about this question?

This is so, even when it means

What should I think about this on the evidence I have?

This must ask what anyone should think about it on that evidence. Equally, what anyone truly believes must be consistent with what others truly believe, and anyone deliberating about the truth is committed, by the nature of the process, to the aim of a consistent set of beliefs, one's own and others'.[19]

It is different with deliberation for action. Practical delibera-tion is in every case first-personal, and the first person is not derivative or naturally replaced by *anyone*. The action I decide on will be mine, and (on the lines of what was said earlier about the aims of action) its being mine means not just that it will be arrived at by this deliberation, but that it will involve changes in the world of which I shall be empirically the cause, and of which these desires and this deliberation itself will be, in some part, the cause. It is true that I can stand back from my desires and reflect on them, and this possibility can indeed be seen as part of the rational freedom at which any rational agent aims. This goes somewhat beyond the considerations about freedom and intentionality acknowledged earlier in the discussion, but it still does not give the required result in relation to morality. The *I* of the reflective practical deliberation is not required to take the result of anyone else's properly conducted deliberation as a datum, nor be committed from the outset to a harmony of everyone's deliberations — that is to say, to making a rule from a standpoint of equality. Reflective deliberation about the truth indeed brings in a standpoint that is impartial and seeks harmony, but this is because it seeks truth, not because it is reflective deliberation, and those features will not be shared by deliberation about what to do simply because it too is reflective. The *I* that stands back in rational reflection from my desires is still the *I* that has those desires and will, empirically and concretely, act; and it is not, simply by standing back in reflection, converted into a being whose fundamental interest lies in the harmony of all interests. It cannot, just by taking this step, acquire the motivations of justice.

Indeed, it is rather hard to explain why the reflective self, if it is conceived as uncommitted to all particular desires, should have a concern that any of them be satisfied. The reflective self of theoretical or factual deliberation has a unity of interest with prereflective belief: each in its way aims at truth, and this is why the prereflective disposition to believe yields so easily, in the standard case, to corrective reflection. But on the model we are considering there is not an identity of interest between the reflective practical self and any particular desires, my own or others'. It is unclear, then, why the reflective self should try to provide for the satisfaction of those desires. This is just another aspect of the mistake that lies in equating, as this argument does, reflection and detachment.

Some deep questions remain about what it is to take the impartial perspective if one *does* possess the motivations of justice. How can an *I* that has taken on the perspective of impartiality be left with enough identity to live a life that respects its own interests? If morality is possible at all, does it leave anyone in particular for me to be? These are important questions about both morality and life: about morality because, as a particular view of the ethical, it raises that question in a particularly acute form, and about life because there are, on any view of ethical questions, real issues about the relations between impartiality and personal satisfactions and aims — or, indeed, personal commitments that are not necessarily egoistic but are narrower than those imposed by a universal concern or respect for rights. Some of these questions will arise later. They concern what happens to personal desire and deliberation under the influence of the impartial standpoint, to the extent that one achieves it. What has been shown in this chapter, I believe, is that there is no route to the impartial standpoint from rational deliberation alone.

CHAPTER 5

Styles of Ethical Theory

THE IMPARTIAL standpoint can be called upon for a different purpose, not to argue someone all the way from bare practical reason to the concerns of justice or benevolence, but to support or demand some ethical conceptions rather than others. The question now is: Given people who are in some general sense committed to thinking in ethical terms, how should they think? Are their ethical thoughts sound?

I am not concerned here with every kind of critique of existing ethical attitudes and beliefs. There are many styles of critique, and the most potent of them rely, as they always have, not so much on philosophical arguments as on showing up those attitudes as resting on myths, falsehoods about what people are like. Even among the criticisms that involve more distinctively philosophical argument, not all of them are my immediate concern. Some of these patterns of argument serve in a local fashion, to bring out the consequences of ethical positions or to convict them of incoherence. They are instruments of ethical argument. In this chapter and the next, I am concerned with a more elaborate, thoroughgoing, and ambitious kind of structure, the *ethical theory*. (Later I shall consider the idea that some of the instruments of ethical argument, thoroughly applied, are themselves enough to generate ethical theory.)

What is an ethical theory? The most helpful use of that expression can best be caught by a rather complex definition. An ethical theory is a theoretical account of what ethical thought and practice are, which account either implies a general test for the correctness of basic ethical beliefs and principles or else implies that there cannot be such a test. It is the first kind of ethical theory, the positive kind, that concerns me here. In this chapter I shall give an account of two leading styles of positive ethical theory, and in the next I shall consider the deeper motivations for theories of this kind and their relation to practice. First, however, I must say something about the negative kind of ethical theory, and about the point of putting the definition in this peculiar way.

It does not matter much how the expression "ethical theory" is used, so long as one's use is made clear. There is a reason, though, for using it in the way suggested by this definition, and it involves a significant philosophical point. Twenty or thirty years ago, it was standard practice to distinguish "ethical" from "meta-ethical" theories. The first made substantive claims about what one should do, how one should live, what was worthwhile, and so on. The second concerned itself with the status of those claims: whether they could be knowledge, how they could be validated, whether they were (and in what sense) objective, and so on. The idea that lay behind the distinction was, naturally enough, that the two types could be taken apart and that a theory of the meta-ethical sort would not, as such, have ethical implications.

It is important to separate this proposed distinction from two other ideas that have often been associated with it. One is that the meta-ethical study should be linguistic, an inquiry into the terms used in ethical discourse. This involves an additional view, about the nature of philosophy — one that has not been very fruitful in moral philosophy. Although the distinction can be separated from this idea, the linguistic formulation probably helped to encourage it, because of a general assumption that it must be possible to distinguish between the means a language provides for saying things and the particular things that happen to be said in it. This assumption was widely made at that time and issued in other distinctions, such as that between analytic and synthetic, which are now also regarded with less favor. But even if the preoccupations of linguistic philosophy encouraged the distinction between the ethical and the meta-ethical, that distinction is not committed to a linguistic formulation.

Another idea that is separable from the distinction, and indeed separable from it even when it takes a linguistic form, is that philosophy should not contain any ethical assertions and should confine itself to the meta-ethical. This policy obviously rests on further assumptions, once more about the nature of philosophy, and they have not universally been made. Thus Moore, whose *Principia Ethica* made an emphatic and influential distinction between saying what goodness is and saying what things are good, allowed himself in that book to try the second as well as the first, and while it was the distinction that was influential with philosophers, it was his account of what things are intrinsically good that impressed others. Moore did, however, have a view about goodness and our knowledge of it, in terms of which it was to some extent appropriate to philosophy that it should try to say what things are good. He thought that goodness was detected by a kind of intellectual discrimination, and part of that process at least (it was too poorly defined to make it clear how much) was enough like intellectual analysis to make it intelligible that philosophy, or the capacities of philosophers, might have something to contribute to it. But someone who thinks that the business of philosophy is primarily analysis, and that what is involved in making substantive ethical judgments is quite different from intellectual analysis, will see no reason why those judgments should be part of philosophy, and will try, as some philosophers did twenty or thirty years ago, to leave them out of it.

The distinction between the ethical and the meta-ethical is no longer found so convincing or important. There are several reasons for this, but the most relevant here is that it is now obvious (once again obvious) that what one thinks about the subject matter of ethical thought, what one supposes it to be about, must itself affect what tests for acceptability or coherence are appropriate to it; and the use of those tests must affect any substantive ethical results. Conversely, the use of certain tests and patterns of argument can imply one rather than another view of what ethical thought is. A theory that combines views on what ethical thought is and how it should be conducted, with substantive consequences of conducting it in that way, is a positive ethical theory.

Some views about the content and nature of ethics, however, imply that there are no tests. The most extreme of these views says that holding an ethical position simply consists of choosing one and sticking to it. There seems to me good reason to call that an ethical theory too, a negative one. But this should be distinguished from a theory about the nature of ethical thought that *leaves open* the question whether there could be such tests. One may be fairly convinced and definite about the account to be given of the ethical, and remain skeptical about the chances of there being these tests; and there are options more complex than that, according to which there may be tests in some cultural circumstances and not in others. That is the kind of account I give in this book, and there is point in not calling it an ethical theory. Ethical theories are philosophical undertakings and commit themselves to the view that philosophy can determine, either positively or negatively, how we should think in ethics — in the negative case, to the effect that we cannot really think much at all in ethics. It is this negative option that philosophers usually had in mind when in the past they said that philosophy could not determine how we should think in ethics.

In contrast, I want to say that we can think in ethics, and in all sorts of ways, unless our historical and cultural circumstances have made it impossible — but that philosophy can do little to determine how we should do so. The purpose of using "ethical theory" in the way I suggest is to bring out the similarity of the positive and the negative theories in the claims they implicitly make for philosophy. It may at this stage of the argument seem a fine point, but I hope that by the end it will not seem so. The aim is to reach an outlook different from that of any of these theories. It is an outlook that embodies a skepticism about philosophical ethics, but a skepticism that is more about philosophy than it is about ethics.

We must now turn to positive ethical theories. There are several kinds of ethical theory, and there are several ways of classifying them, which yield different kinds of kinds. No classification is uniquely illuminating, but one helpful distinction is that between two basic styles, the *contractual* and the *utilitarian*. The central idea of contractualism has been formulated by T. M. Scanlon, in relation to its account of moral wrongness: "An act is wrong if its performance under the circumstances would be disallowed by any system of rules for the general regulation of behaviour which no-one could reasonably reject as a basis for informed, unforced, general agreement."[1] (Scanlon and other writers I shall be discussing usually speak of *morality;* I shall sometimes do the same.) This account of wrongness goes with a particular theory of what moral thought is about, or of what ultimate moral facts there are. On this theory, moral thought is concerned with what agreements people could make in these favored circumstances, in which no one was ignorant or coerced. The theory also gives an account of moral motivation. The basic moral motive is "a desire to be able to justify one's actions to others on grounds they could not reasonably reject."[2] It can be seen how close this complex of ideas is to the Kantian conceptions discussed in the last chapter. Now, however, it is not a matter of trying to show that every rational agent must be a citizen legislator of a notional republic. It is a question of what rules would be acceptable to people who are assumed to be already interested in reaching agreement.

Utilitarianism, by contrast, takes facts of individual welfare as the basic subject matter of ethical thought. There are many species of utilitarianism. They disagree about how welfare is to be assessed, and about other questions: whether, for instance, it is the individual act that should be justified in terms of maximizing welfare, or instead some rule, practice, or institution. (This is the difference between *direct* and *indirect* utilitarianism.) All the variants agree on aggregating welfare,[3] that is to say, adding together in some way the welfare of all the individuals involved (this formula, even the word "involved," raises many difficulties).

I shall look at these styles of ethical theory in greater detail. But even these introductory sketches give some idea of how they might lead to different results. One difference lies in the *constituency* of morality as it is most naturally defined by the theories: that is, those with whom the system is in the first place concerned. The natural constituency for contractualism consists of those to whom you could conceivably try to justify your actions — in the simplest interpretation, other moral agents. This can be extended to a concern for the interests of others who are unable to give or receive justifications — small children, for instance, or the mentally handicapped. In such cases we naturally think, as we do in the law, of trustees acting on those people's behalf. By a further extension, animals may also receive consideration, but they are farther away from the primary constituency. We would expect contractualism to give an account of concern for animals that is different from that given of moral relations between people. The idea of a contract, even in this minimal and schematic form, always brings in as its first concern equal relations between agents who are both the subjects and the objects of moral thought.

Utilitarianism looks in a different direction. One of the most natural interpretations of the welfare with which it is concerned (and historically the earliest) is pleasure and the absence of pain, and the natural utilitarian constituency consists of all creatures capable of feeling pleasure and pain. This basis has been refined by modern work, and the constituency is now likely to be defined in terms of those who have preferences or wants, and can suffer from the frustration of those wants. In most versions, this still includes animals in the primary constituency: in fact, it includes some animals more naturally than some humans (moribund humans, for instance). This conception appeals to one moral motivation, benevolence. At the same time, it introduces a disparity between moral agents, on the one hand, and beneficiaries of morality on the other, the second class being, right from the beginning, larger than the first. This feature of utilitarianism comes from its welfarism.

It has another important feature, which comes from its being a kind of consequentialism and judging actions in terms of their consequences.[4] Any form of consequentialism locates ethical value ultimately in states of affairs. (In the case of utilitarianism, which is welfarist consequentialism,[5] that value is found in differences of welfare located in states of affairs.) This has the result that, for utilitarianism, agency comes in only secondarily: our basic ethical relation to the world, as agents, is that of being the cause of desirable or undesirable states of affairs. Our basic ethical concern is to bring it about, so far as we can, that there is more welfare or utility in the world rather than less, and, in the simplest version of utilitarianism, we should simply act in the most efficient way to bring that about. It is a question of what causal levers are at that moment within reach. Sometimes the causal connections through which I can affect outcomes run through other people's actions,[6] but this makes no special difference. It is simply a matter of what changes produce most welfare. This means that there are states of affairs I can affect with respect to welfare which, because I can do so, turn out to be my concern when, on nonutilitarian assumptions, they would be someone else's concern. Moreover, because the class of beneficiaries is larger than that of agents, there are situations that turn out to be someone's concern when on nonutilitarian assumptions they would have been no one's concern.

These considerations bring out another difference between utilitarianism and contractualism—once more, on the most immediate and natural interpretations of those theories. The demands of utilitarianism for maximum welfare production are boundless. There is no limit to what a given person might be doing to improve the world, except the limits of time and strength. Moreover, because the relations of possible states of affairs to any given person's actions are indeterminate, the demands are boundless in the further sense that there are often no clear boundaries between the demands on me and the demands on someone else. Utilitarian theorists go on (with varying degrees of enthusiasm[7]) to *put back* restrictions on what a given individual may be required to do, saying that it is usually more efficient if you care specially about your own children, for instance, or if you relax occasionally from good works. Contractualists, and many others who are not theorists of either sort, will complain that this gets things back to front: my rights to my own children and my own time are not theirs to give back.

The idea that there should be a limit to "the strains of commitment," as John Rawls puts it, is one thing that helps to form his theory, the richest and most complex contractual account of ethics yet advanced.[8] Rawls's theory of justice aims to find principles to govern social and political life rather than individual conduct. But it starts from a moral basis, and also has important consequences for purely moral thought.

Rawls's theory is an elaboration of a simple idea: a fair system of arrangements is one that the parties can agree to without knowing how it will benefit them personally. This is worked up into a fiction of an Original Position in which people choose social principles behind a "veil of ignorance," which conceals from them their own prospective social positions and indeed their individual tastes and interests. It does not conceal general propositions, such as the findings of the social sciences, so they have some information to work on, but no information that enables any of them to discriminate in his or her own favor. The ignorance is thus less radical than that implied in the last chapter, where I touched on the Kantian idea of people choosing as rational agents "and no more." (The model has the revealing consequence that Rawls must assume, implausibly, that knowledge of history is not essential to social scientific understanding — unless he allows, even less plausibly, that you can know the course of history without knowing your place in it. The fact that the theory, like other such theories, is radically ahistorical is an important fact about it.) The parties have to make, in these circumstances, a self-interested choice of social arrangements. They are not in a good position to do it, since they do not know what selves they are, but it does mean that they do not include any benevolent or altruistic principles in the basis of their choice. Rawls is not to be interpreted here as trying to move to social justice from personal self-interest. The point is that a self-interested choice in ignorance of one's identity is supposed to model in important respects non-self-interested or moral choice under ordinary conditions of knowledge.

The result of the deliberation in the Original Position is that the parties accept two fundamental principles of justice:

(1) Each person is to have an equal right to the most extensive liberty compatible with a similar liberty for others. . . .

(2) Social and economic inequalities are to be arranged so

that they are both (a) to the greatest benefit of the least advantaged and (b) attached to offices and positions open to all under conditions of fair equality of opportunity.[9]

The second of these principles is based on the idea that parties will use in their deliberations a "maximin" rule, a rule that ranks alternatives by their worst possible outcomes. It is a distinctive feature of Rawls's theory. The choice of this principle in the Original Position is supposed to rest not on any peculiarly conservative bias of the parties (who cannot allow for a special taste in that or any other direction), but on the peculiar character of the choice, which consists in the fact that the parties have no probabilities available to them; that they have no very great interest in benefits over the minimum; and that the worst outcomes involve "grave risks" that one could not accept.

This expresses some important ideas about fundamental goods — for instance, that slavery is simply unacceptable, whatever benefits it might confer. Indeed, as Rawls's rejection of all probability calculations shows, he is committed to the conclusion that even a society with a very small number of slaves would be unacceptable. This may be a welcome consequence of a moral theory of justice, but it does not follow naturally from the model of rational choice under ignorance. If self-interested rational choice is what is at issue, it is hard to see how the question of probabilities can altogether be avoided, or how, if the probability of ending up as a slave were small enough, it would not be rational for the parties to choose a system involving slavery if it conveyed large enough other benefits. For reasons of this kind, the decision-theoretical or rational-choice element in Rawls's model has been much criticized.

There is also an important question of what the goods are, in terms of which the parties are supposed to make their rational choice. Rational-choice theory, in its ordinary uses, normally works on a basis of utility or individual welfare, and this is a function of the agents' preferences and tastes (we shall see later that in the hands of the utilitarians welfare does not remain such a simple matter). But the contracting parties do not have any known individual preferences or tastes, so this is not available to them. Rawls makes his parties choose by reference to a list of "primary goods," which are liberty and opportunity, income and wealth, and the bases of self-respect. These goods are given by what he calls "the thin theory of the good"; the idea is that these are goods that everyone is going to want if they want anything. But the question is more complex than this. The list of primary goods does not plausibly look as if it had been assembled simply from the consideration that they are uniquely necessary for pursuing anything. From that consideration we are not likely to derive more than liberty. It is hard to see, also, how the parties could avoid the reflection (available to them from their knowledge of general social facts) that some of these primary goods, notably money, are more important in some societies than in others.

Why are primary goods introduced at all? It is not technically impossible for parties without any known particular preferences to choose one social state over another. We could suppose them to choose a situation in which they (that is to say, anyone they might turn out to be) get more of what they prefer in that situation than they do of what they prefer in other situations. As we shall see, this is what is done by R. M. Hare in constructing a utilitarian theory. Such comparisons may indeed be fanciful, but that is not Rawls's objection to their use in the Original Position. Rather, he has refused to let his parties think merely in terms of what they would prefer in the various social situations. His parties are reluctant, as we actually are, to count a situation as acceptable just because they would find it acceptable if they were in it (we noticed our own reluctance earlier, with "real interests"). So even if the social sciences told us, as in fact they are very unlikely to tell us, that most slaves are content to be free from freedom, this would not give the parties a reason to choose slavery: from the standpoint of free people freely choosing a polity, this is not an option. Rawls has the right, indeed is right, to carry such convictions into his ethical theory, but they are not best represented by the machinery of rational choice deployed under selective conditions of ignorance. The primary goods may perhaps be better seen in terms of a fundamental ethical conception of the person, and Rawls himself has now moved in this direction.[10]

Formally speaking, utilitarianism is itself an option under contractualism. If the contractualist question is asked not about particular principles or practices, but about an entire set of principles, as it is by Rawls, then the parties could choose some utilitarian system as the answer. Granted the kind of differences we have already noticed in the typical outcomes of the two ways of thinking, this is unlikely, but it is not excluded by the machinery. Consider some people asked to select a set of principles. They are armed with utilities (instead of an index of primary goods), and there are no further restrictions on their choice, except that they are subject to the one dimension of ignorance, that they do not know who they will be in the world governed by the principles they select. The idea that certain principles are *impartially acceptable* is then equated with their being those principles that would be selected by someone who believed that he had an equal chance of being anyone in the outcome. (It can now be seen that there need be only one person choosing.) This is the approach of John Harsanyi, who argues that it yields a set of principles that would maximize the average utility of the affected people. This resembles a contractualist argument, but it has a utilitarian outcome.[11]

In its most familiar versions, however, utilitarianism starts from ideas of welfare, or of people's interests. Its project, which (in its simplest form) consists of considering everyone's welfare under various alternative outcomes and compounding it, involves serious technical difficulties as well as deep conceptual ones. One of them is that except in the simplest cases the set of people affected by various outcomes will not be the same, and people who have to be considered under one alternative may well not exist under others.[12] But I shall not pursue technical difficulties here.

I said earlier that for utilitarianism the characteristic moral motive was benevolence. That term is vague, and it can also be misleading, particularly if it suggests warm feelings of personal attachment or, again, any kind of sentiment one naturally feels in greater degree for some people than others. Utilitarian benevolence involves no particular attachments, and it is immune to the inverse square law. The term stands for a positive relation to other people's desires and satisfactions, which the benevolent person has only because they are the desires and satisfactions of others. This rough idea needs work before it can play a part in ethical theory, and the work is done in different ways by different theorists. In considering the important question of utilitarianism's impartial attitude to desire satisfaction, I shall discuss an interesting version of utilitarianism developed by R. M. Hare, who treats the agent's relation to others' desires (what I vaguely called "benevolence") in terms of imaginative identification.

Hare's theory[13] starts from some claims about the nature of moral judgments: they are prescriptive, and they are universal. "Prescriptive" is a term relating to language (I have touched briefly on a possible use of it in Chapter 4 and shall have more to say about it in Chapter 7). A prescriptive utterance is of the type "let so-and-so be done," and Hare takes such an utterance, if sincere, to express a desire or preference. Moreover, every preference can be expressed in a prescription; so any agent who has preferences is in a position to make prescriptions. Yet the agent is not yet committed to making *universal* prescriptions — those come in with moral language, in particular, moral uses of *ought*. Hare thus does not make the claim that the presuppositions of any practical reasoning involve a universal prescription. So far as that goes, Hare and I are in agreement, that the commitments of moral reasoning can be avoided by not engaging in moral reasoning.

The effect of making a universal prescription, in judging that I ought to do a certain thing, is that I accept that anyone else ought to act similarly in similar circumstances. In particular, I accept that this ought to be the case if I were at the receiving end of the action. In considering what I ought to do, therefore, I must consider what it would be like to be the other people affected; in doing this, I apply a "role-reversal test" and think what I would want or prefer if I were in their positions. I should, if thinking ideally, conduct this thought experiment with regard to every person, or indeed every sentient creature, involved in similar situations.

The use of a role-reversal test is not peculiar to utilitarianism. In one form or another it is a basic item of ethical thinking, and a version of it is involved in Kant's Categorical Imperative. The distinctively utilitarian results follow from the special and radical interpretation that Hare's theory gives to the idea of thinking one-self into someone else's position. On this interpretation, an agent will have realized what he would prefer if he were in that position only if he now acquires a corresponding *actual* preference that applies to the hypothetical situation. I shall come later to Hare's reasons for this idea and to criticism of it. First, however, we should see what a crucial part it plays in the transition to utilitarianism. If anyone carried out an ideally complete thought experiment under these requirements, he would actually acquire preferences that would correspond to every preference held by anyone who was affected by the situation. All the preferences would thus be ag-glomerated into one individual. How can the agent decide, given this agglomeration? These are now his preferences, and he can bring to them certain rational requirements that supposedly apply to any first-personal deliberation. But he cannot on ethical grounds discount or downgrade any preferences he has acquired from identification with others — nor, come to that, any of those he started with — since this ideal level of reflection is supposed to criticize all ethical grounds, and none of them can be taken for granted. All that the ideally reflective agent is given, at the ethical level, is the process of additive identification itself. So once the preferences have been adjusted in the light of rational criteria that apply even to first-personal deliberation, there is nothing to do except compare their relative strengths and choose between the various outcomes on the basis of that comparison. The result is utilitarianism.

This structure is equivalent to one version of what has been called Ideal Observer theory. This postulates one omniscient, im-partial, and benevolent observer — he might be called the World Agent — who acquires everybody's preferences and puts them to-gether. The test of what should be done (or, in indirect versions of the theory, of what practices or institutions should be adopted) then becomes what would be chosen by such an observer. As Hare says, his own model comes to the same thing. There is another version of Ideal Observer theory, which leaves out the condition of benevolence and does not imagine the observer actually to take on everyone's preferences. As Roderick Firth put it (perhaps a little quaintly) in a well-known exposition of the theory, the observer is "omniscient, disinterested, dispassionate, but otherwise normal." This version of the theory, in which the various preferences are not aggregated into a World Agent but merely surveyed from outside in a dispassionate spirit, is not supposed to lead necessarily to utilitarianism. Utilitarianism is merely one candidate that might itself be selected by the theory's test. In this form, however, Ideal Observer theory faces the objection that if the observer is not given some motivation in addition to his impartiality, there is no reason why he should choose anything at all; and unless that motivation is benevolent — or positively related to the preferences he knows about — he might as well choose to frustrate as many preferences as possible.[14]

In earlier work Hare did not make the hypothetical identifications so complete, with the result that he was left with what he saw as a problem, the possibility of a "fanatic" who was so wedded to certain ideals that he would accept the hypothetically unpleasant results of the role-reversal argument. Thus a convinced Nazi might accept the prescription "let me be killed if I were a Jew." Hare now regards this problem as having been overcome, by the same process of thought that led him to a utilitarian position. The Nazi, if he engages in the ideal process of thinking, will, in identifying with Jews, lose in relation to the hypothetical situations his antisemitic preferences and will, for each Jew, acquire an actual preference against antisemitism. This process of thought will itself constitute a utilitarian critique (assuming that the sums come out right) of antisemitism. It is of course accepted that an actual racist may refuse to engage in this process of thought, but that does not undermine the argument.

It is striking how strong the claims are that Hare makes for the powers of rational argument in ethics. Why was the fanatic regarded as a problem in the first place? Hare says, "It would expose a gap in the defences of utilitarianism if [a fanatic] could listen to, and understand, all the arguments, and admit all the facts, adduced by a utilitarian, and still sustain his opinion."[15] At first glance, this seems to imply a super-power view of defense, that you are adequately defended only if you can annihilate the other side. As against this, it is surely possible that you might hold a rational, or reasonable, set of ethical beliefs, and yet there be other people who held different ethical beliefs that you might indeed deplore but could not demonstrate to be inconsistent or factually wrong. (Hare himself, in his earliest work, *The Language of Morals*, did believe this.) More interestingly, you may think that some positions that differ from your own are indeed irrational, and racism is one of them; but that their irrationality cannot necessarily be shown by the same arguments in every case, nor by some pattern of argument central to building your own ethical beliefs. There may be something *specially* irrational about racism.

Hare's equation of defense and attack comes from two sources, one rather special to his outlook, the other shared by many ethical theories. The general point is that ethical theories in this style can readily be seen as offensive weapons, aimed against prejudice, so that if there is an important style of prejudice that is immune to them, they are not well designed for their job and are likely to replaced, if not by prejudice, then by an ethical theory with more firepower. To some extent, this is true of all of them, although they differ from one another in their aggressive ambitions.

Hare's special reason for his view of his defenses is that he believes his argument for utilitarianism to follow strictly from the meaning of moral words. It will indeed be a gap in the defenses *of that claim* if there can be someone who correctly uses moral language but consistently refuses the theory: that claim will be not only defenseless but defeated. But the claim is unreasonable. Alternative theories cannot plausibly be shown to misuse or misinterpret moral language. Even if there were one basic characteristic of "moral language" as such, and even if that lay in its being prescriptive and universal, this would still not lead inescapably to the theory. There are other interpretations of what it is to accept a prescription, and of what counts as universalizability, that would lead to different theories. As John Mackie argued, there are various degrees of universalizability less extreme than the ultimate stage represented by Hare's theory, which sinks all the agent's tastes and ideals into the thought experiment of identification. In Mackie's words, "it is at most the first stage, the ruling out of purely numerical differences as morally irrelevant, that is built into the meaning of moral language"[16]

In everyday uses of role-reversal arguments, less ambitious than the attempt to found all moral considerations on them, it is often natural to include personal tastes in the imagined identification, but to leave out ideals or ethical beliefs. Making this distinction involves resisting a characteristic move of utilitarian thought, which has been called *reduction* and defined as "the device of regarding all interests, ideas, aspirations and desires as on the same level, and all representable as preferences, of different degrees of intensity, perhaps, but otherwise to be treated alike."[17] Utilitarian writers often start with a plea for equal consideration of everyone's interests, and then extend this upward (so to speak) to ideals and downward to mere tastes. This assimilation gets things out of proportion in more than one direction. In one way it underestimates the significance of ideals or ethical conceptions, and requires an agent to abandon any stand of principle or deeply held conviction if a large enough aggregate of preferences, of whatever kind, favors a contrary action. The assimilation does not give our convictions enough weight in our own calculations. At the same time, it can give other people's convictions too much weight. While Hare's thought experiments give an argument against the racist fanatic, they do not give the right sort of argument.

There is, first of all, the point that the sums have to come out right. It is naturally characteristic of utilitarianism that its results depend on calculations but, in connections such as this, that feature is particularly undesirable. If racist prejudice is directed toward a small minority by a majority that gets enough satisfaction from it, it could begin to be touch and go whether racism might not be justified. The point is not how likely that is to arise, or in what circumstances, but that the whole question of how many racists are involved cannot begin to be an acceptable consideration on the question whether racism is acceptable (contrast Rawls's treatment of slavery). Moreover, on the utilitarian argument it emerges as *a* consideration — though, if the sums come out right, not a decisive or winning consideration — that racists get some satisfaction out of the sufferings of the Jews; but this cannot be a consideration *at all*. This does not mean that the sufferings of racists never count. It means that sufferings they experience solely because of their racist opinions do not count. Harsanyi, indeed, has built into his system a provision that aims to deal with this kind of problem, by rather briskly excluding "antisocial" preferences from the count. But he does not explain how they are to be defined; his rationale for the provision suggests that what is in question are antiutilitarian preferences.[18]

I have already mentioned the requirement of Hare's theory, that the preferences, when they have all been gathered into one agent, should be modified by reference to criteria of first-personal rationality. What are eventually taken into account are not necessarily the actual preferences of agents (including their actual hypothetical preferences — that is, the preferences they would as a matter of fact have in the hypothetical situations), but rather their "perfectly prudent preferences," which is what they would prefer if they were fully informed and unconfused in their thinking. A similar provision is made by Harsanyi. Moral thinking has been assimilated (in different ways in the two theories) to prudential thinking by a single individual. What it is prudentially rational for an ordinary agent to do does not necessarily correspond to what he actually prefers, since he may be confused or misinformed. Our knowledge of our future preferences also comes into this. We should include among our now-for-then preferences (as Hare calls them in a helpful terminology) our anticipated then-for-then preferences; the way we do this, according to Hare, is that we take on actual now-for-then preferences as surrogates, exactly as the reflective agent takes on other people's preferences.[19] There are many complications involved here. Here I want only to bring out the kind of treatment that Hare's model gives to these aggregated preferences.

This process of correcting preferences (their *idealization,* as we might say) is appropriate to models in which all preferences become notionally one person's preferences, such as the World Agent interpretation of Ideal Observer theory. It is appropriate, though, only if the model is taken literally; and if it is taken literally, even to a slight degree, it becomes clear how bizarre it is. Any one agent who had projects as conflicting, competitive, and diversely based as the World Agent's would be (to put it mildly) in bad shape. He would need a set of values or second-order desires to give some weighting to his array of preferences. But if the World Agent has any of those, and they are still recognizable in the aggregate of preferences, he once again has too many. The truth is that this aggregate of preferences is simply unintelligible unless they are understood to be the preferences of *different people*. The device of the World Agent requires us to forget that fact, to see the ethical world as a sea of preferences. So, in varying degrees, do all forms of utilitarianism. This idea is often criticized in terms of its ethical results, but the fundamental objection is that it makes no sense as an interpretation of the world. It is because of this that it makes no sense of ethics. "The separateness of persons," as John Findlay put it, is "the basic fact for morals."[20]

If utilitarianism is interpreted in terms less drastic than those of the World Agent model, the idealization of preferences becomes less appropriate. Certainly it is never appropriate *merely* because an agent's preferences are based on false information. It will be appropriate if, as a result of action from that preference, the agent and others get less utility than they would get from action based on a correction of preferences. To take a political example, if a utilitarian administration operates not on the basis of what people prefer, but on the basis of what they would prefer if they were better informed, it is possible that those for whom it acts will always be discontented with what is actually done, since they may never lose their errors and, if they do not, will never actually have the idealized preference the policy is designed to satisfy.

The doubtful role of idealization in utilitarian theory is connected with the process of reduction I have already mentioned, by which interests are assimilated to preferences. Idealization or correction is appropriate when one is thinking about people's interests — one of the basic facts about people's interests is that they can be mistaken about them. The question is not whether you can appropriately correct others' preferences when thinking about their interests, but how far you have the right to act on the basis of those corrections if the people concerned do not recognize them. But if you are simply concerned with how much preference-satisfaction the world will contain, the question will be different: whether idealization in a given case will in the long run create more utility. It can be seen how these two different questions will naturally figure in two different conceptions of politics.

Idealization is ambiguously related to the role-reversal test itself. As we have seen, it can be appropriately applied in the World Agent's deliberations, after the preferences have all become his. Yet this result conflicts with the spirit in which the thought experiments of identifying with others were recommended to us in the first place. The original question was "how would it be for me if I were in his position?" This is interpreted by Hare as equivalent to "how would it be for him?"; none of the original *me* is left over in the transfer. (The hypothetical is taken as it is in the well-known reply to the remark "If I had been Roosevelt, I would not have made all those concessions to Stalin": "Don't be silly, if you had been Roosevelt, you would have done whatever Roosevelt did.") But if this is to be the degree of identification (total), then if another's preferences are mistaken, the preferences I imagine myself into are equally mistaken, and if *identification* is the point, they should remain so. In the outcome, however, my total sympathetic identification with the other person issues in my improving his preferences. This is a compact illustration of a truth about all utilitarian politics, that benevolence gets credentials from sympathy and passes them on to paternalism.

At this point we should look back at Hare's reasons for the interpretation that makes each ideally reflective person into a version of the World Agent. Its roots can be found in the relations that Hare sets up between two propositions which, on the face of it, are very different: (1) I now prefer with strength S that if I were in that situation X should happen rather than not. (2) If I were in that situation, I would prefer with strength S that X should happen rather than not. "What I am claiming," Hare writes, "is not that these propositions are identical, but that I cannot know that (2), and what that would be like, without (1) being true."[21] Hare's claim, that is to say, is about knowledge: I cannot now know that in a certain situation I would prefer with a certain strength that X should happen, unless I now prefer with that same strength that X should happen in that situation.

This claim seems hard to accept even if the *I* of the hypothetical situation is straightforwardly *me*, as in cases of buying insurance and other such prudential decisions. I indeed know, for instance, that if my house caught fire, I would prefer, with the greatest possible intensity, that my family and I should get out of it. Since I am a moderately rational agent, I take some action now to make sure that we could do that if the situation arose, and that action comes of course from a preference I have now. But there is no sense at all in which that present prudential preference is of the same strength as the preference I would have if the house were actually on fire (driving almost every other consideration from my mind), and it is not rational that it should be. For one thing, its strength will be formed in part by the probability of the imagined situation.

In the case of the thought experiment that goes with the radical version of the role-reversal test, it might be said that the probability of the imagined situation is always zero, since it is the probability of being someone else. Put like this, that is unfair, since the experiment relates to situations described in general terms, so it is a question of satisfying some general description, not of blankly being another individual. Nevertheless, the probability in many cases will still be zero; and in any case the probability is not supposed to figure in the argument. Granted this, it seems even less plausible that the derived preference should be of the same intensity as the preference that would exist if the situation came about. Indeed it is not even clear what it means to say that it is or that it is not, since there is in general no independent test of the strength of the derived preference.

This is not to say that there are no preferences, of various degrees of intensity, based on sympathetic identification with others. Of course there are, and they are basic to ethical experience. The point is that understanding, identification, and preference are not related to one another as the World Agent model makes out. Confronted with someone in a dire emergency, I will, if I am a humane person, acquire an overriding preference to help him if I can. That operates through consideration of what it is like for him, a consideration in which some part is played by thoughts of what this or something like it would be like for me. My knowledge of what somebody wants (let us say, that I should help him out of the fire) sets off in me, granted a humane disposition, a desire to help him out of the fire. So there are four relevant truths about me in this situation. First, I know how it is for him and that he wants to be helped. Second, I know that if I were in that situation I should want to be helped. Third, I have a preference now, in my own person, for being helped in such situations. Fourth, being of a humane disposition, I want to help him. On Hare's model, the first of these is equivalent to the second, because *being in that situation* is taken to mean total immersion. (This brings out clearly how radical the interpretation is. In ordinary life, they are not taken to be equivalent, and much possible comedy lies in their being confused.) On Hare's model, further, I cannot know the second unless the third is true; and, last, "being of a humane disposition" means being disposed to make rational first-personal calculations in which preferences of that transferred kind are given proper weight (as against my own convenience, and so forth).

These connections cannot all be correct. The operations of sympathetic understanding or, as it is often now called, "empathy" have been much discussed in the history of moral philosophy, and various accounts have been given of it. But one thing that must be true is that the insightful understanding of others' feelings possessed by the sympathetic person is possessed in much the same form by the sadistic or cruel person; that is one way in which the cruel are distinguished from the brutal or indifferent. But the cruel person is someone who has no preference to give help (he is not someone who has a preference to give help but finds it outweighed by a preference for enjoying suffering). Yet he certainly *knows*. Hare indeed says about the connection he makes, that it "is a conceptual truth, in the sense of 'know' that moral thinking demands."[22] But moral thinking demands no sense of "know" except knowledge, and it is a truth, if not a conceptual one, that any knowledge it can use may be turned against it.

I have pursued this question because the operations of sympathy and of the role-reversal test (not necessarily the same thing) are important to ethical thought; and also, more immediately, because they are involved in the influential World Agent interpretation of utilitarianism. This is not the only model for utilitarianism, and other versions of it will escape some of these specific criticisms. But the idea of taking into oneself the world's wants and sufferings and, at an ideal level at least, feeling all of its pains and pleasures as equally close to oneself, is a basic motivation of utilitarianism — the contrast with contractualism is clear in this — and Hare's version of what is in effect the World Agent model brings out with exceptional clarity what is involved.

Utilitarianism is the most ambitious of extant ethical theories. It aims to yield the most definite results and is willing to press them most firmly against everyday ethical beliefs. We must look next at the relation of utilitarianism and of other ethical theories to practice. Why should such theories be granted any authority at all?

CHAPTER 6

Theory and Prejudice

E THICAL THEORIES have to start from somewhere. Earlier I considered ways of their starting outside ethics altogether. I also touched on the idea of starting inside ethics, but merely from the meaning of moral words. I found all of these in varying degrees unpersuasive, and some I rejected altogether. Many would agree with these conclusions, including some writers whose aim it is to construct an ethical theory. They still have to start from somewhere, and the only starting point left is ethical experience itself.

"Ethical experience" can cover many things. There could be a way of doing moral philosophy that started from the ways in which we experience our ethical life. Such a philosophy would reflect on what we believe, feel, take for granted; the ways in which we confront obligations and recognize responsibility; the sentiments of guilt and shame. It would involve a phenomenology of the ethical life. This could be a good philosophy, but it would be unlikely to yield an ethical theory. Ethical theories, with their concern for tests, tend to start from just one aspect of ethical experience, beliefs. The natural understanding of an ethical theory takes it as a structure of propositions, which, like a scientific theory, in part provides a framework for our beliefs, in part criticizes or revises them. So it starts from our beliefs, though it may replace them.

Those initial ethical beliefs are often called in current philosophy *intuitions*, but that term no longer carries quite the implications it once did. Intuition used to be taken as an intellectual power of arriving at abstract truths, and its application to ethics lay in the idea that ethical truths could be grasped *a priori* by such a faculty. The philosophers who used this model[1] differed on various questions: what concepts occurred in the truths given by intuition (whether it was to be goodness or obligation, for example); whether those truths were very particular or very general. But in using the notion of intuition, they all supposed that the way in which we grasped those ethical truths was significantly like the way in which we grasp mathematical and other necessary truths. The ethical truths grasped by intuition could provide a starting point for ethical theory, if there was to be ethical theory, but not all believers in intuition in fact wanted ethical theory, since intuition itself was supposed to provide the test or, rather, make tests unnecessary.

This model of intuition in ethics has been demolished by a succession of critics,[2] and the ruins of it that remain above ground are not impressive enough to invite much history of what happened to it. The charges, briefly put, were that it failed to explain how an eternal truth could provide a practical consideration, and that it was wrong in assimilating ethical truths to necessities. If necessary truths such as those of mathematics were seemingly denied by informants from another culture, one would naturally look in the first instance for a better translator, but the situation with ethical beliefs is not at all like that. Above all, the appeal to intuition as a faculty explained nothing. It seemed to say that these truths were known, but there was no way in which they were known. "Intuition" is not much of an explanation when it is applied to what are necessary truths, but with ethical beliefs it is worse, for reasons that once more have to do with cultural disagreement. Little as we know about it, we already know too much about the explanation of ethical beliefs and their cultural differences to accept a model that says there is not going to be any such explanation.

So intuition in ethics, as a faculty, is no more. But *intuitions* — the beliefs which, when there was supposed to be a faculty, were supposedly given by it — are very much part of the subject. These are spontaneous convictions, moderately reflective but not yet theorized, about the answer to some ethical question, usually hypothetical and couched in general terms. They are often questions about what to do. "What should you do if you could, by switching the points, divert a runaway trolley from one line, where it would certainly kill three old men, to another line on which it would certainly kill one child and a gifted violinist?" This example is not much more fantastic than some that have been offered.[3] But intuitions do not have to be expressed in answers to questions about what to do. Some may be found in our willingness to apply to some imagined situation one of those more substantive ethical concepts, such as those picking out virtues or types of action, that were mentioned in Chapter 1.

There is an analogy that has encouraged the revival of the term "intuition" in these connections. This is its use in linguistics and the philosophy of language to refer to a speaker's spontaneous grasp of what can and cannot be said in his language, or of what can be correctly said in a particular kind of situation. A competent English speaker has the intuition that it is not correct — that is, it is not English — to say (as I once heard an emigré philosopher of language say), "In English we are not using the present continuous to signify a custom or practice." Such intuitions are the raw material of a theory of a natural language. We have good reason to believe that it should be possible to form such a theory, giving an account of the rules that have been internalized by the speaker, just because the speaker can unhesitatingly recognize as correct or incorrect in his language sentences he has never heard before. As Noam Chomsky has emphasized, we do this all the time. Moreover, some theorists, notably Chomsky, believe that since any human being can learn as a child any human language, there are grounds for expecting there to be a theory of rules underlying all natural languages, a universal grammar.

How does this linguistic conception of an intuition apply to ethics? There is one kind of intuition relevant to ethics that certainly fits the model, since it is merely an application of it. In the case of the substantive terms for virtues and kinds of action, there is room for linguistic intuitions about the situations they apply to, just because they are general terms in the language with complex conditions of application. (What ethical consequences, if any, follow from people's capacity to use such terms, differing as they do between one culture and another, is something we shall come to in Chapters 8 and 9.) With terms of this kind there will be disputes about their application at the margin, and these may carry serious practical consequences. They are disputes of the kind familiar in the law, where the issue may be whether a given act constituted theft, for instance. Legal theorists disagree about the exact nature of disputes of that kind and how they are properly decided, so-called legal realists allowing a larger and more explicit role for policy considerations in the decision of hard cases — but all are agreed that there has to be a shared understanding of some core or central cases to make these disputes about hard cases possible. To some extent this must be equally so within the less formal structures of the ethical discussions that involve these substantive terms.

In some traditions great weight is laid on this legalistic strain in ethical thought. It is encouraging to objectivist views of ethics, since the core cases are given in an understanding of these ethical terms, and their application to hard cases, though it is a contentious and ethically fraught matter, is constrained by rational criteria of what is and what is not an adequate similarity to the core cases. There can be rational discussion whether a given extension of the term properly bears the spirit or underlying principle of its application to the core cases. Arguments in this style are, in the Catholic tradition, known as arguments of casuistry (the unfriendly use of that term was a deserved reaction to devious uses made of the technique). The trouble with casuistry, if it is seen as the basic process of ethical thought, is not so much its misuse as the obvious fact that the repertory of substantive ethical concepts differs between cultures, changes over time, and is open to criticism. If casuistry, applied to a given local set of concepts, is to be the central process of ethical thought, it needs more explanation. It has to claim that there are preferred ethical categories that are not purely local. They may be said to come from a theory of human nature; in this form, the explanation leads us back to the concerns of Chapter 3. They may be said to be given by divine command or revelation; in this form, if it is not combined with the grounding in human nature, the explanation will not lead us anywhere except into what Spinoza called "the asylum of ignorance." An exponent of the casuistical method could perhaps fall back simply on the idea that the categories we prefer are the ones we have inherited. This has the merit of facing an important truth, but it will not be able to face it *in* truth unless more is said about ways in which those categories might be criticized.

When we turn away from the use of substantial ethical terms, and merely consider such things as people's answers to questions about the ethically right thing to do in certain situations, the analogy seems much slighter between, on the one hand, the ability to give "intuitive" (assured and unprompted) answers to these questions and, on the other hand, linguistic competence. The ability to give ethical answers does indeed require some explanation. The presented cases are not exactly like previous cases, and the respondent must have internalized something that enables him or her to respond to the new cases. But it is not obvious what that may be. In particular, it is not obvious that it must be a principle, in the sense of a summary and discursively stateable description that does not rely too much on vague references to degree ("too much," "balances out," "does not pay enough attention to . . ."). In fact there is a dispute in the philosophy of language, to what extent linguistic competence itself, particularly on the semantic side, can be captured in some set of stateable rules. In the ethical case, inasmuch as the problem is seen as the explanatory problem of representing people's ability to make judgments about new cases, we do not need to suppose that there is some clear discursive rule underlying that capacity. Aristotle supposed that there was no such rule and that a kind of inexplicit judgment was essentially involved, an ability that a group of people similarly brought up would share of seeing certain cases as like certain others.

This is what followers of Wittgenstein are disposed to believe about all human learning. At some eventual level they must be right: understanding a summary discursive rule would itself involve a shared appreciation of similarities. But this conception of the ability to arrive at shared ethical judgments (and the same thing is going to apply to other kinds of practical judgment as well) goes further than that. It is not merely that the ability to use language requires a shared capacity to see similarities, but that the capacity to see ethical similarities goes beyond anything that can adequately be expressed in language. This is surely true, and it is what Wittgensteinians would predict. It does not mean, however (Wittgensteinians themselves are not always very clear about this) that there is no explanation, at any level, of these human dispositions. All it means is that the explanation does not lie in postulating a stateable rule, which the respondent has internalized and unconsciously consults. Inasmuch as we are concerned at an explanatory level with the ability to respond to new cases, we should not necessarily expect to elicit a rule underlying that ability.

The analogy between ethical and linguistic intuitions seems very weak if one considers the conflict of intuitions. When in the linguistic case there is a conflict between the intuitions of two different people, we recognize that there are two different (if only trivially different) dialects; if one person has conflicting intuitions, this represents an uncertainty that may arise because the answer about what to say in the given case is underdetermined by the language, or perhaps because the speaker has been trained in two dialects. In none of these cases is the theory of the language required to *resolve* the conflict. Linguistic theory will resolve some conflicts, for its own purposes. Indeed, it resolves some conflicts in arriving even at the idealized notion of an intuition, since observation of performance, of how people actually speak, reveals many incoherences due to the conditions of speech, and these are smoothed out in the conception of an intuition as a reflective answer to a question about the language. (Linguistic theorists disagree about the extent to which this is legitimate.) Moreover, it is certainly appropriate for a theory, having formed a principle on the strength of some intuitions, to discount other and conflicting intuitions. To discount them is to regard them as anomalies of performance, for instance, or, again, as yielding a fact about the language that has to be entered into the lexicon as a singularity, without being connected to any general principle. These notions are themselves theoretical devices for dealing with such conflicts.

It is not like this with ethical intuitions. A lot turns on what outlook is to be adopted, and an ethically idiosyncratic outlook will not simply be left alone, inasmuch as it touches on any matters of importance or on the interests of others. Here the aim of theory is not simply, or even primarily, to understand conflict. We have other ways, historical and sociological, of understanding it. The aim of theory is rather to resolve it, in the more radical sense that it should give some compelling reason to accept one intuition rather than another. The question we have to consider is: How can any ethical theory have the authority to do that?

There is one answer to the question that, under some very strong assumptions, makes sense. Let us assume that there are some people who, first, are resolved to reach agreement on important ethical questions, and indeed are more strongly resolved to reach agreement than they are to express different ethical conceptions of the world. They are irreversibly committed to living closely together in one society.[4] Moreover, it is agreement that they are resolved to reach, and they would not be content to end up with the mere domination of one set of beliefs. Next, they see this as a task that requires them to arrive at publicly stateable principles. Last, they want this process to govern the discussion of problems that will arise later from the principles they agree upon, such as conflicts between them. In these circumstances, it is reasonable for them to aim at an ethical theory, and it is also reasonable for them to use a method that tries to save as many of their intuitions as possible, while at the same time it produces a rational structure of principles that will help to make clear what intuitions have to be dropped or modified. An obvious way to do this is to modify theory and intuitions reciprocally until they roughly fit one another. The aims I have just mentioned are, of course, the aims of a contractual theory such as Rawls's, and the method is the one that Rawls recommends, the method of trying to arrive at what he calls *reflective equilibrium* between theory and intuition.[5]

The method is appropriate to constructing an ethical theory under these assumptions, but it is very important how strong these assumptions are. They involve beliefs about what people are like and the ways in which societies can work — *can* work, rather than do work, since it may be that no society has yet worked as the theory requires, but it is essential to the undertaking that it should at least be possible. The assumptions also involve certain ideals, and this type of theory, correspondingly, starts doubly within the ethical world. It not only sets out from the assumption that those involved aspire to be in some ethical world, but it also brings to its task aspirations for one kind of ethical world rather than others. (We saw this in Chapter 5, in the attitude that Rawls's contracting parties implicitly have toward slavery.)

The factual and the ideal are interestingly related in these assumptions. On the one hand, there are assumptions that apply to any society; on the other, there are ideals for a better or more rational society. In between there is a significant, if not clearly defined, area of conditions that apply to a certain kind of society — summarily put, a modern society, where that is to some extent an ethical conception and not merely a historical one.

The first assumption of Rawls's procedure involves one element that must apply to any society, that it should have some degree of homogeneous belief and some ways of resolving conflicts that carry authority and avoid violence. It goes much beyond that minimum condition, however, in aiming at a society where those ways consist overwhelmingly of consensual discussion. This is not a social necessity, and here the question is not whether societies are like this, but whether any could be. In these respects the model is *liberal.* Moreover, it is *rationalistic,* in its requirement that the society represent its values in a set of stateable principles. Once more, it is not a necessity that a society represent its values in that way, and it is again a question whether it could. This aspiration goes a step further than the minimum assumptions of liberalism. It involves not merely the aspiration to consensual discussion, but a rationalistic conception of what consensual discussion is, a conception characteristic of modern societies, or at least of philosophical and sociological representations of them.

It is a further step again, and a development beyond what may be called *expository* rationalism, to insist that conflicts in the society's principles should be resolved by the same kind of procedure. Having taken the first rationalistic step, one might rest with principles that were indeed discursively stated but not systematically ordered. The further requirement is that there should also be a rationalistic decision procedure, a method for resolving conflicts that can itself be discursively laid out. It is this requirement that issues in an ethical theory in the fullest sense. This rejects an approach that has also been called, in a sense different from that considered before, "intuitionism," an approach that offers a set of principles or ethical considerations but allows that conflicts between them, at least beyond a certain point, can be settled only by judgment in the particular case. Many ethical theorists believe that it is reason itself that makes these demands, to go beyond intuitionism into a more fully articulated ethical theory. They think that what I have called rationalism simply follows from being rational.

One important element in these undertakings, and in ethical theory when it is motivated in this way, is the aspiration that society should be *transparent,* in the sense that the working of its ethical institutions should not depend on members of the community misunderstanding how they work.[6] This demand, adopted explicitly by Rawls, fits naturally with liberal contractualism, but it is one that is also made more widely. It marks the distinction not so much between liberals and nonliberals as between any who retain more radical hopes born of the Enlightenment and those who do not. Many Marxist theories embody a version of this, in the aim for a society that can do without false consciousness. This conception can help to sharpen a radical critique. It can be a useful question, for instance, how far accepted relations between the sexes depend upon an imposed ignorance and misunderstanding. Radical critics sometimes press such a question in a spirit of indignant circularity, denouncing a false consciousness that consists (it turns out) in not accepting their ideology. When the critique is used more effectively than that, it will offer other reasons for saying that there is imposed ignorance; the claim that it is ignorance, and the claim that it is imposed, will be to some extent independent of accepting the ideology of the critic. This is, in many interesting cases, a hard condition to meet, but there are also cases in which there is nothing very sophisticated about it: the falsehood of the bad social arrangements is merely falsehood — lies, humbug, polluted speech — just as their cruelty and brutality are often no more than cruelty and brutality.

The aspiration to transparency comes in various forms, some

more ambitious than others. I shall not try to discuss here the questions they raise.[7] One significant point is that while transparency is a natural associate of liberalism, it falls short of implying rationalism. It is one aspiration, that social and ethical relations should not essentially rest on ignorance and misunderstanding of what they are, and quite another that all the beliefs and principles involved in them should be explicitly stated. That these are two different things is obvious with personal relations, where to hope that they do not rest on deceit and error is merely decent, but to think that their basis can be made totally explicit is idiocy.

If it proceeds in this spirit and under these assumptions, the contractualist enterprise is coherent, and so is its use of intuitions in trying to reach a reflective equilibrium. All of this leaves open large questions of how those assumptions are related to reality, how a society would be held together under that degree of self-conscious ethical understanding, and for what actual societies it represents a reasonable aspiration. (I hope these might be, in some part, questions for social science, but it is not clear that any social science has yet given us much help in answering them.)

It is sometimes objected against the method of reflective equilibrium that the intuitions to which theory is being adjusted merely represent our local ethical beliefs, and that those may not be correct. When the enterprise is taken in the way I have described, this is not a relevant objection. The intuitions are supposed to represent our ethical beliefs, because the theory being sought is one of ethical life *for us,* and the point is not that the intuitions should be in some ultimate sense correct, but that they should be ours. Moreover, not only the intuitions that shape and are shaped by the theory are ours, but so are the aspirations that motivate such a theory in the first place.

Still, a problem remains in the method even when one grants its assumptions, and that problem may perhaps be what someone has in mind who raises the question whether the intuitions it endorses are "actually correct." The problem is who *we* are. In describing the theory I have referred to "a society," and it is fairly clear what this means when we are thinking about a contractual theory that is in the first place a theory of social justice. But ethical concerns go beyond such boundaries, as Rawls of course recognizes, and when we turn our attention beyond a possible political order, any concrete conception of a society dissolves; the theory reaches out to that "natural constituency," as I have called it, of everyone who might be subject to an ethical agreement: any moral agent, as the theory might put it. We are led back to the original, Kantian, universalistic concerns of such a theory.

In one way, those concerns fit well with the spirit of the contractualist enterprise and the assumptions I have just described. Its liberal and rationalistic aspirations draw the boundaries outward to include, beyond those with whom we effectively have to make an agreement, those with whom it would be ethically desirable to make an agreement, and ultimately anyone who might exist and with whom we might conceivably make an agreement — the class of rational agents, the citizenry of the notional republic. But in the course of this process two connected things happen. We can less and less appropriately rely on those intuitions that belong distinctively to the local *we,* since the theory is now to be a theory for an *us* that includes agents existing far away from our local folkways. For the same reason, there is less and less to rely on when we try to think out what the ethical theory might contain. In the terms of Scanlon's formula, quoted in Chapter 5, there is an ever thinner basis for deciding what set of rules some agent might "reasonably reject." At the end, there is nothing to bring to that question except, once more, the conception of what any rational agent as such must reject, and this conception is very indeterminate. What the "freedom" of Chapter 4 might yield more specifically, under immense possible differences in bodily constitution, in sentiment, and generally in what Wittgensteinians call "form of life," is a baffling question.

It is so baffling that one must wonder whether it is the right question to ask. If the model is that of coexistence with creatures very different from us, why should that lead us to imagine a universal republic rather than a confederation or — less than that and most appropriately of all — a mere nonaggression treaty? The most schematic code against interference and mutual destruction may be enough for parties who merely have a shared requirement to live, not a requirement to share a life. If that schematic code were taken to provide all the ethical substance of a shared life, it would yield too little: the shared life needs more than a bare defensive individualism. It would be inappropriate to read it back in that way. But then it follows that the universalistic perspective will not determine the content of the ethical theory for a given group, and indeed it will become a question not only whether different ethical content may not be appropriate to different groups, but also how far the liberal and rationalistic assumptions of the contractualist theory are themselves appropriate for determining the content of ethical life for each group.

This was originally a Hegelian problem. Hegel admirably criticized the "abstract" Kantian morality and contrasted it with the notion of *Sittlichkeit,* a concretely determined ethical existence that was expressed in the local folkways, a form of life that made particular sense to the people living in it. The conception inevitably raises the question of how local the view of those folkways can properly remain, and whether they cannot be criticized, ranked, or transcended. Hegel's answer to those questions lay in appealing to a teleological conception of history, as involving the growth of self-consciousness. Few will now trust that, except for the more extravagantly optimistic Marxists who still accept a materialist version of it. But the Hegelian problem is the right problem at least to this extent: it asks how a concretely experienced form of life can be extended, rather than considering how a universal program is to be applied. Moreover, conceptions of self-consciousness are still very relevant to the problem.[8]

Contractual ethical theory cannot provide the basic method of understanding ethics, because it needs itself to be understood. If applied too widely, it does not give any, or enough, results; applied too narrowly, it insistently raises the question of the special conditions required to make it appropriate. There may be circumstances in which aspirations for a better world would most effectively be expressed through the project of thinking about ethical life in terms of a contractual theory—but if there are, the general idea of such a theory cannot by itself tell us what they are.

Turning away from the complexities of contractualism, we see in another direction utilitarianism, seemingly so simple that it may, from this angle, look attractive. It does not have a problem about how far out to go from the folkways, since it has from the start already gone all the way. It does not have a problem of what, having gone so far, we should take into account: it has already told us what alone we should take into account (even if there turns out to be more in the fine print than we expected.) Moreover, it is not bothered, at least at this grand and simple level, with reflective adjustment to intuitions. It sets intuitions aside.

However, while utilitarianism at this level does not waste time fiddling with our more specific intuitions, it should not be thought to rest on no ethical intuitions at all. It rests on two. One of them was well expressed by Henry Sidgwick in his densely argued book *The Methods of Ethics,* in making this very point, that utilitarianism requires at least one intuition:

> I obtain the self-evident principle that the good of any one individual is of no more importance, from the point of view (if I may say so) of the Universe, than the good of any other . . . and it is evident to me that as a rational being I am bound to aim at good generally — so far as it is attainable by my efforts — not merely at a particular part of it.[9]

Sidgwick's self-evident principle is offered as a principle of practical rationality; Hare expresses a similar principle in linguistic form. But it seems clear that what is in question is an ethical principle, and (leaving aside a purely egoistic rejection of it) disagreement will be ethical disagreement. But utilitarianism needs another principle as well, that there are no other basic ethical considerations besides that first one. This, too, is an ethical intuition, and the disagreement it will certainly arouse in many people is, once more, ethical disagreement.

Light can be made to fall on the second principle in such a way that it appears not as an ethical assumption, but as a requirement of theoretical rationality: the principle of simplicity, that assumptions should be made as economically as possible. But this view of it misunderstands, in the first place, the principle of simplicity itself. It is a good idea to make the minimal assumption, one that gives the most economical explanation, but this is not necessarily the same as an assumption of the minimum. The most effective set of assumptions need not be the shortest. A mistake of this kind has been part of the history of empiricism, which works from the assumption that the mind, before any experience, is empty. This assumes a minimal contents of the mind, but in relation to what needs to be explained, it is not a minimal assumption — on the contrary, it involves elaborate and very implausible explanations about evolution and human learning. Similarly, the fact that utilitarianism starts out with so little luggage provides no presumption *at all* in its favor. The question can only be whether it has enough luggage for the journey it must make.

In any case, there is a fundamental question still to be answered about the journey. Why should theoretical simplicity and its criteria be appropriate? Whether they are must surely depend on what an ethical theory is for. Sidgwick, for one, seems sometimes simply to assume the aim of throwing "the morality of commonsense into a scientific form," and it is revealing of his outlook tht he asked "if we are not to systematize human activities by taking universal happiness as their common end, on what principles are we to systematize them?"[10] Some later theorists have also unquestioningly assumed that an ethical system should try to have the same virtues as a scientific theory.

I shall come back to that question. First we must look more closely at ways in which theory, and in particular utilitarian theory, may be related to the "morality of commonsense." It is important that, for utilitarian theorists, systematizing everyday attitudes and dispositions does not necessarily mean replacing them. Theory may sometimes justify those attitudes; moreover, it may sometimes do this even if the attitudes are not themselves utilitarian in spirit. Sidgwick saw that it must be an empirical question what motivations lead to the greatest good; in particular, whether the practice of thinking about the greatest good is likely to lead to the greatest good. The utilitarian consciousness itself becomes an item about which it must think, and Sidgwick came to the conclusion that in many departments of life it should not be too much encouraged. He hoped to save utilitarianism from the old charge that it led to a denial of all natural affections and the stifling of impulse and spontaneity in the interests of a calculative spirit directed toward universal good. (This charge had been originally invited by Godwin, more than anyone else, with his ferociously rational refusal to respect any consideration that an ordinary human being would find compelling.) Sidgwick offered a utilitarian account of many dispositions that are usually thought to have intrinsic or nonutilitarian value. The values of justice, truthtelling, spontaneous affection, loyalty to your friends, a special concern for your own children, and so forth, might seem to involve an outlook that the thoroughgoing utilitarian would not endorse. But, Sidgwick insisted, you must consider the utilitarian value of those values, in the sense of the value of the state of affairs in which people have those values. If you do that, the utilitarian justification will extend much further than had been supposed.

Hare's utilitarianism is similarly indirect. The processes of extensive sympathetic identification are not, for him, a feature of all moral thinking, but only of what he calls "critical" thinking. Most of the time we think at a different, "intuitive," level, where we do not try to work out the complex effects of actions, but rely on schematic and simple principles that have been acquired in childhood. These are not merely rules of thumb, to be laid aside in a particular case if it seems appropriate. They are strongly internalized, and one will depart from them only with the "greatest repugnance," while their violation by others arouses "the highest indignation."[11] The basic reason for this second level of moral thought is that we are not in a position to make the elaborate calculations of critical thinking in everyday situations, and if we try to do so, we are more than likely to get them wrong, particularly through bias in our own favor. These facts, and the consequent value of intuitive thinking, can be recognized from the standpoint of critical thinking. Critical thinking, itself utilitarian, can reach the conclusion, as Sidgwick did, that one does not maximize utility by thinking, most of the time, as a utilitarian.

These styles of indirect utilitarianism involve a special view of the dispositions that are exercised at the everyday or intuitive level; and this raises a serious question: Is there anywhere in the mind or in society that a theory of this kind can be coherently or acceptably located? The theory finds a value for these dispositions, but it is still an instrumental value. The dispositions are seen as devices for generating certain actions, and those actions are the means by which certain states of affairs, yielding the most welfare, come about. This is what those dispositions look like when seen from outside, from the point of view of the utilitarian consciousness. But it is not what they seem from the inside. Indeed, the utilitarian argument implies that they should *not* seem like that from the inside. The dispositions help to form the character of an agent who has them, and they will do the job the theory has given them only if the agent does not see his character purely instrumentally, but sees the world from the point of view of that character. Moreover, the dispositions require the agent to see other things in a noninstrumental way. They are dispositions not simply of action, but of feeling and judgment, and they are expressed precisely in ascribing intrinsic and not instrumental value to such things as truthtelling, loyalty, and so on.

There is a deeply uneasy gap or dislocation in this type of theory, between the spirit of the theory itself and the spirit it supposedly justifies. There is a distinction that is supposed to bridge the gap or, rather, make us accept it: the distinction between theory and practice. But when one asks whose theory is in question, and whose practice, the distinction turns out to have very little power. For Sidgwick, as for many others in the past, the distinction determined two classes of people, one of them a class of theorists who could responsibly handle the utilitarian justification of nonutilitarian dispositions, the other a class who unreflectively deployed those dispositions. This outlook, which accords well with the important colonialist connections of utilitarianism, may be called "Government House utilitarianism." It has some striking consequences, which Sidgwick himself pursued with masochistic thoroughness. There was the question, for instance, of how much should be divulged. Enlightened utilitarians might be able to live by "refined and complicated" rules that admitted exceptions to everyday practice, but others could not, and trying to introduce those rules might "do more harm by weakening current morality than good by improving its quality." So utilitarians must consider seriously how much publicity they should give to "either advice or example":

> Thus, on Utilitarian principles, it may be right to do and privately recommend, under certain circumstances, what it would not be right to advocate openly; it may be right to teach openly to one set of persons what it would be wrong to teach to others; it may be conceivably right to do, if it can be done with comparative secrecy, what it would be wrong to do in the face of the world.

He recognizes that these are likely to be seen as shocking conclusions; but then it is for the best that most people should continue to see them as shocking. "The Utilitarian conclusion would seem to be this," Sidgwick concludes with a certain dry relish, "that the opinion that secrecy may render an action right which would not otherwise be so should itself be kept comparatively secret; and similarly it seems expedient that the doctrine that esoteric morality is expedient should itself be kept esoteric."[12]

Government House utilitarianism is indifferent to the values of social transparency I mentioned when discussing contractualism. It is an outlook that nowadays is likely to do better in practice than in overt theory (something it presumably has no reason to regret). Current versions of indirect utilitarianism, such as Hare's, usually identify the distinction between theory and practice in psychological rather than social terms. They distinguish between the *time* of theorizing and the *time* of practice, and use Bishop Butler's notion of the "cool hour" in which the philosophically disposed moralist reflects on his own principles and practice.[13] There are equally severe difficulties with this version. It is artificial to suppose that a thorough commitment to the values of friendship and so on can merely alternate, on a timetable prescribed by calm or activity, with an alien set of reflections. Moreover, since the reflections are indeed alien, some kind of willed forgetting is needed, an internal surrogate of those class barriers on which Sidgwick relied, to keep the committed dispositions from being unnerved by instrumental reflection when they are under pressure.

Government House utilitarianism had at least the merit of one kind of realism, inasmuch as it tried to find the theory an actual social location. It placed it in a particular body of people, the utilitarian elite (though it had a deluded idea of what such people might be like in reality.) Some versions of indirect utilitarianism fail to provide any location at all for the theory. They treat it as transcendental to life, existing in a space quite outside the practice it is supposed to regulate or justify. In the psychological version, the temptation to do this is found in a certain picture of the time of theory: it is an hour in which the agent leaves himself and sees everything, including his own dispositions, from the point of view of the universe and then, returning, takes up practical life. But any actual process of theorizing of that sort would have to be part of life, itself a particular kind of practice. One cannot separate, except by an imposed and illusory dissociation, the theorist in oneself from the self whose dispositions are being theorized. In the case of indirect utilitarianism, this dissociation helps to disguise a particular difficulty, the conflict between the view the theorist has of these dispositions and the view of the world he has from those dispositions.

Other difficulties arise from any attempt to see philosophical reflection in ethics as a jump to the universalistic standpoint in search of a justification, which is then brought back to everyday practice. They arise even if one requires the justification to be consistent in spirit with what is justified, as contractualism typically does and indirect utilitarianism does not. Any such picture makes in some degree a Platonic assumption that the reflective agent as theorist can make himself independent from the life and character he is examining. The belief that you can look critically at all your dispositions from the outside, from the point of view of the universe, assumes that you could understand your own and other people's dispositions from that point of view without tacitly taking for granted a picture of the world more locally familiar than any that would be available from there; but neither the psychology nor the history of ethical reflection gives much reason to believe that the theoretical reasonings of the cool hour can do without a sense of the moral shape of the world, of the kind given in the everyday dispositions.

What are the attractions of these pictures? What is the pressure toward such theoretical structures? Some of the motivations may be very metaphysical and general, lying for instance in the idea that we consider the world as it really is only when we see it from the outside, *sub specie aeternitatis.* Some of the rational dignity ascribed to trying to see the ethical world from that point of view seems to derive from some such conception of objectivity. There is disagreement in philosophy whether that is a possible view of the world even for science: whether we can, in any ultimate or even very radical sense, detach ourselves from our perspectives on the world to gain what I have elsewhere called an "absolute conception" of it.[14] But, even if it is a proper ambition for science to strive toward such a conception (I shall argue later that it is), this would not make it an attractive or appropriate place in which to rest our ethical consciousness.

In part, this is because of the differences between practical and theoretical reason. In part, it is because the scientific understanding of the world is not only entirely consistent with recognizing that we occupy no special position in it, but also incorporates, now, that recognition.[15] The aim of ethical thought, however, is to help us to construct a world that will be our world, one in which we have a social, cultural, and personal life. That does not mean that we should forget that the natural world is not designed as our home, and some of the stonier expressions of the timeless view, such as Spinoza's, have been devoted to the proper end of getting us to remember that truth and its significance. But this does not mean that it is the proper perspective of ethical thought itself. If it were, we should be strictly committed to thinking about our ethical life not only from that perspective, but using only the concepts available within it. That is certainly impossible. Those concepts are, roughly, the concepts of physics, and it is an unsolved problem how much even of the psychological vocabulary could possess that absolute character.

These metaphysical images may encourage some ethical theory. But the drive to theory has roots in ethical thought itself. For many, it is as if reason itself drew ethical thought in the direction of theory and systematization. To understand properly the hold of theory on ethics, we have to see why that should be so. The important question at this point is why reflection should be taken to require theory. It is too late at this stage to raise the prior question "why reflection?"—too late in terms of this inquiry, since Socrates was given the initiative in Chapter 1 (or at least given the loan of it), and always too late in terms of the question itself, since one could answer it without prejudice only by not considering it. But it is quite wrong to think that the only alternative to ethical theory is to refuse reflection and to remain in unreflective prejudice. Theory and prejudice are not the only possibilities for an intelligent agent, or for philosophy.

What sorts of reflection on ethical life naturally encourage theory? Not all of them do. There is reflection that asks for understanding of our motives, psychological or social insight into our ethical practices, and while that may call for some kinds of theory, ethical theory is not among them. Nor is it merely that this kind of reflection is explanatory, while that which calls for ethical theory is critical. Much explanatory reflection is itself critical, simply in revealing that certain practices or sentiments are not what they are taken to be. This is one of the most effective kinds of critical reflection. It is a different kind of critical reflection that leads to ethical theory, one that seeks *justificatory reasons.* "There cannot any one moral rule be propos'd, whereof a Man may not justly demand a Reason," Locke said,[16] and this maxim, understood in a certain way, naturally leads to theory.

Many people draw a distinction between killing an early fetus and killing a newborn child. Not everyone does. A good many people, in particular Catholics, equate abortion with infanticide and regard both as evil. A very few people equate infanticide with abortion and see both as permitted. In the modern world, the latter seem to consist mostly of enthusiasts for ethical theory,[17] together no doubt with some tough administrators in overcrowded countries. Parents driven by necessity to kill their babies do not, because of that, see the two things as the same. Closely related, though not often mentioned in discussions of abortion, is the fact that few women see a spontaneous abortion or early miscarriage as the same thing as having a child who is stillborn or who dies very soon after birth. For many people, then, the distinction between a fetus and an infant carries enough weight to give a reason in the matter of killing, and for almost everyone it carries enough weight to give a reason for different attitudes in the matter of death. This is one example of a distinction that gives many people a reason. But there is something else for which no reason has yet been given but for which, on one interpretation of Locke's maxim, those people may justly be asked to give a reason. This is their practice of using that distinction as a reason. How do they justify it?

At this point, where a reason is demanded for a given practice of reason-giving, the range of possible answers gets much narrower. There are few considerations that could give an answer, and they already begin to look like the kinds of consideration (welfare, possible contractual agreement) that can figure in an ethical theory. Or if the reasons at this level are not yet of this kind, then the reasons at the next level will be, for the process of course goes on. At the end, if this linear search for reasons is pursued, there will have to be at least one practice of reason-giving for which no reason is given and which holds itself up.[18] Looked at in one way, this result may encourage the simplification principle I mentioned before: if having an unrationalized principle is irrational, it is good to have as little irrationality as possible. Others of a different temper will wonder why, if we are bound to end up with some unjustified reason-giving practice, we should not end up with several. Once we see that it is impossible to rationalize everything, the project of rationalizing as much as possible need not be understood as doing the next best thing. We may conclude instead that we were looking in the wrong direction.

There is not much point, however, in discussing what attitude we should take to the results of this linear model, since the model itself is wrong. No process of reason-giving fits this picture, in the sciences or elsewhere. In theoretical connections, the foundationalist enterprise, of resting the structure of knowledge on some favored class of statements, has now generally been displaced in favor of a holistic type of model, in which some beliefs can be questioned, justified, or adjusted while others are kept constant, but there is no process by which they can all be questioned at once, or all justified in terms of (almost) nothing. In von Neurath's famous image, we repair the ship while we are on the sea.

When we give up the linear model, we might still be left with the possibility that for every practice there is some reason; what we shall have lost is the possibility that there should be some one reason for everything. In the case of ethics, however, even the weaker requirement, that there should be some reason or other for each practice, will have to be taken in some very undemanding way if we expect it to be met. We may be able to show how a given practice hangs together with other practices in a way that makes social and psychological sense. But we may not be able to find anything that will meet a demand for justification made by someone standing outside those practices. We may not be able, in any real sense, to justify it even to ourselves. A practice may be so directly related to our experience that the reason it provides will simply count as stronger than any reason that might be advanced for it.

This is illustrated by some attempts of theorists to replace the categories that give us reasons with others that are supposed to have better systematic credentials. Thus Michael Tooley, the theorist who wants to get us used to the idea of infanticide, urges the category of *person* as the operative notion in these kinds of questions: certain duties are owed just to persons; infants fall out of the favored class at one end, and the senile fall out at the other. This engaging proposal is investing in a deceptive concept. The category of person, though a lot has been made of it in some moral philosophy, is a poor foundation for ethical thought, in particular because it looks like a sortal or classificatory notion while in fact it signals characteristics that almost all come in degrees — responsibility, self-consciousness, capacity for reflection, and so on. It thus makes it seem as if we were dealing with a certain class or type of creature, when in fact we are vaguely considering those human beings who pass some mark on a scale.[19] To make matters worse, the pass mark for some purposes is unsuitable for others. If *person* implies something called "full moral responsibility," the lowest age for entry to the class that has traditionally been entertained is seven, but anyone who has lived with a six-year-old, or a two-year-old, has vivid reasons for thinking of them as persons. Not even Tooley regards them as prepersonal enough to license their being killed.

The defects of *person* as a theoretical category represent a failing in that particular proposal, but they also illustrate failings in the theoretical enterprise more generally. How can we come to see the weaknesses of a theoretical concept except by reference to the every-day distinctions it is supposed to replace or justify, and by a sense of the life it is supposed to help us to lead? So far from having some special authority because of their belonging to a theory, these con-ceptions, in relation to what they are required to do, are likely to be more arbitrary than those they are supposed to replace.

If theory is going to turn out to be a product of *reason itself,* which is the claim I am considering, then it will not do so because every reason requires a reason. Can it be in some other way a product of the demand for rationality? Nothing that has been said should lead us to think that traditional distinctions are beyond criticism; practices that make distinctions between different groups of people may certainly demand justification, if we are not to be content with unreflective traditions which can provide paradigms of prejudice. Those prejudices seem simply irrational; rationality requires them to be criticized and, if not justified, removed; their criticism requires a reason for those discriminations. If this is car-ried far enough, how can it, after all, avoid ethical theory?

The first question is how far what is wrong in such practices is wrong because it is *irrational.* It is wrong, because unjust, to treat blacks or women unfavorably by comparison to whites or men, and when the practices are enforced, it is often cruel as well. It may be said that it is irrational because it is inconsistent. Reasons are not being applied equally, and that offends against a formal principle of universalizability. But this is rarely what is wrong, and if anything is irrational in these matters, this is rarely what it is. The formal and uncontentious principle of universalizability is what I called earlier the "enough is enough" principle, which says that if a certain con-sideration is truly a sufficient reason for a certain action in one case, it is so in another. But discrimination and prejudice can be run on that basis. Someone who counts *being a woman* as in itself a reason for discriminatory treatment is not offending against the "enough is enough" principle merely in doing that. He does offend against it, and is being inconsistent and irrational, if he counts intelligence and reliability as supposedly sufficient grounds for hiring a man and refuses to do so when considering a woman; but he would avoid those charges, at least, if he made it clear that the grounds in the first case were actually that the candidate was intelligent, reliable, and a man. Of course he would be no more just if he put his reasons in this open way, but he would be consistent.

There is another way in which this person may indeed be irrational. Counting *being a man* as a reason may make no sense in the context of what he is doing—in this case, hiring in a job market someone to do a job effectively. Or if it makes sense on some very narrow construction of what he is doing, it makes less sense when he thinks beyond that construction and considers the merits of calling in aid the prejudices of others which are no better than his own. (He may say that he does not dare or cannot afford to go against those prejudices: but then his reason is a different one.) This kind of irrationality is not exposed or cured by invoking an ethical theory, but by getting him to reflect on what he is doing. As before, this may well require some theoretical understandings of other kinds, and it will involve other values.

The investigation of what someone who discriminates is really doing is all the more forceful, and still more removed from ethical theory, in the more usual case where the person practicing it does not admit that "he's black" or "she's a woman" is his reason. Rationalization takes the place of overt discrimination, and some reason will be proferred that may well be relevant but is believed solely because it suits the purpose. This once more is irrationality, and of a deep form, but it is an irrationality of belief, of self-deception, of social deceit, rather than any that lies in resisting the drive of an ethical theory. It is in such areas that the study of irrationality in social practice should lie, and it demands inquiries more detailed and substantive than the schematic considerations of philosophical theory.

The main consequence that this discussion has for ethical argument is that reflective criticism should basically go in a direction opposite to that encouraged by ethical theory. Theory looks characteristically for considerations that are very general and have as little distinctive content as possible, because it is trying to systematize and because it wants to represent as many reasons as possible as applications of other reasons. But critical reflection should seek for as much shared understanding as it can find on any issue, and use any ethical material that, in the context of the reflective discussion, makes some sense and commands some loyalty. Of course that will take things for granted, but as serious reflection it must know it will do that. The only serious enterprise is living, and we have to live after the reflection; moreover (though the distinction of theory and practice encourages us to forget it), we have to live during it as well. Theory typically uses the assumption that we probably have too many ethical ideas, some of which may well turn out to be mere prejudices. Our major problem now is actually that we have not too many but too few, and we need to cherish as many as we can.

"Prejudice" is a powerful and ambiguous word, and its relations to theory are equally ambiguous. It has played a large role in the Cartesian tradition, in which any belief counts as a prejudice that has not yet been given a foundation. In this sense, it is certainly contrasted with theory, but in this sense, as I have already said, everything is a prejudice, in science as in ethics. In another and narrower sense, it means any belief one holds only because one has not reflected on it. In this sense, it may well be that we inevitably have prejudices, but at any rate the reflection demanded, which some beliefs will survive, need not be the reflections of ethical theory. Yet again, a prejudice of the racist or sexist kind is usually a belief guarded against reflection because it suits the interests of the believers that it be held. I have mentioned some kinds of irrationality that may be involved in this kind of belief, and some kinds of reflection that may bear on it. My sketch applies to the situation in which there are materials to hand, such as understanding of the social roles involved, that can be brought to bear in reflection by someone in the society itself. There are other questions that arise when one society is considered from the perspective of another, and the prejudice is seen as a collective one, unbroken from within. This must make for a different kind of reflection, and it is one we shall come to when, in Chapter 9, we consider some problems of relativism.

All these reflections, however, within one society or about

others, will draw on human experience and relate to human interests. If we stop there, some will say, it will represent only another prejudice. Ultimately, equal consideration should extend beyond humanity to everything that could receive consideration. Here one sees how utilitarianism is not only the most ambitious ethical theory, but also the one that carries furthest the ambition of using theory to combat prejudice. This ambition fits with the stance of the Ideal Observer and with its minimal materials: the most it can use is the idea of welfare, which supposedly can be applied to anything that might receive consideration. But we have already seen that this perspective yields too little, and there is no consistent way back that will reinstate the concerns of our local ethical life — that is to say, of our life.

The word "speciesism"[20] has been used for an attitude some regard as our ultimate prejudice, that in favor of humanity. It is more revealingly called "humanism," and it is not a prejudice.[21] To see the world from a human point of view is not an absurd thing for human beings to do. It is sometimes said that such a view implies that we regard human beings as the most important or valuable creatures in the universe. This would be an absurd thing to do, but it is not implied. To suppose that it is, is to make the mistake of identifying the point of view of the universe and the human point of view. No one should make any claims about the importance of human beings to the universe: the point is about the importance of human beings to human beings.

A concern for nonhuman animals is indeed a proper part of human life, but we can acquire it, cultivate it, and teach it only in terms of our understanding of ourselves. Human beings both have that understanding and are the objects of it, and this is one of the basic respects in which our ethical relations to each other must always be different from our relations to other animals. Before one gets to the question of how animals should be treated, there is the fundamental point that this is the only question there can be: how they should be treated. The choice can only be whether animals benefit from our practices or are harmed by them. This is why speciesism is falsely modeled on racism and sexism, which really are prejudices. To suppose that there is an ineliminable white or male understanding of the world, and to think that the only choice is whether blacks or women should benefit from "our" (white, male) practices or be harmed by them: this is already to be prejudiced. But in the case of human relations to animals, the analogues to such thoughts are simply correct.

Our arguments have to be grounded in a human point of view; they cannot be derived from a point of view that is no one's point of view at all. It is not, as the strongest forms of ethical theory would have it, that reason drives us to get beyond humanity. The most urgent requirements of humanity are, as they always have been, that we should assemble as many resources as we can to help us to respect it.

CHAPTER 7

The Linguistic Turn

E ARLIER I discussed several projects for giving ethical thought a foundation. None of those arguments claimed to put us in a position to deduce ethical conclusions, by logically deriving values from facts, for instance, or practical recommendations from mere descriptions of the world, or an *ought* from an *is*. The Kantian approach looked for the preconditions of being a rational agent that supposedly introduced ethical considerations. People who rejected those considerations would be confused in their practical relation to the world, or, if there were a logical conflict involved, it would be not between an *ought* and an *is* but between various *oughts,* each of which they were committed to accepting. Aristotle's concern, again, is basically to determine what we have most reason to pursue. His own account of this borrows from a teleological account of nature that we cannot now accept, but it does not turn on logically deducing values from something else.

There are questions in moral philosophy that connect ethical judgments less directly with practical reason than do most of the issues that have concerned us up to this point. Can there be ethical knowledge? If there is any, how does it compare with scientific knowledge? In considering such questions I shall, once again, not be much concerned with the logical deduction of values from facts. In the next chapter I shall indeed discuss whether there is a distinction between fact and value, and where such a distinction should be located. But the distinction, such as it may be, will not turn out to be primarily logical. Still less will it be found in the use of words.

Until recently these ways of proceeding and these conclusions would have been surprising. Discussions of the deduction of values from facts, or the related question of defining ethical words in nonethical terms, have been prominent in the moral philosophy of this century, sometimes almost to the exclusion of everything else. There is indeed a large idea, or more than one, at the back of these discussions, about the relations among value, knowledge of the world, and freedom. Recent philosophy has often misrepresented these questions by discussing them in terms of questions about the definition of words. I have touched once or twice on that point already. In this chapter I want to discuss more generally the issues raised by a linguistic method. The discussion has to start with a conception that cannot yet be omitted from any general account of moral philosophy, that of the "naturalistic fallacy."

The idea that ethics should pay special attention to definitions was greatly encouraged by Moore, who in his *Principia Ethica* (1903) advanced a set of views about goodness: it was a nonnatural, simple quality that could not be defined.[1] Those who attempted to define goodness were said to commit the naturalistic fallacy. It is hard to think of any other widely used phrase in the history of philosophy that is such a spectacular misnomer. In the first place, it is not clear why those criticized were committing a fallacy (which is a mistake in inference) as opposed to making what in Moore's view was an error, or else simply redefining a word. More important, the phrase appropriated to a misconceived purpose the useful word "naturalism." A naturalistic view of ethics was previously contrasted with a supernaturalistic view, and it meant a view according to which ethics was to be understood in worldly terms, without reference to God or any transcendental authority. It meant the kind of ethical view that stems from the general attitude that man is part of nature. Aristotle's outlook is naturalistic in this sense, so is Mill's utilitarianism, and so are most modern ethical works, including this one. Views that are naturalistic in this broad, useful sense do not necessarily commit the "naturalistic fallacy." Aristotle did not, and I see not much reason to think that Mill (about whom Moore was particularly unpleasant) did so either. What causes even more confusion is that not everyone who, according to Moore, committed this fallacy was also a naturalist in the broad and useful sense. Some of the most conspicuous offenders were antinaturalist in the broad and useful sense, such as those who defined goodness in terms of what is commanded or willed by God.

This last point shows that there is more than a terminological problem with Moore's idea. There is an important theoretical issue, one that gradually emerged from discussions of the naturalistic fallacy after Moore introduced the phrase. If the fallacy is a significant error, what exactly are we required to avoid? There is not simply a ban on defining *good* in naturalistic terms (in the broad and useful sense); as we have just seen, it also bans definitions that are nonnaturalistic. So perhaps it just bans a definition of *good* in terms of anything? This was Moore's own position; but, as I mentioned in Chapter 1, he was prepared to define *right* in terms of *good,* and it was open to others to take one of the alternative reductive routes while at the same time preserving Moore's ban on the naturalistic fallacy. This brings out that the doctrine of the naturalistic fallacy is not, or at least rapidly ceased to be, a ban merely on defining *good.* Rather it was taken as setting up two classes of expressions. One of them contained *good* and *right,* among others, and they were labeled, for instance, "evaluative" terms. The other, nonevaluative, class contained a wide variety of items, such as statements of fact, mathematical truths, and indeed such things as statements about God (unless for some independent reason they were evaluative, as "God is good" was taken to be). The naturalistic fallacy then comes out as the attempt to define any term that belongs to the first class entirely in terms that belong to the second.

It is not only a matter of definitions. The ban prohibits any attempt to deduce an evaluative conclusion from premises that are entirely nonevaluative. (The ban on definitions is a special case of this, since a definition is a kind of logical equivalence or two-way implication.) This wider ban not only excludes attempts to define *good.* It also excludes something that Hume had noticed as suspect, the attempt to derive *ought* from *is.* A change from propositions containing *is* to others containing *ought,* Hume had remarked, is of the last consequence. For as this *ought,* or *ought not,* expresses some new relation or affirmation, 'tis necessary that it shou'd be observ'd and explain'd; and at the same time, that a reason should be given, for what seems altogether inconceivable, how this new relation can be a deduction from others, which are entirely different from it.[2]

It has been reasonably doubted whether Hume himself meant by this passage what has subsequently been made of it.[3] He indeed thought, and explicitly says, that attention to this point would "let us see, that the distinction of vice and virtue is not founded merely on the relations of objects, nor is perceiv'd by reason." But the relation of that kind of conclusion to matters of definition and logical deduction is not straightforward.

The phrase "naturalistic fallacy" is now often used for breaches of this ban on deriving *ought* from *is.* At the same time, it retains its original force with respect to *good* and other such evaluative expressions. Some more theory is needed to explain why a ban involving *ought* will equally yield a ban involving *good.* That theory takes the form of applying the reductionist strategy, treating *good* as definable in terms of *ought.* This is one of the deeper motives for the reductionist strategy. If we are convinced that there must be two fundamental classes of expression, one related to value and the other to fact, it is natural to see one member of the value class as basic, while others are to be defined in terms of it.

This seems all the more natural when we consider a particular way in which modern theorists have tried to explain why we cannot derive the evaluative from the nonevaluative. Moore himself though that goodness was indefinable just because it was a simple nonnatural quality. He also thought that the presence of this quality was detected by intuition, in the sense of that intellectual power discussed in the last chapter as the basis of one kind of "intuitionism." Intuitionism in that sense does not explain anything much, and it does not do a great deal to explain why values cannot be derived from facts.

More recent work has tried to give a better explanation. It takes as central the ban on deriving *ought* from *is.* The central view is *prescriptivism,* developed by Hare, which explains the function of *ought* in terms of prescribing an action, or telling someone what to do. *Ought* is seen as being like an imperative: strictly speaking, a statement employing *ought* used in the normal prescriptive way is a universal expression that entails imperatives applying to all agents in all similar circumstances. (We have already seen the use of this idea in Hare's development of World Agent utilitarianism.) On this interpretation, what I have up to now been calling the *evaluative* will more revealingly be called the *prescriptive,* and it is the prescriptive that cannot be validly derived from the other class of statements — a class that, in this contrast, is appropriately labeled the *descriptive.* The explanation of the ban is now fairly obvious. The prescriptive does something, namely telling people to act in certain ways, which the descriptive, in itself, cannot do. This gives a clear reason for that ban, but if the ban is to be as general as was originally hoped, and is to explain the basic relations between fact and value, then (as I have already said) it has to be extended to *good* and the related concerns of the original argument against the natu-ralistic fallacy. The evaluative in general will have to be reduced to the prescriptive, as that has now been explained; moreover, the resulting theory will have to cover, as Moore's doctrine did, the nonethical as well as the ethical. What has to be shown, then, is that in saying that anything is good or bad, admirable or low, outstand-ing or inferior of its kind, we are in effect telling others or ourselves to do something — as the explanation typically goes, to choose something. All evaluation has to be linked to action.

This result is not at all easy to believe. It seems false to the spirit of many aesthetic evaluations, for instance: it seems to require our basic perspective on the worth of pictures to be roughly that of potential collectors. Even within the realm of the ethical, it is surely taking too narrow a view of human merits to suppose that people recognized as good are people that we are being told to imitate. Hare, in explaining this prescriptive force of evaluation, has written:

> if we say [of a certain hotel] that it is a better hotel than the one on the other side of the road, there is a sense of "better than"

(the prescriptive sense) in which a person who assented orally to our judgment, yet, when faced with a choice between the two hotels (other things such as price being equal) chose the other hotel, must have been saying something he did not really think.[4]

To think something better in the prescriptive sense is, Hare goes on to explain, to prefer it. But this is not quite what he does think, as his own example reveals. It is not, for instance, to prefer a hotel on grounds of price. It must be to prefer it on the grounds of its merits as a hotel. But once you have put in the notion of the merits of a hotel (or whatever the type of thing may be), the logical link with preference seems misguided, and in fact I see no reason to think that there is this *sense* of "better than" at all, at least when what is in question are the merits of a particular thing of a kind, such as a hotel. The merits of hotels are not a very definite matter and leave a good deal of room for personal taste, but even in that case, and even though a hotel is (in principle) something that has a function of ministering to the pleasure of customers, I can distinguish between the merits of a hotel and what I, for perfectly good reasons, happen to prefer. "I simply don't like staying at good hotels" is an intelligible thing to say.

This brings out the basic weakness of prescriptive accounts of the evaluative. When one is evaluating a thing of a certain sort, there will be some standards of merit for things of that sort, even if they may be in a particular case local or vague or indeterminate. While there are many choices that will be appropriately determined by the merits of the thing, because what the chooser is looking for is a good thing of that sort, there is always room for any given person's choice not to be directly related to the way in which that person sees the merits of the thing. For many kinds of thing, you can distinguish between thinking that a given item is good of its kind and liking, wanting, or choosing that item; moreover, your ability to make the distinction shows that you understand that the merits of the thing in question may go beyond your own interests or powers of response. Philosophy cannot make logically compulsory the attitude of a man I knew who, in one of those discussions of what bad music you most enjoy, said "I find I can survive on a diet of masterpieces."

There are serious problems, then, about how much work the distinction between *is* and *ought* can be made to do. This is an important point in relation to the linguistic presentation of a fact-value distinction. The relations of *is* and *ought* provide one of the few places where a clear claim in linguistic terms has been made for a distinction of this kind: it would need to be generalized over the rest of evaluative language if the results were to be as significant as the distinction has been supposed to be.

Besides, we also need to ask exactly how much can be established in relation to *is* and *ought* themselves. There is one clear truth to be found in the *is*–*ought* distinction, though it may not be altogether well expressed in that way. This is a point about practical reasoning. It is true that *ought* cannot be deduced from *is* if the *ought* is taken to be the same as the *should* that occurs in the practical question "what should I do?" and in the "all things considered" answer to it. Such an answer, the conclusion of a piece of practical reasoning, cannot be logically deduced from the premises that support it.[5] This will obviously be so if we do not include in the premises statements about what we want: what we find most reason to do must depend on what we want. But even if we include all relevant statements about what we want; even if we include the general principles of decision theory that we are using (which must themselves be to some extent a matter of choice or of temperament), it will still not be a matter of logical deduction to arrive at a conclusion about what we should do, all things considered. This always requires us to determine what, on this particular occasion, in the light of everything, we judge most important.

On many occasions, it will be entirely obvious what is most important, and "determining" will not require any episodic decision — but there is still a step beyond the input. If I try to include that step in the input, for instance as "I count factors ABC as the most important," then either that is a dispositional remark about me ("that's the sort of person I am"), in which case there remains a determination to be made on this occasion; or else it expresses what the determination on this occasion is, and the statement is not really part of the input, but an anticipation of the conclusion.

Even from this "all-in" conclusion, of course, there is still a step to action, and a gap can open between this conclusion and the intention to act. This constitutes the area of akrasia. But the fact that there can be such a gap does not, so to speak, push the conclusion back into being logically entailed by the input. It is wrong to think that everything is a matter of logical reasoning up to the decision to act. The problems of akrasia concern the relations between intention and one's best judgment about what to do; the point here is that even that best judgment involves judgment.

The question "what should I do?" and its answer, as we saw in Chapter 1, are not necessarily or peculiarly ethical; ethical considerations are one kind of input into the deliberation. Correspondingly, the point just made has nothing especially to do with the ethical. It is a point about input and conclusion in any practical reasoning. Once you get beyond the matter of practical reasoning and its "all-in" conclusions, the deepest questions that have been discussed under the title of the naturalistic fallacy or the *is – ought* distinction could not possibly be solved, or even revealed, by an analysis of language.

Moral philosophy is one area of philosophy in which the "linguistic turn," as it has been called,[6] has not helped to give problems a more tractable shape. This is not to deny that moral philosophy, like other parts of philosophy, is properly concerned with reflection on what we say. Indeed, at one level it might have done better than it has if it had been more concerned with what we say. Its prevailing fault, in all its styles, is to impose on ethical life some immensely simple model, whether it be of the concepts that we actually use or of moral rules by which we should be guided. One remedy to this persistent deformation might indeed have been to attend to the great diversity of things that people do say about how they and other people live their lives.

At one level, if there is to be attention to language, then there should be attention to more of it. But at another, the distinctively linguistic endeavor is not likely to be successful, however it is conducted. One reason for this, as we have already noticed, is that there is no clearly delimited set of linguistic expressions to examine. Theorists have particularly tended to favor the most general expressions used in ethical discussion — *good, right, ought,* and the rest. Our use of these words is of course not confined to ethical thought. That fact in itself would not necessarily wreck the inquiry, but, for two reasons at least, this concentration has helped to do so. One reason lies in the motive for choosing those words, which was the reductionist belief that those notions were contained in more specific ethical conceptions. This conceals the real nature of those conceptions and has helped to hide a truth that a purely linguistic inquiry is unlikely to bring to light in any case: a society that relies on very general ethical expressions is a different sort of society from one that puts greater weight on more specific ones. (In the next chapter I shall consider some important characteristics of more specific ethical concepts, in particular their role in ethical knowledge.) A second reason why the concentration on these general terms has done no good to the linguistic philosophy of ethics is that the theorist, in trying to sort out the relevant uses of them, brings to the inquiry presuppositions that are not only already theoretical but already ethical. The results are usually bad philosophy of language.

They are certainly bad philosophy of ethics. There are genuine ethical, and ultimately metaphysical, concerns underlying the worries about *ought* and *is* and the naturalistic fallacy. At the heart of them is an idea that our values are not "in the world," that a properly untendentious description of the world would not mention any values, that our values are in some sense imposed or projected on to our surroundings. This discovery, if that is what it is, can be met with despair, as can the loss of a teleologically significant world. But it can also be seen as a liberation, and a radical form of freedom may be found in the fact that we cannot be forced by the world to accept one set of values rather than another.

   This set of conceptions does constitute a belief in a distinction, some distinction, between fact and value. Whether some such distinction is sound is certainly a very serious issue. We shall be concerned with it in the next chapter, and with the question of *what* conception of the world would be pure of values. The point that needs to be made now is a preliminary one, but important. It shows why the linguistic turn is likely to be unhelpful. If there is some fundamental distinction of fact and value, it is certainly not a universal feat of humanity to have recognized it — it is instead a discovery, an achievement of enlightenment. But then there is no reason to suppose that our ethical language, insofar as there is any such well-defined thing, *already* presents the distinction to us. It may be that it does not present anything of the sort, either suggestive of such a distinction or concealing it; it may be a mistake to think that language can embody distinctively metaphysical beliefs. But if it does have the capacity to convey anything on such a question, it must be at least as likely to convey an illusion as it is to convey the truth, and indeed more likely to do so, in view of the extent in space and time of the illusion and the recent arrival of enlightenment. If human values are projected from human concerns, and are not a feature of "the world," it does not follow that there is to hand a description of the world — or rather, of enough of the world — that is value-free. (Perhaps there could not be such a thing; but if not, then we should begin to wonder what the talk of projection is really saying. What is the screen?)

This may seem a rather paradoxical way of criticizing the linguistic enterprise. Those who have engaged in it have usually emphasised a fact-value distinction; the distinction between *ought* and *is* has been used to reveal it. So, it seems, either language does not disguise the fact-value distinction, or else the linguistic theorist has managed to penetrate the disguise. But neither of these options is correct. What has happened is that the theorists have brought the fact-value distinction to language rather than finding it revealed there. What they have found are a lot of those "thicker" or more specific ethical notions I have already referred to, such as *treachery* and *promise* and *brutality* and *courage,* which seem to express a union of fact and value. The way these notions are applied is determined by what the world is like (for instance, by how someone has behaved), and yet, at the same time, their application usually involves a certain valuation of the situation, of persons or actions. Moreover, they usually (though not necessarily directly) provide reasons for action. Terms of this kind certainly do not lay bare the fact-value distinction. Rather, the theorist who wants to defend the distinction has to interpret the workings of these terms, and he does so by treating them as a conjunction of a factual and an evaluative element, which can in principle be separated from one another. The clearest account, as so often, is given by Hare: a term of this kind involves a descriptive complex to which a prescription has been attached, expressive of the values of the individual or of the society. A statement using one of these terms can be analyzed into something like "this act has such-and-such a character, and acts of that character one ought not to do." It is essential to this account that the specific or "thick" character of these terms is given in the descriptive element. The value part is expressed, under analysis, by the all-purpose prescriptive term *ought*.

I shall claim in the next chapter that this account is incorrect, and I shall not try to anticipate the argument here. The point here is to suggest, once more, that fact-value theorists who rely on linguistic means are bringing their distinction to language rather than finding it there and, in addition, are unreasonably expecting that when the distinction is revealed it will be found very near the surface of language. There is no reason to expect that to be so. If we are engaged in a fraudulent or self-deceiving business of reading our values into the world, our language is likely to be deeply implicated.

The prescriptivist account claims that the value part of these thick terms is entirely carried by the prescriptive function, which can be analyzed in terms of *ought*. It claims that everything we want to say or think in the ethical domain (and indeed in evaluative areas beyond it) could be said or thought in terms of that very general term. Other theorists say similar things about other general terms: some general, abstract term could do all the work. Indeed, since the thicker ethical terms are only compounds involving this term, it is already doing the work. If this kind of analysis proves to be a mistake, and more generally the impulse to reduce ethical language to such abstract terms is misguided, then they are not doing all the work, and this will leave room for an idea I have already suggested, that a society in which ethical life is understood and conducted in such general terms is socially different from one in which it is not, and the differences require social understanding. If that is a fact, the linguistic approach certainly does not help us to recognize it. It encourages us to neglect it even as a possibility.

It is an obvious enough idea that if we are going to understand how ethical concepts work, and how they change, we have to have some insight into the forms of social organization within which they work. The linguistic approach does not, at some detached level, deny this, but it does not ask any questions that help us to gain that insight or to do anything with it in philosophy if we have gained it. Its concentration on questions of logical analysis have helped to conceal the point, and so has its pure conception of philosophy itself, which indeed emphasizes that language is a social activity but at the same time, oddly enough, rejects from philosophy any concrete interest in societies.[7] But it is at least potentially closer to some understanding of the social and historical dimensions of ethical thought than some other approaches, which see it entirely in terms of an autonomous and unchanging subject matter. To draw attention to our ethical language can at least hold out the prospect of our coming to think about it, and about the ethical life expressed in it, as social practices that can change. The linguistic turn could have helped us, even if it has not actually done so, to recognize that ethical understanding needs a dimension of social explanation.

CHAPTER 8

Knowledge, Science, Convergence

So far I have not said much about objectivity, though earlier chapters have had a good deal to do with it. If an Archimedean point could be found and practical reason, or human interests, could be shown to involve a determinate ethical outlook, then ethical thought would be objective, in the sense that it would have been given an objective foundation. Those are possibilities — or they might have turned out to be possibilities — within the perspective of practical reason. Very often, however, discussions of objectivity come into moral philosophy from a different starting point, from an interest in comparing ethical beliefs with knowledge and claims to truth of other kinds, for instance with scientific beliefs. Here a rather different conception of objectivity is involved. It is naturally associated with such questions as what can make ethical beliefs true, and whether there is any ethical knowledge. It is in this field of comparisons that various distinctions between fact and value are located.

Discussions of objectivity often start from considerations about disagreement. This makes it seem as if disagreement were surprising, but there is no reason why that should be so (the earliest thinkers in the Western tradition found conflict at least as obvious a feature of the world as concord). The interest in disagreement comes about, rather, because neither agreement nor disagreement is universal. It is not that disagreement needs explanation and agreement does not, but that in different contexts disagreement requires different sorts of explanation, and so does agreement.

The way in which we understand a given kind of disagreement, and explain it, has important practical effects. It can modify our attitude to others and our understanding of our own outlook. In relation to other people, we need a view of what is to be opposed, rejected, and so forth, and in what spirit; for ourselves, disagreement can raise a warning that we may be wrong, and if truth or correctness is what we are after, we may need to reform our strategies.

Disagreement does not necessarily have to be overcome. It may remain an important and constitutive feature of our relations to others, and also be seen as something that is merely to be expected in the light of the best explanations we have of how such disagreement arises. There can be tension involved here, if we at once feel that the disagreement is about very important matters and that there is a good explanation of why the disagreement is only to be expected. The tension is specially acute when the disagreement is not only important but expresses itself in judgments that seem to demand assent from others. (As we shall see in the next chapter, there is a special problem for relativism, of trying to understand our outlook in a way that will accommodate both sides of the tension.)

Among types of disagreement, and the lessons that can be learned from them, there is a well-known polarity. At one extreme there is the situation of two children wanting one bun or two heroes wanting one slave girl. The disagreement is practical, and its explanation is not going to cast much doubt on the cognitive powers of the people involved. It may be said that this kind of case is so primitively practical that it hardly even introduces any judgment over which there is disagreement. Even at the most primitive level, of course, there is disagreement about *what is to be done,* but this is so near to desire and action that no one is going to think that the disagreement shows any failure of knowledge or understanding. It is simply that two people want incompatible things. But the conflict may well not remain as blank as that, and if the parties want to settle it by ordered speech rather than by violence, they will invoke more substantive judgments, usually of justice, and the children will talk about fairness or the heroes about precedence.

In their most basic form, at least, these disagreements need not make anyone think that someone has failed to recognize or understand something, or that they cannot speak the language. At the opposite pole of the traditional contrast are disagreements that do make one think this. What these typically are depends on the theory of knowledge favored by the commentator, but they often involve the observation under standard conditions of what the Oxford philosopher J. L. Austin used to called "middle-sized dry goods." An important feature of these examples is that the parties are assumed to share the same concepts and to be trained in the recognition of furniture, pens, pennies, or whatever.

Around these paradigms there have been formed various oppositions: between practical and theoretical, or value and fact, or *ought* and *is*. Each of these has been thought to represent a fundamental difference in what disagreement means, and they are often taken to suggest contrasting hopes for resolving it. But it is a mistake to suppose that these oppositions are different ways of representing just one distinction. Indeed, the two examples I have mentioned significantly fail to correspond to the two ends of any one of these contrasts. The quarrel about the allocation of a good is certainly an example of the practical, but until one gets to the stage of taking seriously the claims of justice, it is not yet a disagreement about value. A disagreement in the perception of furniture is without doubt a disagreement about a matter of fact, but is not yet a disagreement about what is most often contrasted with the practical, namely the theoretical. To assemble these kinds of example into some one contrast requires more work. It has been done, characteristically, by reducing the evaluative to the practical and extending the factual to the theoretical. Both these maneuvers are of positivist inspiration, and they are both suspect. It is not surprising that some philosophers now doubt whether there is any basic distinction at all that can be constructed to the traditional pattern.[1]

I accept that there is no one distinction in question here. I also accept that the more positivistic formulations that have gone into defining each side of such a distinction are misguided. Still I believe that in relation to ethics there is a genuine and profound difference to be found, and also — it is a further point — that the difference is enough to motivate some version of the feeling (itself recurrent, if not exactly traditional) that science has some chance of being more or less what it seems, a systematized theoretical account of how the world really is, while ethical thought has no chance of being everything it seems. The tradition is right, moreover, not only in thinking that there is such a distinction, but also in thinking that we can come to understand what it is through understanding disagreement. However, it is not a question of how much disagreement there is, or even of what methods we have to settle disagreement, though that of course provides many relevant considerations. The basic difference lies rather in our reflective understanding of the best hopes we could coherently entertain for eliminating disagreement in the two areas. It is a matter of what, under the most favorable conditions, would be the best explanation of the end of disagreement: the explanation — as I shall say from now on — of convergence.

The fundamental difference lies between the ethical and the scientific. I hope to explain why one end of the contrast should be labeled "the scientific" rather than, say, "the factual." The other end is labeled "the ethical" because the ethical is what we are considering, and it would require a good deal of discussion either to extend the field or to narrow it. It is not called "the evaluative" because that additionally covers at least the area of aesthetic judgment, which raises many questions of its own. It is not called "the normative," a term that covers only part of the interest of the ethical (roughly, the part concerned with rules) and also naturally extends to such things as the law, which again raises different questions. More significantly, it is not called "the practical." This would displace a large part of the problem, for a reason we have already noticed in considering prescriptions and the *is–ought* distinction. It is not hard to concede that there is a distinction between the practical and the nonpractical. There is clearly such a thing as practical reasoning or deliberation, which is not the same as thinking about how things are. It is *obviously* not the same, and this is why positivism thought it had validated the traditional distinction by reducing the evaluative to the practical. But the reduction is mistaken, and it makes the whole problem look easier than it is.[2]

The basic idea behind the distinction between the scientific and the ethical, expressed in terms of convergence, is very simple. In a scientific inquiry there should ideally be convergence on an answer, where the best explanation of the convergence involves the idea that the answer represents how things are; in the area of the ethical, at least at a high level of generality, there is no such coherent hope. The distinction does not turn on any difference in whether convergence will actually occur, and it is important that this is not what the argument is about. It might well turn out that there will be convergence in ethical outlook, at least among human beings. The point of the contrast is that, even if this happens, it will not be correct to think it has come about because convergence has been guided by how things actually are, whereas convergence in the sciences might be explained in that way if it does happen. This means, among other things, that we understand differently in the two cases the existence of convergence or, alternatively, its failure to come about.

I shall come back to ways in which we might understand ethical convergence. First, however, we must face certain arguments suggesting that there is really nothing at all in the distinction, expressed in these terms. There are two different directions from which this objection can come. In one version, the notion of a convergence that comes about because of how things are is seen as an empty notion. According to the other, the notion of such a convergence is not empty, but it is available as much in ethical cases as in scientific — that is to say, the notion has some content, but it does nothing to help the distinction.

I have already said that the point of the distinction and of its explanation in terms of convergence does not turn on the question whether convergence actually occurs. On the scientific side, however, it would be unrealistic to disconnect these ideas totally from the ways in which the history of Western science since the seventeenth century is to be understood. The conception of scientific progress in terms of convergence cannot be divorced from the history of Western science because it is the history of Western science that has done most to encourage it. It is quite hard to deny that that history displays a considerable degree of convergence; what has been claimed is that this appearance has no real significance because it is a cultural artifact, a product of the way in which we choose to narrate the history of science. Richard Rorty has written:

> It is less paradoxical . . . to stick to the classic notion of "better describing what was already there" for physics. This is not because of deep epistemological or metaphysical considerations, but simply because, when we tell our Whiggish stories about how our ancestors gradually crawled up the mountain on whose (possibly false) summit we stand, we need to keep some things constant throughout the story . . . Physics is the paradigm of "finding" simply because it is hard (at least in the West) to tell a story of changing universes against the background of an unchanging Moral law or poetic canon, but very easy to tell the reverse sort of story.[3]

There are two notable faults in such a description of scientific success and what that success means. One is its attitude to the fact that it is easy to tell one kind of story and hard to tell the other. *Why* is the picture of the world "already there," helping to control our descriptions of it, so compelling? This seems to require some explanation on Rorty's account, but it does not get one. If the reference to "the West" implies a cultural or anthropological explanation, it is totally unclear what it would be: totally unclear, indeed, what it could be, if it is not going itself to assume an already existing physical world in which human beings come into existence and develop their cultures.

The point that an assumption of this kind is going to lie behind any explanations of what we do leads directly to the second fault in Rorty's account: it is self-defeating. If the story he tells were true, then there would be no perspective from which he could express it in this way. If it is overwhelmingly convenient to say that science describes what is already there, and if there are no deep metaphysical or epistemological issues here but only a question of what is convenient (it is "simply because" of this that we speak as we do), then what everyone should be saying, including Rorty, is that science describes a world already there. But Rorty urges us not to say that, and in doing so, in insisting, as *opposed to* that, on our talking of what it is convenient to say, he is trying to reoccupy the transcendental standpoint outside human speech and activity, which is precisely what he wants us to renounce.[4]

A more effective level of objection lies in a negative claim that Rorty and others make, that no convergence of science, past or future, could possibly be explained in any meaningful way by reference to the way the world is, because there is an insoluble difficulty with the notion of "the world" as something that can determine belief. There is a dilemma. On the one hand, "the world" may be characterized in terms of our current beliefs about what it contains; it is a world of stars, people, grass, or tables. When "the world" is taken in this way, we can of course say that our beliefs about the world are affected by the world, in the sense that for instance our beliefs about grass are affected by grass, but there is nothing illuminating or substantive in this — our conception of the world as the object of our beliefs can do no better than repeat the beliefs we take to represent it. If, on the other hand, we try to form some idea of a world that is prior to any description of it, the world that all systems of belief and representation are trying to represent, then we have an empty notion of something completely unspecified and unspecifiable.[5] So either way we fail to have a notion of "the world" that will do what is required of it.

Each side of this dilemma takes all our representations of the world together, in the one case putting them all in and in the other leaving them all out. But there is a third and more helpful possibility, that we should form a conception of the world that is "already there" in terms of some but not all of our beliefs and theories. In reflecting on the world that is there *anyway*, independent of our experience, we must concentrate not in the first instance on what our beliefs are about, but on how they represent what they are about. We can select among our beliefs and features of our world picture some that we can reasonably claim to represent the world in a way to the maximum degree independent of our perspective and its peculiarities. The resultant picture of things, if we can carry through this task, can be called the "absolute conception" of the world.[6] In terms of that conception, we may hope to explain the possibility of our attaining the conception itself, and also the possibility of other, perspectival, representations.

This notion of an absolute conception can serve to make effective a distinction between "the world as it is independent of our experience" and "the world as it seems to us." It does this by understanding "the world as it seems to us" as "the world as it seems peculiarly to us"; the absolute conception will, correspondingly, be a conception of the world that might be arrived at by any investigators, even if they were very different from us. What counts as a relevant difference from us, and indeed what for various levels of description will count as "us," will, again, be explained on the basis of the conception itself; we shall be able to explain, for instance, why one kind of observer can make observations that another kind cannot make. It is centrally important that these ideas relate to science, not to all kinds of knowledge. We can *know* things whose content is perspectival: we can know that grass is green, for instance, though *green*, for certain, and probably *grass* are concepts that would not be available to every competent observer of the world and would not figure in the absolute conception. (As we shall see, people can know things even more locally perspectival than that.) The point is not to give an account of knowledge, and the contrast with value should be expressed not in terms of knowledge but of science. The aim is to outline the possibility of a convergence characteristic of science, one that could meaningfully be said to be a convergence on how things (anyway) are.

That possibility, as I have explained it, depends heavily on notions of explanation. The substance of the absolute conception (as opposed to those vacuous or vanishing ideas of "the world" that were offered before) lies in the idea that it could nonvacuously explain how it itself, and the various perspectival views of the world, are possible. It is an important feature of modern science that it contributes to explaining how creatures with our origins and characteristics can understand a world with properties that this same science ascribes to the world. The achievements of evolutionary biology and the neurological sciences are substantive in these respects, and their notions of explanation are not vacuous. It is true, however, that such explanations cannot themselves operate entirely at the level of the absolute conception, because what they have to explain are psychological and social phenomena, such as beliefs and theories and conceptions of the world, and there may be little reason to suppose that they, in turn, could be adequately characterized in nonperspectival terms. How far this may be so is a central philosophical question. But even if we allow that the explanations of such things must remain to some degree perspectival, this does not mean that we cannot operate the notion of the absolute conception. It will be a conception consisting of nonperspectival materials available to any adequate investigator, of whatever constitution, and it will also help to explain to us, though not necessarily to those alien investigators, such things as our capacity to grasp that conception. Perhaps more than this will turn out to be available, but no more is necessary in order to give substance to the idea of "the world" and to defeat the first line of objection to the distinction, in terms of possible convergence, between the scientific and the ethical.

The opposite line of objection urges that the idea of "converging on how things are" is available, to some adequate degree, in the ethical case as well. The place where this is to be seen is above all with those substantive or thick ethical concepts I have often mentioned. Many exotic examples of these can be drawn from other cultures, but there are enough left in our own: *coward, lie, brutality, gratitude,* and so forth. They are characteristically related to reasons for action. If a concept of this kind applies, this often provides someone with a reason for action, though that reason need not be a decisive one and may be outweighed by other reasons, as we saw with their role in practical reasoning in Chapter 1. Of course, exactly what reason for action is provided, and to whom, depends on the situation, in ways that may well be governed by this and by other ethical concepts, but some general connection with action is clear enough. We may say, summarily, that such concepts are "action-guiding."

At the same time, their application is guided by the world. A concept of this sort may be rightly or wrongly applied, and people who have acquired it can agree that it applies or fails to apply to some new situation. In many cases the agreement will be spontaneous, while in other cases there is room for judgment and comparison. Some disagreement at the margin may be irresoluble, but this does not mean that the use of the concept is not controlled by the facts or by the users' perception of the world. (As with other concepts that are not totally precise, marginal disagreements can indeed help to show how their use *is* controlled by the facts.) We can say, then, that the application of these concepts is at the same time world-guided and action-guiding. How can it be both at once?

The prescriptivist account discussed in the last chapter gives a very simple answer to this question. Any such concept, on that account, can be analyzed into a descriptive and a prescriptive element: it is guided round the world by its descriptive content, but has a prescriptive flag attached to it. It is the first feature that allows it to be world-guided, while the second makes it action-guiding. Some of the difficulties with this picture concern the prescriptive element and how it is supposed to guide action in the relevant sense (telling yourself to do something is not an obvious model for recognizing that you have a reason to do it). But the most significant objection applies to the other half of the analysis. Prescriptivism claims that what governs the application of the concept to the world is the descriptive element and that the evaluative interest of the concept plays no part in this. All the input into its use is descriptive, just as all the evaluative aspect is output. It follows that, for any concept of this sort, you could produce another that picked out just the same features of the world but worked simply as a descriptive concept, lacking any prescriptive or evaluative force.

Against this, critics have made the effective point that there is no reason to believe that a descriptive equivalent will necessarily be available.[7] How we "go on" from one application of a concept to another is a function of the kind of interest that the concept represents, and we should not assume that we could see how people "go on" if we did not share the evaluative perspective in which this kind of concept has its point. An insightful observer can indeed come to understand and anticipate the use of the concept without actually sharing the values of the people who use it: this is an important point, and I shall come back to it. But in imaginatively anticipating the use of the concept, the observer also has to grasp imaginatively its evaluative point. He cannot stand quite outside the evaluative interests of the community he is observing, and pick up the concept simply as a device for dividing up in a rather strange way certain neutral features of the world.

It is very plausible, and it is certainly possible, that there should be ethical concepts that make these demands on understanding. It does not need, in fact, to be much more than possible to play an important part in this argument, by reminding moral philosophy of what the demands made by an adequate philosophy of language or by the philosophy of social explanation may turn out to be. If it is not only possible but plausible, moral philosophy will be well advised to consider what must be said if it is true.

The sympathetic observer can follow the practice of the people he is observing; he can report, anticipate, and even take part in discussions of the use they make of their concept. But, as with some other concepts of theirs, relating to religion, for instance, or to witchcraft, he may not be ultimately identified with the use of the concept: it may not really be his.[8] This possibility, of the insightful but not totally identified observer, bears on an important question, whether those who properly apply ethical concepts of this kind can be said to have ethical knowledge.

Let us assume, artificially, that we are dealing with a society that is maximally homogeneous and minimally given to general reflection; its members simply, all of them, use certain ethical concepts of this sort. (We may call it the "hypertraditional" society.) What would be involved in their having ethical knowledge? According to the best available accounts of propositional knowledge,[9] they would have to believe the judgments they made; those judgments would have to be true; and their judgments would have to satisfy a further condition, which has been extensively discussed in the philosophy of knowledge but which can be summarized by saying that the first two conditions must be nonaccidentally linked: granted the way that the people have gone about their inquiries, it must be no accident that the belief they have acquired is a true one, and if the truth on the subject had been otherwise, they would have acquired a different belief, true in those different circumstances. Thus I may know, by looking at it, that the die has come up 6, and this roughly[10] involves the claim that if it had come up 4, I would have come to believe, by looking at it, that it had come up 4 (the alternative situations to be considered have to be restricted to those moderately like the actual one). Taking a phrase from Robert Nozick, we can say that the third requirement — it involves a good deal more elaboration than I have suggested — is that one's belief should "track the truth."

The members of the hypertraditional society apply their thick concepts, and in doing so they make various judgments. If any of those judgments can ever properly be said to be true, then their beliefs can track the truth, since they can withdraw judgments if the circumstances turn out not to be what was supposed, can make an alternative judgment if it would be more appropriate, and so on. They have, each, mastered these concepts, and they can perceive the personal and social happenings to which the concepts apply. If there is truth here, their beliefs can track it. The question left is whether any of these judgments can be true.

An objection can be made to saying that they are. If they are true, the observer can correctly say that they are; letting F stand in for one of their concepts, he can say, "The headman's statement, 'The boy is F,' is true." Then he should be able to say, in his own person, "the boy is F." But he is not prepared to do that, since F is not one of his concepts.

How strong is this objection? It relies on the following principle: A cannot correctly say that B speaks truly in uttering S unless A could also say something tantamount to S. This may seem to follow from a basic principle about truth, the *disquotation principle*,[11] to the effect that P is true if and only if P. But that principle cannot be applied so simply in deciding what can be said about other people's statements. For a naive example, we may imagine a certain school slang that uses special names for various objects, places, and institutions in the school. It is a rule that these words are appropriately used only by someone who is a member of the school, and this rule is accepted and understood by a group outside the school (it would have to be, if it were to be *that* rule at all). People know that if they use these terms in their own person they will be taken for members of the school, or else criticized, and so forth. Suppose that in this slang "Weeds" were the name of some school building. Under the imagined rules, an observer could not, entirely in his own person and not playing a role, properly say "Robertson is at Weeds." But he could say, "Smith said 'Robertson is at Weeds,' " and he could then add to that, "and what Smith said is true." (Indeed—though this is not necessary to the argument—it seems quite natural for him to go one step further than that and say, "Smith truly said that Robertson was at Weeds.")

In this simple case, it is of course true that the observer has other terms that refer to the same things as the slang terms. Presumably, so do the local users; but there are other examples in which this is not so, as with languages in which males and females use different names for the same thing. In the school case, both the observer and the locals have verbal means to factor out what makes a given slang statement true from what, as contrasted with that, makes it appropriate for a particular person to make it. Where the gender of the speaker determines the correct term that he or she should use, it is more complicated. In the case of the thick ethical concept, it is more complicated still, because the observer does not have a term that picks out just the same things as the locals' term picks out and, at the same time, is entirely independent of the interest that shapes their use. (He has, of course, an expression such as "what they call *F*," and the fact that he can use it, although it is not independent of their term, is important: his intelligent use of it shows that he can indeed understand their use of their term, although he cannot use it himself.)

Despite its differences from the simple case of school slang, however, we can see the case of the ethical concept as only a deeper example of the same thing. In both cases, there is a condition that has to be satisfied if one is to speak in a certain way, a condition satisfied by the locals and not by the observer, and in both cases it is a matter of belonging to a certain culture. When we compare those cases with each other, and both of them with the situation in which vocabulary is affected by the speaker's gender, we can understand why the observer is barred from saying just what the locals say, and we can also see that he is not barred from recognizing that what they say can be true. The disquotation principle, then, does not lead to the conclusion that the locals' statements, involving their thick ethical concepts, cannot be true.

There is a different argument for the conclusion that the locals' statements may not be true. This claims, more bluntly, that they may be false: not because they can be mistaken in ways that the locals themselves could recognize, but because an entire segment of the local discourse may be seen from outside as involving a mistake. This possibility has been much discussed by theorists. Social anthropologists have asked whether ritual and magical conceptions should be seen as mistaken in our terms, or rather as operating at a different level, not commensurable with our scientific ideas. Whatever may be said more generally, it is hard to deny that magic, at least, is a causal conception, with implications that overlap with scientific conceptions of causality.[12] To the extent this is so, magical conceptions can be seen from the outside as false, and then no one will have known to be true any statement claiming magical influence, even though he may have correctly used all the local criteria for claiming a given piece of magical influence. The local criteria do not reach to everything that is involved in such claims. In cases of this sort, the problem with conceding truth to the locals' statements is the opposite of the one discussed before. The earlier claim was that their notions were so different from the observer's that he could not assert what they asserted. Now the problem is that their statements may imply notions similar enough to some of his for him to deny what they assert.

We may see the local ethical statements in a way that raises this difficulty. On this reading, the locals' statements imply something that can be put in the observer's terms and is rejected by him: that it is *right,* or *all right,* to do things he thinks it is not right, or all right, to do. Prescriptivism sees things in this way. The local statements entail, together with their descriptive content, an all-purpose *ought*. We have rejected the descriptive half of that analysis — is there any reason to accept the other half?

Of course, there is a minimal sense in which the locals think it "all right" to act as they do, and they do not merely imply this, but reveal it, in the way they live. To say that they "think it all right" at this level is not to mention any further and disputable judgment of theirs; it is merely to record their practice. Must we agree that there is a judgment, to be expressed by using some universal moral notion, which they accept and the observer may very well reject?

I do not think we have to accept this idea. More precisely, I do not think we can decide whether to accept it until we have a more general picture of the whole question; this is not an issue that in itself can force more general conclusions on us. The basic question is how we are to understand the relations between practice and reflection. The very general kind of judgment that is in question here — a judgment using a very general concept — is essentially a product of reflection, and it comes into question when someone stands back from the practices of the society and its use of these concepts and asks whether this is the right way to go on, whether these are good ways in which to assess actions, whether the kinds of character that are admired are rightly admired. In many traditional societies themselves there is some degree of reflective questioning and criticism, and this is an important fact. It is for the sake of the argument, to separate the issues, that I have been using the idea of the hypertraditional society where there is no reflection.

In relation to this society, the question now is: Does the practice of the society, in particular the judgments that members of the society make, imply answers to reflective questions about that practice, questions they have never raised? Some judgments made by members of a society do indeed have implications, which they have never considered, at a more general or theoretical level. This will be true of their magical judgments if those are taken as causal claims; it is true of their mathematical judgments and of their judgments about the stars. We may be at some liberty whether to construe what they are saying as expressing mathematical judgments or opinions about the stars; but if we do take them to be making those judgments and expressing those opinions, their statements will have more general implications. If what a statement expresses is an opinion about the stars, it follows that it can be contradicted by another opinion about the stars.

There are two different ways in which we can see the activities of the hypertraditional society. They depend on different models of ethical practice. One of them may be called an "objectivist" model. According to this, we shall see the members of the society as trying, in their local way, to find out the truth about values, an activity in which we and other human beings, and perhaps creatures who are not human beings, are all engaged. We shall then see their judgments as having these general implications, rather as we see primitive statements about the stars as having implications that can be contradicted by more sophisticated statements about the stars. On the other model we shall see their judgments as part of their way of living, a cultural artifact they have come to inhabit (though they have not consciously built it). On this, nonobjectivist, model, we shall take a different view of the relations between that practice and critical reflection. We shall not be disposed to see the level of reflection as implicitly already there, and we shall not want to say that their judgments have, just as they stand, these implications.

The choice between these two different ways of looking at their activities will determine whether we say that the people in the hypertraditional society have ethical knowledge. It is important to be quite clear what ethical knowledge is in question. It is knowledge involved in their making judgments in which they use their thick concepts. We are not considering whether they display knowledge *in using those concepts rather than some others:* this would be an issue at the reflective level. The question "does the society possess ethical knowledge?" is seriously ambiguous in that way. The collective reference to the society invites us to take the perspective in which its ethical representations are compared with other societies' ethical representations, and this is the reflective level, at which they certainly do not possess knowledge. There is another sense of the question in which it asks whether members of the society could, in exercising their concepts, express knowledge about the world to which they apply them, and the answer to that might be yes.

The interesting result of this discussion is that the answer will be yes if we take the nonobjectivist view of their ethical activities: various members of the society will have knowledge, when they deploy their concepts carefully, use the appropriate criteria, and so on. But on the objectivist view they do not have knowledge, or at least it is most unlikely that they do, since their judgments have extensive implications, which they have never considered, at a reflective level, and we have every reason to believe that, when those implications are considered, the traditional use of ethical concepts will be seriously affected.

The objectivist view, while it denies knowledge to the unreflective society, may seem to promise knowledge at the reflective level. Characteristically, it expects the demands of knowledge to be satisfied only by reflection. No doubt there are some ethical beliefs, universally held and usually vague ("one has to have a special reason to kill someone"), that we can be sure will survive at the reflective level. But they fall far short of any adequate, still less systematic, body of ethical knowledge at that level, and I think that the outcome of my earlier discussion of ethical theory has shown that, at least as things are, no such body of knowledge exists. Later I shall suggest that, so far as propositional knowledge of ethical truths is concerned, this is not simply a matter of how things are. Rather, at a high level of reflective generality there could be no ethical knowledge of this sort—or, at most, just one piece.

If we accept that there can be knowledge at the hypertraditional or unreflective level; if we accept the obvious truth that reflection characteristically disturbs, unseats, or replaces those traditional concepts; and if we agree that, at least as things are, the reflective level is not in a position to give us knowledge we did not have before—then we reach the notably un-Socratic conclusion that, in ethics, *reflection can destroy knowledge.* In the next chapter, when I turn to the concerns of relativism, we shall see what this conclusion means.

Another consequence, if we allow knowledge at the unreflective level, will be that not all propositional knowledge is additive. Not all pieces of knowledge can be combined into a larger body of knowledge. We may well have to accept that conclusion anyway from other contexts that involve perspectival views of the world. A part of the physical world may present itself as one color to one kind of observer, and another to another; to another, it may not exactly be a color at all. Call those qualities perceived by each kind of observer A, B, C. Then a skilled observer of one kind can know that the surface is A, of another kind that it is B, and so on, but there is no knowledge that it is A and B and C. This result would disappear if what A or B or C meant were something relational — if, when observers said "that is A" they meant "A to observers like us." It is very doubtful that this is the correct account.[13] If it is not, the coherence of those pieces of knowledge is secured at a different level, when the various perceived qualities are related to the absolute conception. Their relation to the conception is also what makes it clear that the capacities that produce these various pieces of knowledge are all forms of *perception*. Of course we have good reason to believe this before we possess any such theoretical conception, and certainly before we possess its details. This is because our everyday experience, unsurprisingly, reveals a good deal of what we are and how we are related to the world, and in this way leads us toward the theoretical conception.[14]

Some think of the knowledge given by applying ethical concepts as something like perception. But we can now see a vital asymmetry between the case of the ethical concepts and the perspectival experience of secondary qualities such as colors. This asymmetry shows, moreover, that the distinction between the scientific and the ethical has wider implications. It is not merely a matter of distinguishing between an ideally nonperspectival science on the one hand and ethical concepts on the other. Not all perspectival concepts are ethical, and there are significant differences between ethical and other perspectival concepts, such as those of sense perception.

The main difference is that, in the case of secondary qualities, what explains also justifies; in the ethical case, this is not so. The psychological capacities that underly our perceiving the world in terms of certain secondary qualities have evolved so that the physical world will present itself to us in reliable and useful ways. Coming to know that these qualities constitute our form of perceptual engagement with the world, and that this mode of presentation works in a certain way, will not unsettle the system.[15] In the ethical case, we have an analogy to the perceptual just to this extent, that there is local convergence under these concepts: the judgments of those who use them are indeed, as I put it before, world-guided. This is certainly enough to refute the simplest oppositions of fact and value. But if it is to mean anything for a wider objectivity, everything depends on what is to be said *next*. With secondary qualities, it is the explanation of the perspectival perceptions that enables us, when we come to reflect on them, to place them in relation to the perceptions of other people and other creatures; and that leaves everything more or less where it was, so far as our perceptual judgments are concerned. The question is whether we can find an ethical analogy to that. Here we have to go outside local judgments to a reflective or second-order account of them, and here the analogy gives out.

There is, first, a problem of what the second-order account is to be. An *explanation* of those local judgments and of the conceptual differences between societies will presumably have to come from the social sciences: cultural differences are in question. Perhaps no existing explanation of such things goes very deep, and we are not too clear how deep an explanation might go. But we do know that it will not look much like the explanation of color perception. The capacities it will invoke are those involved in finding our way around in a social world, not merely the physical world, and this, crucially, means *in some social world or other,* since it is certain both that human beings cannot live without a culture and that there are many different cultures in which they can live, differing in their local concepts.

In any case, an explanatory theory is not enough to deal with the problems of objectivity raised by the local ethical concepts. In the case of secondary qualities, the explanation also justifies, because it can show how the perceptions are related to physical reality and how they can give knowledge of that reality, which is what they purport to do. The question with them is: Is this a method of finding our way around the physical world? The theoretical account explains how it is. In the ethical case, this is not the kind of question raised by reflectiion. If we ask the question "is this a method of finding our way around the social world?" we would have to be asking whether it was a method of finding our way around some social world or other, and the answer to that must obviously be yes (unless the society were extremely disordered, which is not what we were supposing). The question raised is rather "is this a good way of living compared with others?"; or, to put it another way, "is this the best kind of social world?"

When these are seen to be the questions, the reflective account we require turns out to involve reflective *ethical* considerations. These are the considerations that some believe should take the form of an ethical theory. The reflective considerations will have to take up the job of justifying the local concepts once those have come to be questioned. An ethical theory might even, in a weak sense, provide some explanations. It might rationalize some cultural differences, showing why one local concept rather than others was ethically appropriate in particular circumstances (we can recall here the possibilities and perils of indirect utilitarianism). But while it might explain why it was reasonable for people to have these various ethical beliefs, it would not be the sort of theory that could explain why they did or did not have them. It could not do something that explanations of perception can do, which is to generate an adequate theory of error and to account generally for the tendency of people to have what, according to its principles, are wrong beliefs.[16]

If a wider objectivity were to come from all this, then the reflective ethical considerations would themselves have to be objective. This brings us back to the question whether the reflective level might generate its own ethical knowledge. If this is understood as our coming to have propositional knowledge of ethical truths, then we need some account of what "tracking the truth" will be. The idea that our beliefs can track the truth at this level must at least imply that a range of investigators could rationally, reasonably, and unconstrainedly come to converge on a determinate set of ethical conclusions. What are the hopes for such a process? I do not mean of its actually happening, but rather of our forming a coherent picture of how it might happen. If it is construed as convergence on a body of ethical truths which is brought about and explained by the fact that they are truths — this would be the strict analogy to scientific objectivity — then I see no hope for it. In particular, there is no hope of extending to this level the kind of world-guidedness we have been considering in the case of the thick ethical concepts. Discussions at the reflective level, if they have the ambition of considering all ethical experience and arriving at the truth about the ethical, will necessarily use the most general and abstract ethical concepts such as "right," and those concepts do not display world-guidedness (which is why they were selected by prescriptivism in its attempt to find a pure evaluative element from which it could *detach* world-guidedness).

I cannot see any convincing theory of knowledge for the convergence of reflective ethical thought on ethical reality in even a distant analogy to the scientific case. Nor is there a convincing analogy with mathematics, a case in which the notion of an independent reality is at least problematical. Besides the reasons mentioned in Chapter 6, there is the important point that every noncontradictory piece of mathematics is part of mathematics, though it may be left aside as too trivial or unilluminating or useless. But not every noncontradictory structure of ethical reflection can be part of one such subject, since bodies of ethical thought can conflict with one another in ways that not only lack the kinds of explanation that could form a credible theory of error, but have too many credible explanations of other kinds.

I do not believe, then, that we can understand reflection as a process that substitutes knowledge for beliefs attained in unreflective practice. We must reject the objectivist view of ethical life as in that way a pursuit of ethical truth. But this does not rule out all forms of objectivism. There is still the project of trying to give an objective grounding or foundation to ethical life. For this, we should look in the direction of the ideas about human nature discussed in Chapter 3. Those ideas should be now freed from the Socratic requirement that they should provide a reason to *each* person to lead an ethical life rather than not. For the purposes we are now considering, it would be significant enough if such considerations could give us a schema of an ethical life that would be the best ethical life, the most satisfactory for human beings in general. The question to be answered is: Granted that human beings need to share a social world, is there anything to be known about their needs and their basic motivations that will show us what this world would best be?

I doubt that there will turn out to be a very satisfying answer. It is probable that any such considerations will radically underdetermine the ethical options even in a given social situation (we must remember that what we take the situation to be is itself, in part, a function of what ethical options we can see). Any ethical life is going to contain restraints on such things as killing, injury, and lying, but those restraints can take very different forms. Again, with respect to the virtues, which is the most natural and promising field for this kind of inquiry, we only have to compare Aristotle's catalogue of the virtues with any that might be produced now to see how pictures of an appropriate human life may differ in spirit and in the actions and institutions they call for. We also have the idea that there are many and various forms of human excellence which will not all fit together into a one harmonious whole, so any determinate ethical outlook is going to represent some kind of specialization of human possibilities. That idea is deeply entrenched in any naturalistic or, again, historical conception of human nature—that is, in any adequate conception of it—and I find it hard to believe that it will be overcome by an objective inquiry, or that human beings could turn out to have a much more determinate nature than is suggested by what we already know, one that timelessly demanded a life of a particular kind.

The project of giving to ethical life an objective and determinate grounding in considerations about human nature is not, in my view, very likely to succeed. But it is at any rate a comprehensible project, and I believe it represents the only intelligible form of ethical objectivity at the reflective level. It is worth asking what would be involved in its succeeding. We should notice, first, how it would have to be human beings that were primarily the subject of our ethics, since it would be from their nature that its conclusions would be drawn. Here this project joins hands with contractualism, in seeing other animals as outside the primary constituency of ethics, and at most beneficiaries of it, while it expects less than contractualism does of our relations to extraterrestrials, who would be connected with it simply through the rules of mutual restraint that might figure in a nonaggression treaty.

If the project succeeded, it would not simply be a matter of agreement on a theory of human nature. The convergence itself would be partly in social and psychological science, but what would matter would be a convergence to which scientific conclusions provided only part of the means. Nor, on the other hand, would there be a convergence directly on ethical truths, as in the other objectivist model. One ethical belief might be said to be in its own right an object of knowledge at the reflective level, to the effect that a certain kind of life was best for human beings. But this will not yield other ethical truths directly. The reason, to put it summarily, is that the excellence or satisfactoriness of a life does not stand to beliefs involved in that life as premise stands to conclusion. Rather, an agent's excellent life is characterized by *having* those beliefs, and most of the beliefs will not be about that agent's dispositions or life, or about other people's dispositions, but about the social world. That life will involve, for instance, the agent's using some thick concepts rather than others. Reflection on the excellence of a life does not itself establish the truth of judgments using those concepts or of the agent's other ethical judgments. Instead it shows that there is good reason (granted the commitment to an ethical life) to live a life that involves those concepts and those beliefs.[17]

The convergence that signaled the success of this project would be a convergence of practical reason, by which people came to lead the best kind of life and to have the desires that belonged to that life; convergence in ethical belief would largely be a part and consequence of that process. One very general ethical belief would, indeed, be an object of knowledge at that level. Many particular ethical judgments, involving the favored thick concepts, could be known to be true, but then judgments of this sort (I have argued) are very often known to be true anyway, even when they occur, as they always have, in a life that is not grounded at the objective level.

The objective grounding would not bring it about that judgments using those concepts were true or could be known: this was so already. But it would enable us to recognize that certain of them were the best or most appropriate thick concepts to use. Between the two extremes of the one very general proposition and the many concrete ones, other ethical beliefs would be true only in the oblique sense that they were the beliefs that would help us to find our way around in a social world which — on this optimistic program — was shown to be the best social world for human beings.

This would be a structure very different from that of the objectivity of science. There would be a radical difference between ethics and science, even if ethics were objective in the only way in which it intelligibly could be. However, this does not mean that there is a clear distinction between (any) fact and (any) value; nor does it mean that there is no ethical knowledge. There is some, and in the less reflective past there has been more.

The problems I have discussed here are not merely hypothetical questions, of whether ethics might eventually turn out to be objective and, if so, how. They are problems about the nature of ethical thought, the way in which it can understand its own nature and the exent to which it can consistently appear to be what it really is. Those are serious problems on any showing, and would be so even if ethical thought turned out to be objective in the only way that is intelligible. We shall see them more distinctly when we have looked at them from a different angle, that of relativism.

CHAPTER 9

Relativism and Reflection

I F WE REFLECT on disagreements of a certain kind and come to the conclusion that they cannot be objectively settled, we may react by adopting some form of relativism. Relativism is not peculiar to ethics; it can be found in many places, even in the philosophy of science. Its aim is to take views, outlooks, or beliefs that apparently conflict and treat them in such a way that they do not conflict: each of them turns out to be acceptable in its own place. The problem is to find a way of doing this, in particular by finding for each belief or outlook something that will be its own place.

The simplest method, and the one that is in the most precise sense relativistic, is to interpret the original claims as each introducing a relation to a different item. The Greek thinker Protagoras, generally acknowledged to have been the first relativist, started from conflicting sensory appearances, as when I find the wind cold and you find it warm, and claimed that there was no answer to the question whether the wind was really "in itself" warm or cold — the fact of the matter is simply that it is cold for me and warm for you. It was this relational treatment that I mentioned in the last chapter as a way, though not the most convincing way, of treating variations in the perception of secondary qualities, not (as in Protagoras' original case) between individuals but between different kinds of perceiver.

The aim of relativism is to *explain away* a conflict, and this involves two tasks. It has to say why there is no conflict and also why it looked as if there were one. Strict relational relativism performs the first task very crisply, by finding in the two statements a logical form that makes them straightforwardly compatible, so that there is no problem in accepting both. It tends to have less success with the second task because, the more convincing it is to claim that the statements are really relational, the more puzzling it is that people should have thought there was a conflict. Relational relativism introduces a clearly compatible structure and then has to say what disguised it. It may be helpful to approach relativism from the other direction, and ask what happens if we start by conceding that two beliefs or outlooks do indeed conflict and are genuinely exclusive. The problem will then be to find a sense in which each may still be acceptable in its place.

One idea that requires us to think in a broader way about relativism is *incommensurability*. Some philosophers of science hold that scientific theories may be incommensurable with one another because they differ in the concepts they use, the reference they give to various terms, and what they count as evidence. These theories will not straightforwardly contradict one another. Yet they do exclude one another. If they did not, there would be no difficulty in combining them, as one can combine the topography of separate places. They cannot be combined, and it was this fact that started the discussion in the first place. Those supporting one of the theories try to find reasons for rejecting the other; one of them may drive out the other in the course of the history of science. How can this be? Some radical philosophers of science will say that you cannot combine the two theories merely because you cannot combine accepting both theories: the research activities characteristic of each theory, the direction of attention appropriate to each, and so on, cannot be combined. You cannot work within both of them.

This account of rival scientific theories makes them sound like two cultures or forms of life. As an account of science, it seems to me a wild exaggeration, but a story of this kind may be appropriate to what really are different cultures or forms of life, such as that of the hypertraditional society considered in the last chapter. The outlook of one such society might to an important extent be incommensurable with that of another, but they would still exclude one another. The conflict would lie in what was involved in living within them.

If two cultures, or outlooks, or ways of life exclude one another, is there any room for relativism? Not instantly. Someone who has certain dispositions and expectations as a member of one culture will often be unwilling, when confronted with an alternative way of life, to do what is done in the other culture. Moreover, it is part of what makes his responses ethical responses that they are deeply internalized enough for his reaction, in some cases, to be not merely unwillingness but rejection. For rejection to be appropriate, it is not necessary that the parties conceptualize in the same way the actions in question, and, granted the situation we are supposing, they will not do so. Thus members of a culture that does not admit human sacrifice encounter members of another that does. They conceptualize differently the ritual killings, but this does not mean that the first group, if horrified, are laboring under an anthropological misunderstanding. It is, as they might put it, a deliberate killing of a captive, which is enough for their ethically hostile sentiments to extend to it. (It does not follow that they have to blame anyone: that is another question.)

The dispositions and reactions that are exercised within one culture are not merely diverted or shown to be inappropriate by the fact that its members are presented with the behavior of another culture. In any case, it is artificial to treat these matters as if they always involved two clearly self-contained cultures. A fully individuable culture is at best a rare thing. Cultures, subcultures, fragments of cultures, constantly meet one another and exchange and modify practices and attitudes. Social practices could never come forward with a certificate saying that they belonged to a genuinely different culture, so that they were guaranteed immunity to alien judgments and reactions.

So instant relativism is excluded. For similar reasons, strict relational relativism in ethics is excluded altogether. It has had able defenders,[1] but it is implausible to suppose that ethical conceptions of right and wrong have a logically inherent relativity to a given society. Consider once more the hypertraditional society, and suppose that it does have some rules expressed in terms of something like "right" and "wrong." When it is first exposed to another culture and invited to reflect, it cannot suddenly discover that there is an implicit relativization hidden in its language. It will always be, so to speak, too early or too late for that. It is too early, when they have never reflected or thought of an alternative to "us." (A question from Chapter 7 applies here: how could this have come into their language?) It is too late, when they confront the new situation; that requires them to see beyond their existing rules and practices.

It now looks as if relativism may be excluded altogether. The fact that people can and must react when they are confronted with another culture, and do so by applying their existing notions— also by reflecting on them—seems to show that the ethical thought of a given culture can always stretch beyond its boundaries. It is important that this is a point about the content or aspirations of ethical thought, not about its objectivity. Even if there is no way in which divergent ethical beliefs can be brought to converge by independent inquiry or rational argument, this fact will not imply relativism. Each outlook may still be making claims it intends to apply to the whole world, not just to that part of it which is its "own" world.

Nevertheless, while it is true that nonobjectivity does not imply any relativistic attitude, there does seem something blank and unresponsive in merely stopping at that truth. If you are *conscious* of nonobjectivity, should that not properly affect the way in which you see the application or extent of your ethical outlook? If so, how? This consciousness cannot just switch off your ethical reactions when you are confronted with another group, and there is no reason why it should. Some people have thought that it should, believing that a properly relativistic view requires you to be equally well disposed to everyone else's ethical beliefs. This is seriously confused, since it takes relativism to issue in a nonrelativistic morality of universal toleration.[2] But the confused reaction is certainly a reaction to something. If we become conscious of ethical variation and of the kinds of explanation it may receive, it is incredible that this consciousness should just leave everything where it was and not affect our ethical thought itself. We can go on, no doubt, simply saying that we are right and everyone else is wrong (that is to say, on the nonobjectivist view, affirming our values and rejecting theirs), but if we have arrived at this stage of reflection, it seems a remarkably inadequate response. What else is possible? In trying to answer this, we once again turn the question of relativism around. The question has traditionally been whether we *have* to think in a relativistic way, for conceptual or logical reasons, or whether that is impossible. We should rather ask how much room we can coherently find for thinking like this, and how far it provides a more adequate response to reflection.

All the ideas we have considered so far assume that there is one basic distinction, between the outlook of one group and the outlook of all others. The relativist thinks that the judgments of one group apply just to that group, and the other party thinks that any group's judgments must apply to everybody. They are both wrong. If we are going to accommodate the relativist's concerns, we must not simply draw a line between ourselves and others. We must not draw a line at all, but recognize that others are at varying distances from us. We must also see that our reactions and relations to other groups are themselves part of our ethical life, and we should understand these reactions more realistically in terms of the practices and sentiments that help to shape our life. Some disagreements and divergences matter more than others. Above all, it matters whether the contrast of our outlook with another is one that makes a difference, whether a question has to be resolved about what life is going to be lived by one group or the other.

We should distinguish between *real* and *notional* confrontations.[3] A real confrontation between two divergent outlooks occurs at a given time if there is a group of people for whom each of the outlooks is a real option. A notional confrontation, by contrast, occurs when some people know about two divergent outlooks, but at least one of those outlooks does not present a real option. The idea of a "real option" is largely, but not entirely, a social notion. An outlook is a real option for a group either if it already is their outlook or if they could go over to it; and they could go over to it if they could live inside it in their actual historical circumstances and retain their hold on reality, not engage in extensive self-deception, and so on. The extent to which they can do this depends on what features of their present social situation are assumed to remain constant if they go over to the other outlook. Something might become possible for people if their situation were changed, and the question whether it is a real option for them involves the question whether their situation could be changed. People can be mistaken about these questions. They may think an outlook is a real option when it is not, because they are ill informed or optimistic or in the grip of a fantasy, and this may be a social or political mistake, not just a personal one. In the other direction, they may not have realized what going over to the outlook could offer them.

Many outlooks that human beings have had are not real options for us now. The life of a Bronze Age chief or a medieval samurai are not real options for us: there is no way of living them. This is not to deny that reflection on those value systems might inspire some thoughts relevant to modern life, but there is no way of taking on those outlooks. Even utopian projects among a small band of enthusiasts could not reproduce *that* life. Still more, the project of reenacting it on a social scale in the context of modern industrial life would involve a vast social illusion. The prospect of removing the conditions of modern industrial life altogether is something else again — another, though different, impossibility.

It is important that options may be asymmetrically related. Some version of modern technological life has become a real option for members of surviving traditional societies, but their life is not a real option for us, despite the passionate nostalgia of many. The theories we have about the nature of such asymmetries, and how far they extend, affect our views about the possibilities of radical social and political action.

A relativist view of a given type of outlook can be understood as saying that for such outlooks it is only in real confrontations that the language of appraisal — good, bad, right, wrong, and so on — can be applied to them; in notional confrontations, this kind of appraisal is seen as inappropriate, and no judgments are made. When relativism is rejected for a given area, this does not mean that there are no notional confrontations. The confrontation between phlogiston theory and any contemporary theory of combustion is without doubt notional, and phlogiston theory is not now a real option; but on the nonrelativist view of such theories there is something to be said in appraisal of phlogiston theory, that it is false. It is not merely that to try to live the life of a convinced phlogiston theorist in contemporary academia is as incoherent an enterprise as trying to live the life of a Teutonic Knight in 1930's Nuremberg. Phlogiston theory is not a real option because it cannot be squared with a lot that we know to be true.

I shall call relativism seen in this way *the relativism of distance*. There is room for it in a reflective ethical outlook. The distance that makes confrontation notional, and makes this relativism possible, can lie in various directions. Sometimes it is a matter of what is elsewhere, and the relativism is applied to the exotic. It is naturally applied to the more distant past. It can also be applied to the future, and I shall turn to that at the end of this chapter.

In introducing this kind of relativism, I have mentioned ethical outlooks rather than particular practices, and it is to fairly large-scale systems or bodies of beliefs and attitudes that it has to be applied. If we are to take seriously the relativistic suspension of ethical judgment, we have to conceive of the society in question as a whole. There are some ethical concepts that we can apply to people and their actions — virtue and vice concepts, for instance — even when the outlook of the society in which they lived is not in real confrontation with ours. This involves taking the people in abstraction from the social practices in which they lived, and so, often, we do not see them realistically. A special case is the historical figure who was a criminal or a dissenter, so that neither we nor his contemporaries see him as living entirely by the local values. In this case, the dissenter and the society can in principle be concretely understood, though they rarely are.[4]

If the relativist suspension of assessment is to be taken seriously, we have to think of the society itself realistically and concretely. Many ethical stories we tell about the past or the exotic have little to do with the reality of those times or places. They are fantasies, serving some of the same ethical ends as fairy tales, and if they offend against anything, it is against a realistic view of human life and human possibilities, rather than against any seriously proposed relativism. They do not really think about other societies, but use them as a source of emblems and aspirations.[5]

Relativism over merely spatial distance is of no interest or application in the modern world. Today all confrontations between cultures must be real confrontations, and the existence of exotic traditional societies presents quite different, and difficult, issues of whether the rest of the world can or should use power to preserve them, like endangered species; anthropological and other field workers find themselves in the role of game wardens.[6] Thoughts about the past and the future raise different problems because we are caused by the one and cause the other. Moreover, the past and our understanding of it are specially related to the reflectiveness that starts off these problems. I take it that the modern world is marked by a peculiar level of reflectiveness, and while that fact was expressed by Hegel, and these discussions in good part started by him, the range of explanatory frameworks in which we can set our own and others' cultures is now much greater.

The growth of reflective consciousness has not been even or always positive. Still less should we believe that up to a certain point there was in the Western world an integrated, concrete, familiar, community life that was shattered by something which, according to taste, is identified with 1914, the Industrial Revolution, Galileo, the Reformation, or some yet earlier item. These various versions of the Fall are equally mythical and equally expressive of a yearning for a state of absolute identity with the environment, a yearning for something dimly remembered. One does not have to accept the myth in order to grant two things, that the urge to reflective understanding of society and our activities goes deeper and is more widely spread in modern society than it has ever been before; and that the thicker kinds of ethical concept have less currency in modern society than they did in more traditional societies, even if their use in those societies did not guarantee, as the myth has it, communal identity, lack of conflict, and a sense of completeness.[7]

There is no route back from reflectiveness. I do not mean that nothing can lead to its reduction; both personally and socially, many things can. But there is no *route* back, no way in which we can consciously take ourselves back from it. Even in the individual case, though we can consciously embark on a course to reduce reflection, we cannot consciously pursue that course, and if we are successful, we will have had to forget it. But in the social case, there will be people who do not want to pursue it, and they will try not to let the others forget it. This phenomenon of self-consciousness, together with the institutions and processes that support it, constitute one reason why past forms of life are not a real option for the present, and why attempts to go back often produce results that are ludicrous on a small scale and hideous on a larger one. This can be seen, above all, with reactionary projects to recreate supposedly contented hierarchical societies of the past. These projects in any case face the criticism that their pictures of the past are fantasies; but even if there have been contented hierarchies, any charm they have for us is going to rest on their having been innocent and not having understood their own nature. This cannot be recreated, since measures would have to be taken to stop people raising questions that are, by now, there to be raised.[8]

But if the questions are there to be raised, should we not — or, at any rate, may we not — raise them about those societies as they existed in the past? In particular, may we not ask whether those societies, however unaware they may have been, were unjust? Can a relativism of distance put them beyond this question? There is a question we can usefully ask first. In being less reflective and self-conscious than modern society, what was it that these societies did not know?

It is tempting to say that they did not know of alternatives to their social arrangements and thought that their social order was necessary. Of some traditional societies, isolated and nonliterate, it may have been straightforwardly true that they did not know that there were alternatives, but many sophisticated hierarchical societies, those of the European Middle Ages for instance, certainly knew of alternatives, inasmuch as they knew that human beings had organized societies in other ways and did so at that time elsewhere. What they did not know, we shall have to say, is that there was an alternative *for them.* But then it is far from clear that there was an alternative for them. We need some firmer hold than we presently have on *what might have been* to say (at any interesting level, at least) that they might have had a different social organization,[9] and some even more robust views about freedom to say that they could have attained it. They may not have been wrong in thinking that their social order was necessary for them. It is rather the way in which they saw it as necessary — as religiously or metaphysically necessary — that we cannot now accept. Where we see them as wrong was in the myths that legitimated their hierarchies. We see our view of our society and ourselves as more naturalistic than their view of themselves. This naturalistic conception of society, expressed by Hobbes and Spinoza at the beginning of the modern world, represents one of the ways in which the world has become *entzaubert,* in Max Weber's famous phrase: the magic has gone from it. (The current attempts by Islamic forces in particular to reverse that process — if that is what those attempts really are — do not show that the process is local or reversible, only that it can generate despair.)

The legitimations of hierarchy offered in past societies, and the ways in which we now see them, are relevant to what we say about the justice or injustice of those societies. This is important for the relativism of distance. "Just" and "unjust" are central terms that can be applied to societies as a whole, and in principle, at least, they can be applied to societies concretely and realistically conceived. Moreover, an assessment in terms of justice can, more obviously than others, be conducted without involving the unhelpful question of whether anyone was to blame. The combination of these features makes social justice a special case in relation to relativism. Justice and injustice are certainly ethical notions and arguably can be applied to past societies as a whole, even when we understand a good deal about them.

One can defend a relativistic view of justice. There is some pressure, if one thinks historically at all, to see modern conceptions of social justice, in terms of equal rights, for instance, as simply not applying to hierarchical societies of the past. The obvious fact that those societies would not satisfy the conditions I quoted from Rawls in Chapter 5 seems relevant neither to those societies nor to the merits of Rawls's criteria as proposed for modern societies.[10] Yet there are strong pressures for the justice or injustice of past societies not merely to evaporate in the relativism of distance. Even if we refuse to apply to them determinately modern ideas, some conceptions of justice were used in those societies themselves, and it is not a pun or a linguistic error to call them that. One can see some modern conceptions of social justice as more radical — conservatives may say, misguided — applications of ideas that have existed elsewhere and informed other societies; equally, historical continuities may be put to ethical use in the opposite direction. Earlier conceptions, in some form, are still with us. We know, or should know, that there is no going back and that the legitimations of hierarchy in earlier societies are not available to us. But if radicals can identify more egalitarian modern conceptions as descendants of past conceptions of justice, so can conservatives try to find some less egalitarian analogue of the old conceptions to serve them now, freed from the past legitimations, which (unless they are benightedly reactionary) they as well as everyone else can see will no longer do.

It matters a great deal to ethical thought, in what way past legitimations are seen as discredited. The growth of reflection and the naturalistic view of society leads to their being intellectually discredited; they are explained or understood, and not in the way that they themselves would have wished. But some explanations of them may mean that they are ethically discredited. Critical theory[11] rightly urges us to raise particular kinds of question about their explanation, asking whether the acceptance of the legitimation may not have been merely an effect of the power it was supposed to legitimate. This is potentially an ethical argument, not merely an explanatory one. Such arguments help to keep questions of the justice of past societies alive within the boundaries of modern ethical thought, and to make the relativism of distance seem less appropriate.

There is much more that should be said on these issues.[12] It may be that considerations of justice are a central element of ethical thought that transcends the relativism of distance. Perhaps this, too, comes from a feature of the modern world. We have various conceptions of social justice, with different political consequences;

each has comprehensible roots in the past and in our sentiments. Since we know that we do not accept their past legitimations, but otherwise are not sure how to read them, we are disposed to see past conceptions of justice as embodiments of ideas that still have a claim on modern people. To this extent, we see them as in real confrontation with each other and with modern ideas.

I come back now to reflection itself and its relations to ethical knowledge. Earlier I said that reflection might destroy knowledge, because thick ethical concepts that were used in a less reflective state might be driven from use by reflection, while the more abstract and general ethical thoughts that would probably take their place would not satisfy the conditions of propositional knowledge. To say that knowledge is destroyed in such a case is not to say that particular beliefs that once were true now cease to be true. Nor is it to say that people turn out never to have known the things they thought they knew. What it means is that these people once had beliefs of a certain kind, which were in many cases pieces of knowledge; but now, because after reflection they can no longer use concepts essential to those beliefs, they can no longer form beliefs of that kind. A certain kind of knowledge with regard to particular situations, which used to guide them round their social world and helped to form it, is no longer available to them. Knowledge is destroyed because a potentiality for a certain kind of knowledge has been destroyed; moreover, if they think about their earlier beliefs, they will now see them as the observer saw them, as knowledge they do not share.

It is not unknown for reflection to destroy knowledge. It is a platitude that a practical skill can, in an individual case, be destroyed by reflection on how one practices it (though equally, in favorable circumstances, it can be enhanced). But that case is very different from this. First, that is only a point about the individual's own consciousness: observers can theoretically inquire into the ways in which the skilled performer performs, and their conclusions, correctly deployed, can certainly help his performance. A second difference is that his reflection concerns something he undoubtedly can do, and while it may bring it about that he can no longer do it, it does not imply that this should be so. In the ethical case, however, while it is true that before reflection people could genuinely find their way around a social world by using these concepts, the implication of the reflection is that they should now be doing something else. Unlike the unsettling reflections of the bicyclist or the tightrope walker, ethical reflection becomes part of the practice it considers, and inherently modifies it.

Socrates thought of these issues only in terms of an individual's reflection on his own practice. He thought it impossible that reflection should destroy knowledge, since nothing unreflective could be knowledge in the first place. He believed that reflection led, if anything did, to knowledge and that knowledge was what mattered (one must be in a better state with knowledge than without it). If one has the second of these beliefs without the first, the idea that reflection can destroy knowledge will turn against reflection and express itself in the kind of conservatism, or worse, that praises rootedness, unspoken grasp, and traditional understandings. There is certainly more to be said for these things than much progressive thought has allowed; indeed, there is more to be said for them than there is for much progressive thought. But even if one grants value to traditional knowledge, to try to suppress reflection in that interest can lead to nothing but disaster, rather as someone who finds that having children has disrupted her life cannot regain her earlier state by killing them.

But we should not accept Socrates' second belief. If we are going to accept the un-Socratic paradox, we should reject both his assumptions. Ethical knowledge, though there is such a thing, is not necessarily the best ethical state. Here we must remember that, in the process of losing ethical knowledge, we may gain knowledge of other kinds, about human nature, history, what the world is actually like. We can gain knowledge about, or around, the ethical. Inside the ethical, by the same process, we may gain understanding.

This is not merely another name for the knowledge we shall have lost. Above all, it is not related in the same way to conviction. One reason why conservatives and traditionalists attack reflection is that they fear the uncertainty that seems to follow from it, the situation in which the best lack all conviction. The result they fear is something to be feared, and they are right to detest a certain liberal posture that makes a virtue out of uncertainty itself and, in place of conviction, enjoys the satisfactions — the equally intellectualist satisfactions — of a refined indecision. But those traditionalists and those liberals share the error of thinking that what conviction in ethical life has to be is knowledge, that it must be a mode of certainty.

If ethical conviction is not to be identified with knowledge or certainty, what is it? There are those who reject the account of it as certainty, but replace this account with another that is no more sound and rather less plausible. Believing that besides the intellect there can only be the will, they think that the source of ethical conviction must be a *decision,*[13] to adopt certain moral principles or to live in one way rather than another. This cannot be right because ethical conviction, like any other form of *being convinced,* must have some aspect of passivity to it, must in some sense come to you. Some decisions can seem like that, but this is because they are particularly compelling decisions. You could not have an ethical conviction, and be conscious that it was the product of a decision, unless that decision itself appeared inescapable. But then this is what would need to be explained.

Kant indeed believed that morality required autonomy and that no moral principle could properly be *yours* — or, to put it another way, nothing that was yours could be a moral principle — unless you had freely acknowledged or adopted it. But, as we saw in Chapter 4, that was a view Kant applied equally to theoretical conclusions, and he held it at the level of his transcendental psychology. He was not concerned with any decision that was a psychological feature of our everyday experience. Indeed, as we shall see in the next chapter, he needed to find in everyday experience something that had just the opposite character, something that stood in for the acknowledgments of reason, and this presented itself in the mode of passivity, as a feeling that seemed to be determined from outside, which he called "the sense of reverence for the Law."

Neither the decision model nor the certainty model looks very helpful in face of actual lack of ethical conviction. Some people argue in favor of the certainty model by saying that we need ethical conviction and that only knowledge can bring it. They ignore the obvious fact that no amount of faith in cognitive certainty will actually bring about ethical conviction if we cannot agree on what we are supposed to be certain about. Seeing the force of this, those who favor the other model say that we have been looking in the wrong direction: ethics is a matter for decision, and we must face the responsibility and take up the burden of making those decisions. This ignores the equally obvious point that if ethics is a matter of decision, and we are uncertain, then we are uncertain what to decide.

We need a third conception, for which the best word is perhaps *confidence.* It is basically a social phenomenon. This is not to deny that when it exists in a society, it does so because individuals possess it in some form, nor that it can exist in some individuals when it is lacking in society. When this happens, however, it is in a different form, since the absence of social confirmation and support for the individual's attitudes must affect the way in which he holds those attitudes — in the first place, by making him conscious of them. The point of bringing in this conception is not that philosophy, which could not tell us how to bring about conviction, can tell us how to bring about confidence. It is rather that this conception makes it clearer than the other models did why philosophy cannot tell us how to bring it about. It is a social and psychological question what kinds of institutions, upbringing, and public discourse help to foster it. The first questions that should come to mind about ethical confidence are questions of social explanation. This does not mean that it has nothing to do with rational argument. Social states can be affected, one way or another, by rational argument. Moreover, if we try to generate confidence without rational argument or by suppressing it, we are quite likely to fail, but, besides that, we shall be sacrificing other goods. Confidence is merely one good among others: it has a price, and the price should not be set too high.

Confidence is both a social state and related to discussion, theorizing, and reflection; correspondingly, these activities are themselves forms of practice, which take up social space, just as in

the individual they take up psychological space. We are led to forget
that fact by a series of intellectualist conceptions: that our fundamental aim must be to arrive at the answers to ethical questions;
that the way to do this must be to pay as much attention as possible
to reasons bearing on those questions; and that the demands of
practice limiting those activities are simply that, a practical limitation. The truth is that the basic question is how to live and what to
do; ethical considerations are relevant to this; and the amount of
time and human energy to be spent in reflecting on these considerations must itself depend on what, from the perspective of the
ethical life we actually have, we count as a life worth living and on
what is likely to produce people who find life worth living. One
question we have to answer is how people, or enough people, can
come to possess a practical confidence that, particularly granted
both the need for reflection and its pervasive presence in our world,
will come from strength and not from the weakness of self-deception and dogmatism. (Confidence is not the same as optimism; it
could rest on what Nietzsche called the pessimism of strength.)

This discussion suggests a conclusion about the future of ethical
thought and practice. We should recall the idea, which I considered
at the end of the last chapter, of human beings arriving at an
objective foundation of ethical life; or, to put it in a way that will be
most helpful here, of their arriving at an ethical life they know to be
objectively founded. This may not be a likely prospect, but there is
something more to be learned from the idea of it. The process
would involve a practical convergence, on a shared way of life. In
the case of science, my account of objectivity involved the idea of a
convergence that would be *uncoerced*: if it were not uncoerced, we
could not explain it as a process that arrives at the truth. In the
practical, ethical, case convergence would need to be explained in
terms of basic desires or interests, and this also requires the process
to be uncoerced. It raises the question of what would count as that.

Some processes would obviously not count. If Martians arrived and made it clear that if human beings did not bring about a
high level of agreement on a certain form of ethical life, they would
destroy our planet, it might be that in a couple of generations,

perhaps with the help of some technology they provided, this agreement would be established. This would certainly involve basic desires and interests, but not in a way relevant to the idea of giving our life an objective grounding. It would merely be that, because of these sanctions, the life would have been accepted. After we had arrived at the required state of affairs, the aliens would have to keep us conscious of the terror; or destroy the power of reflection; or provide a powerful legitimating myth. If, without any of these, they could leave the system to run satisfactorily, then they must have given us a satisfactory way of life (not one that was uniquely so, perhaps) — but what made it so would be the fact that we could live stably and reflectively in it, not that we were forced to converge on it.

If the agreement were to be uncoerced, it would have to grow from inside human life. It would have to be influenced at the same time by theoretical inquiry. Such a process implies free institutions, ones that allow not only for free inquiry but also for diversity of life and some ethical variety. Here, however, we have to guard once again against the error, in its social version, of assuming that reflection takes up no psychological space. A society given over to "experiments in living," in Mill's phrase, is not one that simply increases the chances of living in the best way. It is one sort of society rather than another, and there are various forms of living that it rules out; indeed, those ruled out could include those most worth living. However, this means only that diversity and freedom of inquiry are, like confidence, some goods to be encouraged among others, not that they fail to be goods. Those who believe in objectivity, and see that the only intelligible form of objectivity is an objective grounding, have reason to accept that they are important goods.

One also has reason to accept that they are important goods if one does not believe in objectivity. This is because of a relativism of distance directed toward the future. The case of people in a future society is the unique case in which we can have both a purely notional confrontation with another set of values and also some responsibility for them — a responsibility at least to the extent that we can try or refuse to try to seal our values into future generations.

To be confident in trying to make sure that future generations shared our values, we would need, it seems to me, not only to be confident in those values — which, if we can achieve it, is a good thing to be — but also convinced that they were objective, which is a misguided thing to be. If we do not have this conviction, then we have reason to stand back from affecting the future, as we have reason to stand back from judging the past. We should not try to seal determinate values into future society.

We also have reason to take some positive steps. We should try to leave resources for an adequate life and, as means to that and as part of it, we shall try to transmit what we take to be our knowledge. We cannot consistently leave out the reflective consciousness itself and practices of free inquiry needed to sustain it and to make use of it. Of course, there is some tension between these two aims, the negative and the positive. To try to transmit free inquiry and the reflective consciousness is to transmit something rather than nothing, and something that demands some forms of life rather than others.

To our immediate successors, our children at least, we have reason to try to transmit more: it is a mark of our having ethical values that we aim to reproduce them. But this does not affect very determinately what remoter generations will hold. If new developments were to give us more influence on their outlooks, we would do better not to use it, beyond sending them, if we can, free inquiry and reflection, a legacy we can see as created by our knowledge. That will be enough of a legacy, and it will show a proper respect for the relativism of distance that we should not try to send them more.

CHAPTER 10

Morality, the Peculiar Institution

EARLIER I referred to morality as a special system, a particular variety of ethical thought. I must now explain what I take it to be, and why we would be better off without it.

The important thing about morality is its spirit, its underlying aims, and the general picture of ethical life it implies. In order to see them, we shall need to look carefully at a particular concept, *moral obligation*. The mere fact that it uses a notion of obligation is not what makes morality special. There is an everyday notion of obligation, as one consideration among others, and it is ethically useful. Morality is distinguished by the special notion of obligation it uses, and by the significance it gives to it. It is this special notion that I shall call "moral obligation." Morality is not one determinate set of ethical thoughts. It embraces a range of ethical outlooks; and morality is so much with us that moral philosophy spends much of its time discussing the differences between those outlooks, rather than the difference between all of them and everything else. They are not all equally typical or instructive examples of the morality system, though they do have in common the idea of moral obligation. The philosopher who has given the purest, deepest, and most thorough representation of morality is Kant. But morality is not an invention of philosophers. It is the outlook, or, incoherently, part of the outlook, of almost all of us.

In the morality system, moral obligation is expressed in one especially important kind of deliberative conclusion—a conclusion that is directed toward what to do, governed by moral reasons, and concerned with a particular situation. (There are also general obligations, and we shall come back to them later.) Not every conclusion of a particular moral deliberation, even within the morality system, expresses an obligation. To go no further, some moral conclusions merely announce that you *may* do something. Those do not express an obligation, but they are in a sense still governed by the idea of obligation: you ask whether you are under an obligation, and decide that you are not.

This description is in terms of the output or conclusion of moral deliberation. The moral considerations that go into a deliberation may themselves take the form of obligations, but one would naturally say that they did not need to do so. I might, for instance, conclude that I was under an obligation to act in a certain way, because it was for the best that a certain outcome should come about and I could bring it about in that way. However, there is a pressure within the morality system to represent every consideration that goes into a deliberation and yields a particular obligation as being itself a general obligation; so if I am now under an obligation to do something that would be for the best, this will be because I have some general obligation, perhaps among others, to do what is for the best. We shall see later how this happens.

The fact that moral obligation is a kind of practical conclusion explains several of its features. An obligation applies to someone with respect to an action — it is an obligation to do something — and the action must be in the agent's power. "*Ought* implies *can*" is a formula famous in this connection. As a general statement about *ought* it is untrue, but it must be correct if it is taken as a condition on what can be a particular obligation, where that is practically concluded. If my deliberation issues in something I cannot do, then I must deliberate again. The question of what counts as in the agent's power is notoriously problematical, not only because of large and unnerving theories claiming that everything (or everything psychological) is determined, but also because it is simply unclear what it means to say that someone can act, or could have acted, in a certain way. To say anything useful about these problems needs a wide-ranging discussion that I shall not attempt in this book.[1] What I shall have to say here, however, will suggest that morality, in this as in other respects, encounters the common problems in a peculiarly acute form.

Another feature of moral obligations in this sense is that they cannot conflict, ultimately, really, or at the end of the line. This will follow directly from the last point, that what I am obliged to do must be in my power, if one grants a further principle (it has been called the "agglomeration principle"), that if I am obliged to do X and obliged to do Y, then I am obliged to do X and Y. This requirement, too, reflects the practical shape of this notion of obligation. In an ordinary sense of "obligation," not controlled by these special requirements, obligations obviously can conflict. One of the most common occasions of mentioning them at all is when they do.[2]

The philosopher David Ross invented a terminology, still sometimes used, for discussing the conflict of obligations, which distinguished between *prima facie* and actual obligations. A *prima facie* obligation is a conclusion, supported by moral considerations, which is a candidate for being one's actual obligation. It will be the proper conclusion of one's moral deliberation if it is not outweighed by another obligation. Ross tried to explain (without much success) why a merely *prima facie* obligation — one that is eventually outweighed — is more than an apparent obligation. It is to be seen as exerting some force on the place of decision, but not enough, granted the competition, to get into that place. The effect, in more concrete terms, is that the considerations that supported the defeated *prima facie* obligation can come to support some other, actual, obligation. If I have for good and compelling reasons broken a promise, I may acquire an actual obligation to do something else because of that, such as compensate the person who has been let down.

It is not at all clear why I should be under this further obligation, since it is one's own business, on this view of things, to observe one's obligations, and I shall have done that. No actual obligation has been broken. This has a comforting consequence, that I should not blame myself. I may blame myself for something else, such as getting into the situation, but it is mistaken to blame or reproach myself for not doing the rejected action: self-reproach belongs with broken obligations, and, it has turned out, there was no obligation. It is conceded that I may reasonably feel bad about it, but this feeling is distinguished by the morality system from remorse or self-reproach, for instance under the title "regret," which is not a moral feeling. This reclassification is important, and very characteristic of what happens when the ethical is contracted to the moral. To say that your feelings about something done involuntarily, or as the lesser of two evils, are to be understood as regret, a nonmoral feeling, implies that you should feel toward those actions as you feel toward things that merely happen, or toward the actions of others. The thought *I did it* has no special significance; what is significant is whether I voluntarily did what I ought to have done. This turns our attention away from an important dimension of ethical experience, which lies in the distinction simply between what one has done and what one has not done. That can be as important as the distinction between the voluntary and the nonvoluntary.[3]

Moral obligation is inescapable. I may acquire an obligation voluntarily, as when I make a promise: in that case, indeed, it is usually said that it has to be voluntarily made to be a promise at all, though there is a gray area here, as with promises made under constraint. In other cases, I may be under an obligation through no choice of mine. But, either way, once I am under the obligation, there is no escaping it, and the fact that a given agent would prefer not to be in this system or bound by its rules will not excuse him; nor will blaming him be based on a misunderstanding. Blame is the characteristic reaction of the morality system. The remorse or self-reproach or guilt I have already mentioned is the characteristic first-personal reaction within the system, and if an agent never felt such sentiments, he would not belong to the morality system or be a full moral agent in its terms. The system also involves blame between persons, and unless there were such a thing, these first-personal reactions would doubtless not be found, since they are formed by internalization. But it is possible for particular agents who belong to the system never to blame anyone, in the sense of expressing blame and perhaps even of feeling the relevant sentiments. They might, for instance, be scrupulously skeptical about what was in other people's power. The point that self-blame or remorse requires one's action to have been voluntary is only a special application of a general rule, that blame of anyone is directed to the voluntary. The moral law is more exigent than the law of an actual liberal republic, because it allows no emigration, but it is unequivocally just in its ideas of responsibility.

In this respect, utilitarianism is a marginal member of the morality system. It has a strong tradition of thinking that blame and other social reactions should be allocated in a way that will be socially useful, and while this might lead to their being directed to the voluntary, equally it might not. This follows consistently from applying the utilitarian criterion to all actions, including the social actions of expressing blame and so forth. The same principle can be extended to unexpressed blame and critical thoughts; indeed, at another level, a utilitarian might well ask whether the most useful policy might not be to forget that the point of blame, on utilitarian grounds, was usefulness. These maneuvers do seem to receive a check when it comes to self-reproach and the sense of moral obligation. Utilitarians are often immensely conscientious people, who work for humanity and give up meat for the sake of the animals. They think this is what they morally ought to do and feel guilty if they do not live up to their own standards. They do not, and perhaps could not, ask: How useful is it that I think and feel like this? It is because of such motivations, and not only because of logical features, that utilitarianism in most versions is a kind of morality, if a marginal one.

The sense that moral obligation is inescapable, that what I am obliged to do is what I *must* do, is the first-personal end of the conception already mentioned, that moral obligation applies to people even if they do not want it to. The third-personal aspect is that moral judgment and blame can apply to people even if, at the limit, they want to live outside that system altogether. From the perspective of morality, there is nowhere outside the system, or at least nowhere for a responsible agent. Taking Kant's term, we may join these two aspects in saying that moral obligation is *categorical*.

I shall come back later to people outside the system. There is more that needs to be said first about what a moral obligation is for someone within the system. It is hard to agree that the course of action which, on a given occasion, there is most moral reason to take must necessarily count as a moral obligation. There are actions (also policies, attitudes, and so on) that are either more or less than obligations. They may be heroic or very fine actions, which go beyond what is obligatory or demanded. Or they may be actions that from a ethical point of view it would be agreeable or worthwhile or a good idea to do, without one's being required to do them. The point is obvious in terms of people's reactions. People may be greatly admired, or merely well thought of, for actions they would not be blamed for omitting. How does the morality system deal with the considerations that seemingly do not yield obligations?

One way in which the central, deontological, version of morality deals with them is to try to make as many as possible into obligations. (It has a particular motive for the reductivist enterprise of trying to make all ethical considerations into one type.) There are some instructive examples of this in the work of Ross, whose terminology of *prima facie* obligations I have already mentioned. He lists several types of what he regards as general obligations or, as he also calls them, duties.[4] The first type includes what everyone calls an obligation, keeping promises and, by a fairly natural extension, telling the truth. The second class involves "duties of gratitude": to do good to those who have done services for you. But it is not really clear that these are *duties,* unless the benefactor (as the word "services" may imply) has acquired a right to expect a return —in which case, it will follow from some implied promise, and the obligation will belong with the first type. Good deeds I have not asked for may indeed be oppressive, but I should not simply take that oppression for obligation.[5]

What Ross is trying to force into the mold of obligation is surely a different ethical idea, that it is a sign of good character to want to return benefits. This characteristic is not the same thing as a disposition to do what one is morally obliged to do. A different ethical thought, again, is disguised in Ross's third class, which he calls "duties of justice." What he says about this is extraordinary:

[these duties] rest on the fact or possibility of a distribution of pleasure or happiness or the means thereto which is not in accordance with the merits of the persons concerned; in which case there arises a duty to upset or prevent such a distribution.

There are such things as duties or obligations of justice, but this incitement to insurrection against the capitalist economy (or any other, come to that) can hardly be the right account of what they are. The requirements of justice concern, in the first place, *what ought to happen.* The way in which a given requirement of justice relates to what a given person has reason to do, or more specifically is under an obligation to do, is a matter of how that person stands to the requirement. In politics, the question of how far personal action stands from the desirable — the *utopia measure,* as it might be called — is itself one of the first, and one of the first ethical, questions.

It is a mistake of morality to try to make everything into obligations. But the reasons for the mistake go deep. Here we should recall that what is *ordinarily* called an obligation does not necessarily have to win in a conflict of moral considerations. Suppose you are under an everyday obligation — to visit a friend, let us say (a textbook example), because you have promised to. You are then presented with a unique opportunity, at a conflicting time and place, to further significantly some important cause. (To make the example realistic, one should put in more detail; and, as often in moral philosophy, if one puts in the detail the example may begin to dissolve. There is the question of your friend's attitude toward the cause and also toward your support of the cause. If he or she favors both, or merely the second, and would release you from the promise if you could get in touch, only the stickiest moralist would find a difficulty. If the friend would not release you, you may wonder what sort of friend you have . . . But it should not be hard for each person reading this to find some example that will make the point.) You may reasonably conclude that you should take the opportunity to further the cause.[6] But obligations have a moral stringency, which means that breaking them attracts blame. The only thing that can be counted on to cancel this, within the economy of morality, is that the rival action should represent another and more stringent obligation. Morality encourages the idea, *only an obligation can beat an obligation.*[7]

Yet how can this action of yours have been an obligation, unless it came from some more general obligation? It will not be easy to say what the general obligation is. You are not under an unqualified obligation to pursue this cause, nor to do everything you possibly can for causes you have adopted. We are left with the limp suggestion that one is under an obligation to assist some important cause on occasions that are specially propitious for assisting it. The pressure of the demand within the morality system to find a general obligation to back a particular one — what may be called the *obligation-out, obligation-in* principle — has a clearer result in those familiar cases where some general ethical consideration is focused on to a particular occasion by an emergency, such as the obligation to try to assist someone in danger. I am not under an obligation to assist all people at risk, or to go round looking for people at risk to assist. Confronted[8] with someone at risk, many feel that they are under an obligation to try to help (though not at excessive danger to themselves, and so on: various sensible qualifications come to mind). In this case, unlike the last, the underlying obligation seems ready made. The immediate claim on me, "In this emergency, I am under an obligation to help," is thought to come from, "One is under this general obligation: to help in an emergency." If we add the thought that many, perhaps any, moral considerations could overrule some obligation on some occasion, we find that many, perhaps all, such considerations are related to some general obligations, even if they are not the simple and unqualified ones suggested by Ross's reductionism.

Once the journey into more general obligations has started, we may begin to get into trouble — not just philosophical trouble, but conscience trouble — with finding room for morally indifferent actions. I have already mentioned the possible moral conclusion that one *may* take some particular course of action. That means that there is nothing else I am obliged to do. But if we have accepted general and indeterminate obligations to further various moral objectives, as the last set of thoughts encourages us to do, they will be waiting to provide work for idle hands, and the thought can gain a footing (I am not saying that it has to) that I could be better employed than in doing something I am under no obligation to do, and, if I could be, then I ought to be: I am under an obligation not to waste time in doing things I am under no obligation to do. At this stage, certainly, only an obligation can beat an obligation, and in order to do what I wanted to do, I shall need one of those fraudulent items, a duty to myself. If obligation is allowed to structure ethical thought, there are several natural ways in which it can come to dominate life altogether.

In order to see around the intimidating structure that morality has made out of the idea of obligation, we need an account of what obligations are when they are rightly seen as merely one kind of ethical consideration among others. This account will help to lead us away from morality's special notion of moral obligation, and eventually out of the morality system altogether.

We need, first, the notion of *importance*. Obviously enough, various things are important to various people (which does not necessarily mean that those things are important for those people's interests). This involves a relative notion of importance, which we might also express by saying that someone *finds* a given thing important. Beyond this merely relative idea, we have another notion, of something's being, simply, important (important *überhaupt*, as others might put it, or important *period*). It is not at all clear what it is for something to be, simply, important. It does not mean that it is important to the universe: in that sense, nothing is important. Nor does it mean that it is as a matter of fact something that most human beings find important; nor that it is something people ought to find important. I doubt that there can be an incontestable account of this idea; the explanations people give of it are necessarily affected by what they find important.

It does not matter for the present discussion that this notion is poorly understood. I need only three things of it. One is that there is such a notion. Another is that if something is important in the relative sense to somebody, this does not necessarily imply that he or she thinks it is, simply, important. It may be of the greatest importance to Henry that his stamp collection be completed with a certain stamp, but even Henry may see that it is not, simply, important. A significant ideal lies in this: people should find important a number of things that are, simply, important, as well as many things that are not, and they should be able to tell the difference between them.

The third point is that the question of importance, and above all the question of what is, simply, important, needs to be distinguished from questions of *deliberative priority*. A consideration has high deliberative priority for us if we give it heavy weighting against other considerations in our deliberations. (This includes two ideas, that when it occurs in our deliberations, it outweighs most other considerations, and also that it occurs in our deliberations. There are some reasons for treating the second idea separately, and I shall touch on one later, but in general it is simpler to consider them together.)

Importance has some connections with deliberative priority, but they are not straightforward. There are many important things that no one can do much about, and very many that a given person can do nothing about. Again, it may not be that person's business to do anything: there is a deliberative division of labor. Your deliberations are not connected in a simple way even with what is important to you. If you find something important, then that will affect your life in one way or another, and so affect your deliberations, but those effects do not have to be found directly in the content of your deliberations.

A consideration may have high deliberative priority for a particular person, for a group of people, or for everyone. In this way priority is relativized, to people. But it should not be relativized in another way: it should not be marked for subject matter, so that things will have moral or prudential deliberative priority. This would be a misunderstanding. It may be said that moral considerations have a high priority from a moral point of view. If this is so, what it will mean is that someone within the moral system gives those considerations a high priority. It does not define a kind of priority. A major point about deliberative priority is that it can relate considerations of different types.[9] The same thing is true of importance. In a sense, there are kinds of importance, and we naturally say that some things are morally important, others aesthetically important, and so on. But there must be a question at the end, in a particular case or more generally, whether one kind of importance is more important than another kind.

Those who are within the morality system usually think that morality is important. Moreover, morality has by definition something to do with personal conduct, so here importance is likely to have something to do with deliberation. But what it has to do with it depends crucially on the way one understands morality and morality's importance. For utilitarians, what is important is that there should be as much welfare as possible. The connection with deliberation is a subsequent question, and it is entirely open. We saw when we considered indirect utilitarianism how the question is open of what moral considerations should occur in a utilitarian agent's deliberations. More than that, it is open whether any moral considerations at all should occur in them. Some kinds of utilitarian thought have supposed that the best results would follow if people did not think in moral terms at all, and merely (for instance) acted selfishly. With less faith in the invisible hand, others give moral considerations some priority, and some of them, as we have seen, take a highly conscientious line. But for any utilitarian it should always be an empirical question: What are the implications for deliberation of welfare's being important? In this respect, however, there are many utilitarians who belong to the morality system first and are utilitarians second.

At the other extreme, the purest Kantian view locates the importance of morality in the importance of moral motivation itself. What is important is that people should give moral considerations the highest deliberative priority. This view was relentlessly and correctly attacked by Hegel, on the grounds that it gave moral thought no content and also that it was committed to a double-mindedness about the improvement of the world. The content of the moral motivation was the thought of obligation to do certain things, as against mere inclination; the need for that thought implied that individuals were not spontaneously inclined to do those things; its supreme importance implied that it was better so.

Neither view is adequate, and a better view is not going to consist of any simple compromise. Ethical life itself is important, but it can see that things other than itself are important. It contains motivations that indeed serve these other ends but at the same time be seen from within that life as part of what make it worth living.

On any adequate showing, ethical motivations are going to be important, and this has consequences for how we should deliberate. One consequence is that some kinds of ethical consideration will have high deliberative priority. This is only one way in which ethical motivations may affect people's deliberations. They may equally affect their style and their occasion, among other things.[10]

There is one kind of ethical consideration that directly connects importance and deliberative priority, and this is obligation. It is grounded in the basic issue of what people should be able to rely on. People must rely as far as possible on not being killed or used as a resource, and on having some space and objects and relations with other people they can count as their own. It also serves their interests if, to some extent at least, they can count on not being lied to. One way in which these ends can be served, and perhaps the only way, is by some kind of ethical life; and, certainly, if there is to be ethical life, these ends have to be served by it and within it. *One* way in which ethical life serves them is by encouraging certain motivations, and *one* form of this is to instill a disposition to give the relevant considerations a high deliberative priority—in the most serious of these matters, a virtually absolute priority, so that certain courses of action must come first, while others are ruled out from the beginning. An effective way for actions to be ruled out is that they never come into thought at all, and this is often the best way. One does not feel easy with the man who in the course of a discussion of how to deal with political or business rivals says, "Of course, we could have them killed, but we should lay that aside right from the beginning." It should never have come into his hands to be laid aside. It is characteristic of morality that it tends to overlook the possibility that some concerns are best embodied in this way, in deliberative silence.

Considerations that are given deliberative priority in order to secure reliability constitute obligations; corresponding to those obligations are rights, possessed by people who benefit from the obligations. One type of obligations is picked out by the basic and standing importance of the interests they serve. These are all negative in force, concerning what we should not do. Another, and now positive, sort involves the obligations of immediacy. Here, a high deliberative priority is imposed by an emergency, such as the rescue case we considered before. A general ethical recognition of people's vital interests is focused into a deliberative priority by immediacy, and it is immediacy to *me* that generates *my* obligation, one I cannot ignore without blame. Two connected things follow from understanding the obligations of emergency in this way. First, we do not after all have to say that the obligation comes from a more general obligation. The point of the negative obligations does lie in their being general; they provide a settled and permanent pattern of deliberative priorities. In the positive kind of case, however, the underlying disposition is a general concern, which is not always expressed in deliberative priority, and what produces an obligation from it is, precisely, the emergency. We need not accept the *obligation-out, obligation-in* principle.

More important, there are ethical consequences of understanding these obligations in this way. Some moralists say that if we regard immediacy or physical nearness as relevant, we must be failing in rationality or imagination; we are irrational if we do not recognize that those starving elsewhere have as big a claim on us as those starving here. These moralists are wrong, at least in trying to base their challenge simply on the structure of obligations. Of course this point does not dispose of the challenge itself. We should be more concerned about the sufferings of people elsewhere. But a correct understanding of what obligation is will make it clearer how we should start thinking about the challenge. We should not banish the category of immediacy, but we must consider what for us, in the modern world, should properly count as immediacy, and what place we have in our lives for such concerns when they are not obligations.

The obligations considered so far involve (negatively) what is fundamentally important and (positively) what is important and immediate. They are both based ultimately on one conception, that each person has a life to lead. People need help but (unless they are very young, very old, or severely handicapped) not all the time. All the time they need not to be killed, assaulted, or arbitrarily interfered with. It is a strength of contractualism to have seen that such positive and negative obligations will follow from these basic interests.[11]

The obligations that are most familiarly so called, those of promises, differ from both of these because what I am obliged to do, considered in itself, may not be important at all. But just because of that, they are an example of the same connection, between obligation and reliability. The institution of promising operates to provide portable reliability, by offering a formula that will confer high deliberative priority on what might otherwise not receive it. This is why it is odd for someone to promise not to kill you — if he does not already give it high priority, why should his promising be relied upon to provide it? (There are answers to this question, in special cases, and considering what they might be will help to show how the system works.)

Obligation works to secure reliability, a state of affairs in which people can reasonably expect others to behave in some ways and not in others. It is only one among other ethical ways of doing this. It is one that tries to produce an expectation *that* through an expectation *of.* These kinds of obligation very often command the highest deliberative priority and also present themselves as important — in the case of promises, because they are promises and not simply because of their content. However, we can also see how they need not always command the highest priority, even in ethically well-disposed agents. Reflecting that some end is peculiarly important, and the present action importantly related to it, an agent can reasonably conclude that the obligation may be broken on this occasion, as we noticed before, and indeed this conclusion may be acceptable,[12] in the sense that he can explain within a structure of ethical considerations why he decided as he did. But there is no need for him to call this course another and more stringent obligation. An obligation is a special kind of consideration, with a general relation to importance and immediacy. The case we are considering is simply one in which there is a consideration important enough to outweigh this obligation on this occasion,[13] and it is cleaner just to say so. We should reject morality's other maxim, that only an obligation can beat an obligation.

When a deliberative conclusion embodies a consideration that has the highest deliberative priority and is also of the greatest importance (at least to the agent), it may take a special form and become the conclusion not merely that one should do a certain thing, but that one *must*, and that one cannot do anything else. We may call this a conclusion of practical necessity. Sometimes, of course, "must" in a practical conclusion is merely relative and means only that some course of action is needed for an end that is not at all a matter of "must." "I must go now" may well be completed ". . . . if I am to get to the movies" where there is no suggestion that I have to go to the movies: I merely am going to the movies. We are not concerned with this, but with a "must" that is unconditional and *goes all the way down.*

It is an interesting question, how a conclusion in terms of what we must do, or equally of what we cannot do, differs from a conclusion expressed merely in terms of what we have most reason to do; in particular, how it can be stronger, as it seems to be. (How, in deliberation, can anything stronger be concluded in favor of a course of action than that we have most reason to take it?) I shall not try to discuss this question here.[14] What is immediately relevant is that practical necessity is in no way peculiar to ethics. Someone may conclude that he or she unconditionally must do a certain thing, for reasons of prudence, self-protection, aesthetic or artistic concern, or sheer self-assertion. In some of these cases (basic self-defense, for instance), an ethical outlook may itself license the conclusion. In others, it will disapprove of it. The fundamental point is that a conclusion of practical necessity is the same sort of conclusion whether it is grounded in ethical reasons or not.

Practical necessity, and the experience of reaching a conclusion with that force, is one element that has gone into the idea of moral obligation (this may help to explain the sense, which so many people have, that moral obligation is at once quite special and very familiar). Yet practical necessity, even when it is grounded in ethical reasons, does not necessarily signal an obligation. The course of action the agent "must" take may not be associated with others' expectations, or with blame for failure. The ethically outstanding or possibly heroic actions I mentioned before, in being more than obligations, are not obligatory, and we cannot usually be asked to do them or be blamed for not doing them. But the agent who does such a thing may feel that he must do it, that there is no alternative for him, while at the same time recognizing that it would not be a demand on others. The thought may come in the form that it is a demand on him, but not on others, because he is different from others; but the difference will then typically turn out to consist in the fact that he is someone who has this very conviction. His feelings, indeed, and his expectations of feelings he will have if he does not act, may well be like those associated with obligations (more like them than morality admits[15]).

I have already mentioned Kant's description of morality as categorical. When he claimed that the fundamental principle of morality was a Categorical Imperative, Kant was not interested in any purely logical distinction between forms of what are literally imperatives. He was concerned with the recognition of an *I must* that is unconditional and goes all the way down, but he construed this unconditional practical necessity as being peculiar to morality. He thought it was unconditional in the sense that it did not depend on desire at all: a course of action presented to us with this kind of necessity was one we had reason to take *whatever we might happen to want,* and it was only moral reasons that could transcend desire in that way. As I have introduced it, however, practical necessity need not be independent of desire in so strong a sense. I distinguished a "must" that is unconditional from one that is conditional on a desire *that the agent merely happens to have;* but a conclusion of practical necessity could itself be the expression of a desire, if the desire were not one that the agent merely happened to have, but was essential to the agent and had to be satisfied. The difference between this conception of practical necessity and Kant's is not of course merely a matter of definition or of logical analysis. Kant's idea of practical necessity is basically this more familiar one, but it is given a particularly radical interpretation, under which the only necessary practical conclusions are those absolutely unconditioned by any desire. For Kant there could be a practical conclusion that was radically unconditioned in this way, because of his picture of the rational self as free from causality, and because there were reasons for action which depended merely on rational agency and not on anything (such as a desire) that the agent might not have had.[16]

Kant also describes the conclusion of practical necessity, understood as peculiar to morality, as a recognition of the demands of moral law, and when he speaks of this in psychological terms, he refers to a special feeling or sentiment, a "sense of reverence for the law." Modern moralists are not likely to use those words, but they do not find it hard to recognize what Kant was describing. (Some of them still want to invoke a conception of moral law. Others, reluctant to do so, are using ideas that implicitly involve it.) Kant did not think that the compelling sense of moral necessity, regarded as a feeling, was itself what provided the reason for moral action. As a feeling, it was just a feeling and had no more rational power than any other merely psychological item had. The reason lay not in what that feeling was, but in what it represented, the truth that moral universality was a requirement of practical reason itself.

That truth, as Kant took it to be, meant that morality had an objective foundation, as we saw in Chapter 4, and he took the experience of the moral demand to represent this foundation. However, it must be said that it also significantly misrepresents it. The experience is like being *confronted* with something, a law that is part of the world in which one lives.[17] Yet the power of the moral law, according to Kant, does not lie and could not conceivably lie in anything outside oneself. Its power lies in its objective foundation, and no experience could adequately represent that kind of objectivity. The objectivity comes from this, that the requirements of practical reason will be met only by leading a life in which moral considerations play a basic and characteristic role; and that role is one they perform only if, unlike other motivations, they present themselves in the form of an objective demand. But then what is it for a consideration to present itself as an objective demand? It cannot consist in its presenting itself as so related to that very argument. It must have some other psychological form, and the form will be, to that extent, misleading.

On Kant's assumptions, however, one can at least come to understand how, and why, such an experience is bound to be misleading, and this will help to make it stable to reflection. If Kant is right, I can come to understand what the "sense of reverence for the law" is, and not lose my respect for it or for the moral law. This stability is helped by a further thought, that there is one sense in which the law is rightly represented by the experience as being outside me: it is equally in other people. The moral law is the law of the notional republic of moral agents. It is a notional republic, but they are real agents and, because it is rationally self-imposed by each of them, it is a real law.

Once we have ceased to believe in Kant's own foundation or anything like it, we cannot read this experience in this way at all. It is the conclusion of practical necessity, no more and no less, and it seems to come "from outside" in the way that conclusions of practical necessity always seem to come from outside — from deeply inside. Since ethical considerations are in question, the agent's conclusions will not usually be solitary or unsupported, because they are part of an ethical life that is to an important degree shared with others. In this respect, the morality system itself, with its emphasis on the "purely moral" and personal sentiments of guilt and self-reproach, actually conceals the dimension in which ethical life lies outside the individual.

When we know what the recognition of obligation is, if we still make it the special center of ethical experience, we are building ethical life around an illusion. Even in Kant's own view, this experience involves a misrepresentation, but it is a necessary and acceptable one, a consequence of transposing objectivity from the transcendental level to the psychological. But if this experience is special only in the psychological mode, then it is worse than a misrepresentation: there is nothing (or nothing special) for it to represent.

Kant's construction also explains how the moral law can unconditionally apply to all people, even if they try to live outside it. Those who do not accept his construction, but still accept the morality system, need to say how moral obligation binds those who refuse it. They need to say how there can be a moral *law* at all.[18] The fact that a law applies to someone always consists in more than a semantic relation; it is not merely that the person falls under some description contained in the law. The law of a state applies to a person because he belongs to a state that can apply power. The law of God applied because God applied it. Kant's moral law applied because as a rational being one had a reason to apply it to oneself. For the moral law to apply now, it can only be that we apply it.

When we say that someone ought to have acted in some required or desirable way in which he has not acted, we sometimes say that *there was a reason* for him to act in that way — he had promised, for instance, or what he actually did violated someone's rights. Although we can say this, it does not seem to be connected in any secure way with the idea that *he had a reason* to act in that way. Perhaps he had no reason at all. In breaking the obligation, he was not necessarily behaving irrationally or unreasonably, but badly. We cannot take for granted that he had a reason to behave well, as opposed to our having various reasons for wishing that he would behave well. How do we treat him? We recognize in fact, very clumsily in the law, less clumsily in informal practice, that there are many different ways in which people can fail to be what we would ethically like them to be. At one extreme there is general deliberative incapacity. At another extreme is the sincere and capable follower of another creed. Yet again there are people with various weaknesses or vices, people who are malicious, selfish, brutal, inconsiderate, self-indulgent, lazy, greedy. All these people can be part of our ethical world. No ethical world has ever been free of those with such vices (though their classification will be a matter of the culture in question); and any individual life is lined by some of them. There are, equally, various negative reactions to them, from hatred and horror in the most extreme cases, to anger, regret, correction, blame. When we are not within the formal circumstances of the state's law, there is the further dimension of who is reacting: not everyone can or should sustain every complaint. It is another consequence of the fiction of the moral law that this truth does not occur to us. It is as if every member of the notional republic were empowered to make a citizen's arrest.

Within all this there is a range, quite a wide one, of particular deviations that we treat with the machinery of everyday blame. They include many violations of obligations, but not all of them: some of the most monstrous proceedings, which lie beyond ordinary blame, involve violations of basic human rights. Nor, on the other hand, is there blame only for broken obligations; particularly in bringing up children, actions that merely manifest imperfect dispositions are blamed. But blame always tends to share the particularized, practical character of moral obligation in the technical sense. Its negative reaction is focused closely on an action or omission, and this is what is blamed. Moreover — though there are many inevitable anomalies in its actual working — the aspiration of blame is that it should apply only to the extent that the undesired outcome is the product of voluntary action on the particular occasion.

This institution, as opposed to other kinds of ethically negative or hostile reaction to people's doings (it is vital to remember how many others there are), seems to have something special to do with the idea that the agent had a reason to act otherwise. As I have already said, this is often not so.[19] The institution of blame is best seen as involving a fiction, by which we treat the agent as one for whom the relevant ethical considerations are reasons. The "ought to have" of blame can be seen as an extension into the unwilling of the "ought to have" we may offer, in advice, to those whose ends we share. This fiction has various functions. One is that if we treat the agent as someone who gives weight to ethical reasons, this may help to make him into such a person.

The device is specially important in helping to mediate between two possibilities in people's relations. One is that of shared deliberative practices, where to a considerable extent people have the same dispositions and are helping each other to arrive at practical conclusions. The other is that in which one group applies force or threats to constrain another. The fiction underlying the blame system helps at its best to make a bridge between these possibilities, by a process of continuous recruitment into a deliberative community. At its worst, it can do many bad things, such as encouraging people to misunderstand their own fear and resentment — sentiments they may quite appropriately feel — as the voice of the Law.

The fiction of the deliberative community is one of the positive achievements of the morality system. As with other fictions, it is a real question whether its working could survive a clear understanding of how it works. This is part of the much larger question of what needs to be, and what can be, restructured in the light of a reflective and nonmythical understanding of our ethical practices. It is certain that the practices of blame, and more generally the style of people's negative ethical reactions to others, will change. The morality system, in my view, can no longer help them to do so in a desirable way. One reason is that morality is under too much pressure on the subject of the voluntary.

To the extent that the institution of blame works coherently, it does so because it attempts less than morality would like it to do. When we ask whether someone acted voluntarily, we are asking, roughly, whether he really acted, whether he knew what he was doing, and whether he intended this or that aspect of what happened. This practice takes the agent together with his character, and does not raise questions about his freedom to have chosen some other character. The blame system, most of the time, closely concentrates on the conditions of the particular act; and it is able to do this because it does not operate on its own. It is surrounded by other practices of encouragement and discouragement, acceptance and rejection, which work on desire and character to shape them into the requirements and possibilities of ethical life.

Morality neglects this surrounding and sees only that focused, particularized judgment. There is a pressure within it to require a voluntariness that will be total and will cut through character and psychological or social determination, and allocate blame and responsibility on the ultimately fair basis of the agent's own contribution, no more and no less. It is an illusion to suppose that this demand can be met (as opposed to the less ambitious requirements of voluntariness that take character largely as given). This fact is known to almost everyone, and it is hard to see a long future for a system committed to denying it. But so long as morality itself remains, there is danger in admitting the fact, since the system itself leaves us, as the only contrast to rational blame, forms of persuasion it refuses to distinguish in spirit from force and constraint.

In truth, almost all worthwhile human life lies between the extremes that morality puts before us. It starkly emphasizes a series of contrasts: between force and reason, persuasion and rational conviction, shame and guilt, dislike and disapproval, mere rejection and blame. The attitude that leads it to emphasize all these contrasts can be labeled its *purity*. The purity of morality, its insistence on abstracting the moral consciousness from other kinds of emotional reaction or social influence, conceals not only the means by which it deals with deviant members of its community, but also the virtues of those means. It is not surprising that it should conceal them, since the virtues can be seen as such only from outside the system, from a point of view that can assign value to it, whereas the morality system is closed in on itself and must consider it an indecent misunderstanding to apply to the system any values other than those of morality itself.

The purity of morality itself represents a value. It expresses an ideal, presented by Kant, once again, in a form that is the most unqualified and also one of the most moving: the ideal that human existence can be ultimately just. Most advantages and admired characteristics are distributed in ways that, if not unjust, are at any rate not just, and some people are simply luckier than others. The ideal of morality is a value, moral value, that transcends luck. It must therefore lie beyond any empirical determination. It must lie not only in trying rather than succeeding, since success depends partly on luck, but in a kind of trying that lies beyond the level at which the capacity to try can itself be a matter of luck. The value must, further, be supreme. It will be no good if moral value is merely a consolation prize you get if you are not in worldly terms happy or talented or good-humoured or loved. It has to be what ultimately matters.

This is in some ways like a religious conception. But it is also unlike any real religion, and in particular unlike orthodox Christianity. The doctrine of grace in Christianity meant that there was no calculable road from moral effort to salvation; salvation lay beyond merit, and men's efforts, even their moral efforts, were not the measure of God's love.[20] Moreover, when it was said by Christianity that what ultimately mattered was salvation, this was thought to involve a difference that anyone would recognize as a difference, as *the* difference. But the standpoint from which pure moral value has its value is, once more, only that of morality itself. It can hope to transcend luck only by turning in on itself.

The ideals of morality have without doubt, and contrary to a vulgar Marxism that would see them only as an ideology of unworldliness, played a part in producing some actual justice in the world and in mobilizing power and social opportunity to compensate for bad luck in concrete terms. But the idea of a value that lies beyond all luck is an illusion, and political aims cannot continue to draw any conviction from it. Once again, the other conceptions of morality cannot help us. They can only encourage the idea, which always has its greedy friends, that when these illusions have gone there can be no coherent ideas of social justice, but only efficiency, or power, or uncorrected luck.

Many philosophical mistakes are woven into morality. It misunderstands obligations, not seeing how they form just one type of ethical consideration. It misunderstands practical necessity, thinking it peculiar to the ethical. It misunderstands ethical practical necessity, thinking it peculiar to obligations. Beyond all this, morality makes people think that, without its very special obligation, there is only inclination; without its utter voluntariness, there is only force; without its ultimately pure justice, there is no justice. Its philosophical errors are only the most abstract expressions of a deeply rooted and still powerful misconception of life.

Postscript

THERE ARE two tensions to which the argument of this book has constantly returned. In terms of philosophy's questions and its centers of interest, there is a tension between ancient and modern. In actual life, the tension is between reflection and practice. I have suggested that in some basic respects the philosophical thought of the ancient world was better off, and asked more fruitful questions, than most modern moral philosophy. Although it had its own limiting concerns, such as the desire to reduce life's exposure to luck, it was typically less obsessional than modern philosophy, less determined to impose rationality through reductive theory. The hopes for philosophy that some of those philosophers could entertain have gone, however, and the world to which ethical thought now applies is irreversibly different, not only from the ancient world but from any world in which human beings have tried to live and have used ethical concepts.

The resources of most modern moral philosophy are not well adjusted to the modern world. I have tried to show that this is partly because it is too much and too unknowingly caught up in it, unreflectively appealing to administrative ideas of rationality. In other ways, notably in its more Kantian forms, it is not involved enough; it is governed by a dream of a community of reason that is too far removed, as Hegel first said it was, from social and historical reality and from any concrete sense of a particular ethical life—farther removed from those things, in some ways, than the religion it

198 Ethics and the Limits of Philosophy

replaced. These various versions of moral philosophy share a false image of how reflection is related to practice, an image of theories in terms of which they uselessly elaborate their differences from one another.

It is not a paradox that in these very new circumstances very old philosophies may have more to offer than moderately new ones, and a historical story could be told to show why this is so. It would involve the coming and departure of Christianity (which helps to explain why the ancient world is nearer than it may seem) and the failures of the Enlightenment (which make its characteristic philosophies so unhelpful). Some, perhaps most, who have reached this kind of conclusion — notably Nietzsche, to the extent that he is caught by any such description — have taken it to be destructive of the values of the Enlightenment; or, if not, have interpreted those values in a conservative way, like many Hegelians. I do not think we are forced to join them. A respect for freedom and social justice and a critique of oppressive and deceitful institutions may be no easier to achieve than they have been in the past, and may well be harder, but we need not suppose that we have no ideas to give them a basis. We should not concede to abstract ethical theory its claim to provide the only intellectual surroundings for such ideas.

This has been a book about what is rather than about what might be, and the hopes I have expressed are, for now, hopes. They rest on assumptions that some people will think optimistic. They can be compressed into a belief in three things: in truth, in truthfulness, and in the meaning of an individual life. I shall end by saying something briefly about each.

I have claimed that the natural sciences, at least, are capable of objective truth. The error of people who deny this characteristically expresses itself in a misplaced rhetoric of comfort. They say that those who believe that science can tell us how the world really is are superstitiously clutching on to science, in a desperate faith that it is the only solid object left. But equally one may say that comfort is being sought in the opposite direction, and that skepticism against science serves, as it did in the seventeenth century, to warm those whose own claims to knowledge or rational practice look feeble by comparison. The idea that modern science is what absolute knowl-edge should be like can be disquieting, and it can be a relief if one represents science as merely another set of human rituals, or as dealing with merely another set of texts.

These claims about what provides comfort or takes it away can be made in any direction one likes, and none of them is in the least interesting. What matters more, and may have something to do with comfort or with optimism, is how far notions of objective truth can be extended to social understanding. As I mentioned in Chapter 8, it need not seek to join the natural sciences in providing an absolute conception of the world, but we need to have some reflective social knowledge, including history, that can command unprejudiced assent if the better hopes for our self-understanding are to be realized. We shall need it if we are to carry out the kind of critique that gives ethical insight into institutions through explana-tions of how they work and, in particular, of how they generate belief in themselves. It is worth repeating here something that has come out at various points in the discussion of positive ethical theory: it should not suppose that it can do without such social understanding, or that by a pure moralistic stand it can detach itself from these issues. It needs this understanding in order to answer questions about itself that it cannot ultimately avoid, about its relations to social life, its social or psychological connections with practice, and the ways in which it might hope to turn its supposed rational authority into power.

The hope for truthfulness, next, is essentially that ethical thought should stand up to reflection, and that its institutions and practices should be capable of becoming transparent. I have tried to say why ethical thought has no chance of being everything it seems. Even if ethical thought had a foundation in determinate concep-tions of well-being, the consequences of that could lie only in justifying a *disposition to accept* certain ethical statements, rather than in showing, directly, the truth of those statements: but this is not how it would naturally appear to those who accepted them. Moreover, it is unlikely that we can achieve this foundation.

While ethical thought will never entirely appear as what it is, and can never fully manifest the fact that it rests in human dispositions, this will present greater obstacles to reflection in some conditions of ethical thought than in others. One thing that will make a difference is the extent to which ethical life can still rely on what I have called thick ethical concepts. They are indeed open to being unseated by reflection, but to the extent that they survive it, a practice that uses them is more stable in face of the general, structural reflections about the truth of ethical judgments than a practice that does not use them. The judgments made with these concepts can straightforwardly be true, and, for the people who have those concepts, the claim involved in assenting to them can correspondingly be honored.

I hope I have made it clear that the ideal of transparency and the desire that our ethical practice should be able to stand up to reflection do not demand total explicitness, or a reflection that aims to lay everything bare at once. Those demands are based on a misunderstanding of rationality, both personal and political. We must reject any model of personal practical thought according to which all my projects, purposes, and needs should be made, discursively and at once, considerations *for* me. I must deliberate *from* what I am. Truthfulness requires trust in that as well, and not the obsessional and doomed drive to eliminate it.

How truthfulness to an existing self or society is to be combined with reflection, self-understanding, and criticism is a question that philosophy, itself, cannot answer. It is the kind of question that has to be answered through reflective living. The answer has to be discovered, or established, as the result of a process, personal and social, which essentially cannot formulate the answer in advance, except in an unspecific way. Philosophy can play a part in the process, as it plays a part in identifying the question, but it cannot be a substitute for it. This is why it is a misunderstanding to ask, in the way that ethical theorists often ask, "what alternative" one has to their formulations. They mean, what formulation does one have as an alternative to their formulations, either of the answer or of some determinate heuristic process that would yield the answer; and there is none. There might turn out to be an answer to the real question, and this would indeed be an alternative to their formulations; but it would not be an answer produced in the way that their demand requires an answer, as a piece of philosophy. To suppose that, if their formulations are rejected, we are left with *nothing* is to take a strange view of what in social and personal life counts as something.

The picture I give as the background to these various hopes does require, last, that there be individuals with dispositions of character and a life of their own to lead. (As I said in Chapter 1, this does not commit us to the biographical perspective favored by the Greeks, in which it is a whole natural life that is ethically basic.) In one sense, the primacy of the individual and of personal dispositions is a necessary truth — necessary, at least, up to drastic technological changes such as cloning, pooling of brainstores, and so on. This is the sense in which even radical structuralist descriptions of society, whatever they may say, suppose there to be individuals who acquire certain dispositions and aims and express them in action. If the structuralists are right, then these dispositions will be more thoroughly determined by social factors such as class, more uniform in content, and less understood by the individuals than has been traditionally supposed; but those claims cannot deny the existence and causal role of dispositions. No set of social structures can drive youths into violence at football games except by being represented, however confusedly or obscurely, in those youths' desires and habits of life. In this sense, social or ethical life must exist in people's dispositions. It is the content of the dispositions, their intelligibility and their degree of particularity, that differs between societies and is at issue between different interpretations of modern society.

Yet an individualism rather less formal than that is surely necessary if distinctively ethical thought is to be possible, as opposed to social planning or communal ritual; and with regard to the hopes I am expressing here, it will be obvious that a more substantial individualism is in question. It has been so in other parts of the book, in the account I have given of obligation as one ethical consideration among others, for instance, and in some of the things said about practical necessity. My third optimistic belief is in the continuing possibility of a meaningful individual life, one that does not reject society, and indeed shares its perceptions with other people to a considerable depth, but is enough unlike others, in its opacities and disorder as well as in its reasoned intentions, to make it *somebody's*. Philosophy can help to make a society possible in which most people would live such lives, even if it still needs to learn how best to do so. Some people might even get help from philosophy in living such a life—but not, as Socrates supposed, each reflective person, and not from the ground up.

NOTES

INDEX

Notes

1. Socrates' Question

1. Plato, *Republic*, 352D.
2. See Chapter 3, note 6, for more on Aristotle's work.
3. Martha C. Nussbaum, *The Fragility of Goodness* (New York: Cambridge University Press, 1985), explores this and related notions in ancient literature and philosophy. For the idea of morality as transcending luck, see Chapter 10.
4. If some philosophers have found difficulty with this obvious account, it may be because they assume that this "altogether" question would have to be answered by appealing to just one kind of consideration. I shall argue later in this chapter that the assumption is wrong.
5. F. H. Bradley, "My Station and Its Duties", in *Ethical Studies,* 2nd ed. (Indianapolis: Bobbs-Merrill, 1951); first published in 1876.
6. The point is made by Alasdair MacIntyre, *After Virtue* (Notre Dame: University of Notre Dame Press, 1981), and by Michael Sandel, *Liberalism and the Limits of Justice* (New York: Cambridge University Press, 1982). Sandel's emphasis on a "socially constituted self" encounters difficulties familiar in neo-Hegelian writers. See also Chapter 10, note 16, and, on MacIntyre, note 13 below.
7. P. T. Geach, *The Virtues: The Stanton Lectures, 1973 – 74* (New York: Cambridge University Press, 1977); Philippa Foot, *Virtues and Vices* (Berkeley: University of California Press, 1978); James D. Wallace, *Virtues and Vices* (Ithaca: Cornell University Press, 1978); MacIntyre, *After Virtue.* The reasons for the neglect chiefly lie in a narrow view of ethical concerns and a concentration on the preoccupations of morality; it may also be that the study of the virtues has been associated with religious assumptions (which are emphati-

cally present in Geach's work). There is an objection worth taking seriously to the idea of a virtue, which is that it calls on the notion of character, and this is a notion that no longer has any, or enough, sense for us. I touch on this question in the Postscript. I believe that the objection, if developed, is an objection to ethical thought itself rather than to one way of conducting it.

8. For example, Harry Frankfurt, "Freedom of the Will and the Concept of a Person", *Journal of Philosophy,* 67 (1971); Amartya Sen, "Choice, Orderings and Morality", in Stephan Körner, ed., *Practical Reason* (New Haven: Yale University Press, 1974); R. C. Jeffery, "Preference among Preferences", *Journal of Philosophy,* 71 (1974); A. O. Hirschman, *Shifting Involvements* (Princeton: Princeton University Press, 1982), chap. 4.

9. The doctrine is part of Kant's theory of freedom, which, if it can be made intelligible at all, is notoriously difficult to save from inconsistency. For further comment on it, see Chapter 4.

10. I have discussed this in *Morality: An Introduction to Ethics* (New York: Harper and Row, 1972).

11. The distinction between deontological and teleological is very roughly introduced here. The interest of the distinction is probably to be found at a different level, in a disagreement about where the importance of morality lies: see Chapter 10. The distinction is only one of many that have been drawn. For a luxuriant classification, see W. K. Frankena, *Ethics,* 2nd ed. (Englewood Cliffs: Prentice-Hall, 1973).

12. G. E. Moore, *Principia Ethica* (New York: Cambridge University Press, 1959), sections 17 and 89; *Ethics* (New York: Oxford University Press, 1967), pp. 246 – 248 and elsewhere. He seems to qualify this view to some extent in "A Reply to My Critics," in P. A. Schilpp, ed., *The Philosophy of G. E. Moore* (La Salle: Open Court Publishing Co., 1942), pp. 558 – 571.

13. In certain forms, the demand for explicit discursive rationality is as old as Socrates, and does not represent any modern influence, but the most powerful models of justification now active, and the demands for a single currency of reasons, are certainly expressions of modern bureaucratic rationality. The question is related to that of the history of the "bare" self, not socially defined, which was referred to in note 6 above: MacIntyre exaggerates the extent to which this is a purely modern conception. On the question of what rationality may reasonably demand of a decision system, even when that is expressed in formal terms, see Amartya Sen, *Collective Choice and Social Welfare* (San Francisco: Holden Day, 1970), and "Rational Fools", reprinted in his *Choice, Welfare and Measurement* (Oxford: Blackwell, 1982); A. Sen and B. Williams, eds., *Utilitarianism and Beyond* (New York: Cambridge University Press, 1982), Introduction, pp. 16 – 18.

14. This is denied by Edward J. Bond, *Reason and Value* (New York: Cambridge University Press, 1983).

15. Discussion of akrasia include: Donald Davidson, "How Is Weakness of the Will Possible?" in Joel Feinberg, ed., *Moral Concepts* (New York: Oxford University Press, 1969); David Pears, *Motivated Irrationality* (New York. Oxford University Press, 1984).

16. This is not to forget "what shall *we* do?" That is first-personal too; the basic question is who the speaker is taking as the plural first person — a speaker who, it is essential to remember, is once more an *I*.

2. The Archimedean Point

1. Robert Nozick, *Philosophical Explanations* (Cambridge: Harvard University Press, 1981), p. 408.

2. G. E. Moore, "Proof of an External World," reprinted in his *Philosophical Papers* (Atlantic Highlands, N.J.: Humanities Press, 1977). On the force of the Moorean answer to skepticism, see Thompson Clarke, "The Legacy of Skepticism," *Journal of Philosophy,* 69 (1972).

3. Renford Bambrough, *Moral Scepticism and Moral Knowledge* (Atlantic Highlands, N.J.: Humanities Press, 1979), p. 15.

4. See Myles Burnyeat, "Can the Sceptic Live his Scepticism?", in Malcolm Schofield, Myles Burnyeat, and Jonathan Barnes, eds., *Doubt and Dogmatism: Studies in Hellenistic Epistemology* (New York: Oxford University Press, 1980); reprinted in Myles Burnyeat, ed., *The Skeptical Tradition* (Berkeley: University of California Press, 1983).

5. Cf "The Analogy of City and Soul in Plato's *Republic*," in E. N. Lee, A. P. Mourelatos, and R. M. Rorty, eds., *Exegesis and Argument, Studies in Greek Philosophy presented to Gregory Vlastos* (Assen: Van Gorcum, 1973).

6. A precise formulation of such instabilities is to be found in the problem of the Prisoners' Dilemma: see e.g. Robert D. Luce and Howard Raiffa, *Games and Decisions* (New York: John Wiley, 1957). The political theory of Hobbes is based on one way of dealing with this problem. For the relevance of such issues to ethics, see Edna Ullmann-Margalit, *The Emergence of Norms* (New York: Oxford University Press, 1977).

3. Foundations: Well-Being

1. The Greek word *dikaiosyne* of which this is the translation ranges more widely in Plato's use than the English expression does. I have given a fuller account of some ancient views on these matters in an article on Greek

philosophy in M. I. Finley, ed., *The Legacy of Greece* (New York: Oxford University Press, 1981), with which the present discussion partly overlaps.

2. An assumption that Greek ideas in ethics compare unfavorably with modern, and in particular Kantian, ideas is an unhelpful feature of A. W. Adkins' well-known book, *Merit and Responsibility* (Chicago: Univesity of Chicago Press, 1975).

3. Aristotle's claim is actually rather weaker than this: see below, p. 39f.

4. For some recent material, see Paul Helm, ed., *Divine Commands and Morality* (New York: Oxford University Press, 1981). On the egoism point, see "God, Morality and Prudence", in *Morality*. On deriving *ought* from *is* see Chapter 7.

5. "'How are we to bury you?' said Crito. 'However you like,' said Socrates, 'provided that you can catch me.'" Plato, *Phaedo* 115 C-D.

6. There are two books with "Ethics" in their titles that go under the name of Aristotle, the Nicomachean and the Eudemian. Some material is common to both. The usual view is that the Nicomachean is the more authentic, but see Anthony Kenny, *The Aristotelian Ethics* (New York: Oxford University Press, 1978). For some general issues, see John Cooper, *Reason and Human Good in Aristotle* (Cambridge: Harvard University Press, 1975). Amelie Rorty, ed., *Essays on Aristotle's Ethics* (Berkeley: University of California Press, 1981), is a useful collection.

7. Aristotle does say that the good man's friend is "another himself" (*Nicomachean Ethics* 1166 a 31), a phrase that expresses genuine tensions in his thought between friendship and self-sufficiency. However, I now think that a criticism of Aristotle's outlook I made elsewhere (*Moral Luck,* New York: Cambridge University Press, 1981, p. 15), emphasizing this phrase, was exaggerated. I am indebted to Martha Nussbaum on this question: see her *Fragility of Goodness* (New York: Cambridge University Press, 1985), part 3. See also John Cooper, "Aristotle on Friendship," in Rorty, *Essays on Aristotle's Ethics*.

8. See P. F. Strawson, "Freedom and Resentment", reprinted in *Freedom and Resentment and Other Essays* (New York: Methuen, 1976). I discuss the peculiarities of morality, and its conception of blame, in Chapter 10.

9. *Nicomachean Ethics* 1113 b 18. On Aristotle and free will, see Richard Sorabji, *Necessity, Cause and Blame: Perspectives on Aristotle's Theory* (Ithaca: Cornell University Press, 1980), esp. part 5.

10. Although Aristotle says they are, emphasizing those cases in which people ruin their characters by bad practices: *Nic. Eth.* 1114 a 3–8, 1114 b 25–1115 a 2; in the latter passage he does say that actions and states of character are not "voluntary in the same way." See Myles Burnyeat, "Aristotle

on Learning to Be Good," in Rorty, *Essays on Aristotle's Ethics,* which discusses the nature of Aristotle's inquiry.

11. For example, John Rawls, *A Theory of Justice* (Cambridge: Harvard University Press, 1972), sec. 45, pp. 293–298; see also sec. 63, pp. 409–411, and sec. 64, pp. 416–424. For a contrary view, see Derek Parfit, *Reasons and Persons* (Oxford: Clarendon Press, 1984).

12. There is an analogy between the suggested account of real interests and certain considerations in the theory of purely cognitive interests. In many circumstances of potential error, inquiries conducted in those circumstances will improve your information. One result is that you can learn not to be deceived. There are other circumstances of error, however, such as dreaming, in which that is not possible (hence their special role in generating philosophical skepticism). The account of what is wrong in those circumstances also explains why that account cannot itself be applied in those circumstances. See my *Descartes: The Project of Pure Enquiry* (Atlantic Highlands, N.J.: Humanities Press, 1978) chap. 2 and appendix 3.

13. John Maynard Smith, *Evolution and the Theory of Games* (New York: Cambridge University Press, 1982). Michael Ruse, *Sociobiology: Sense or Nonsense?* (Hingham, Mass.: Kluwer Boston, 1979) gives a good critical account of some central issues. For the definition of "fitness" used in the text and its significance, see Richard M. Burian "Adaptation," in Marjorie Grene, ed., *Dimensions of Darwinism* (New York: Cambridge University Press, 1983). For some further considerations about evolutionary biology and ethics, especially the point about possible restrictions on institutions, see "Evolution, Ethics and the Representation Problem," in D. S. Bendall, ed., *Evolution from Molecules to Men* (New York: Cambridge University Press, 1983).

14. For this dimension in Freud's thought, see Philip Rieff, *Freud: The Mind of the Moralist,* 3rd ed. (Chicago: University of Chicago Press, 1979).

15. An outstanding statement of this is Hannah Arendt, *Eichmann in Jerusalem: A Report on the Banality of Evil* (New York, 1963; Penguin Books, 1977). With good, the effect is the opposite.

16. See the work of Noam Chomsky, in particular *Language and Mind* (New York: Harcourt Brace Jovanovich, 1972). For a general account, see John Lyons, *Noam Chomsky* (London, 1970; New York: Penguin Books, 1978).

17. I have discussed this in more detail in "Egoism and Altruism," in *Problems of the Self* (New York: Cambridge University Press, 1973).

18. The importance of this requirement—that an outside viewpoint from which I can understand my dispositions should not alienate me from them—comes out in a different connection (a different sense of "understand") in Chapter 6.

4. Foundations: Practical Reason

1. Kant's approach can perhaps best be summarized by saying that he gives an account of morality and an account of practical reason, and takes them to arrive at the same place.

2. The argument I shall develop is similar in several respects to that offered by Alan Gewirth in *Reason and Morality* (Chicago: University of Chicago Press, 1977). Gewirth says: "Although the importance of action for moral philosophy has been recognized since the ancient Greeks, it has not hitherto been noted that the nature of action enters into the very content and justification of the supreme principle of morality" (p. 26). While Gewirth's account contains many original features, I think that this underestimates the affinity of his project to Kant's. Although Gewirth's treatment of the issues differs in some respects from that considered here, I believe it fails for the same general reasons.

3. It is not enough to say: the desired outcome includes your doing something. That formula could apply just as well to the previous kind of case—for instance, you want the outcome to include not just her falling in love with you, but your then making love to her. For some further complications, and the relevance of all this to consequentialism, see "A Critique of Utilitarianism," in J. J. C. Smart and Bernard Williams, *Utilitarianism: For and Against* (New York: Cambridge University Press, 1973), sec. 2.

4. See my *Descartes: The Project of Pure Enquiry,* chap. 1.

5. Structures of this kind are characteristic of the phenomena of intentionality. See in particular H. P. Grice "Meaning," *Philosophical Review,* 66 (1957), and John Searle, *Intentionality* (New York: Cambridge University Press, 1983).

6. As Gewirth points out, p. 53.

7. Hobbes may have thought it did, but it is not easy to distinguish between what he thought was necessarily involved in wanting anything and the grim view he took of what would be involved, without a sovereign, in getting or keeping anything.

8. Gewirth takes this path.

9. The point is not that a desire is not enough to give one a reason for acting. I have already said that it is enough (Chapter 1). The truth is that not every reason for action is grounded in an evaluation.

10. For more on prescription, see my discussion of R. M. Hare's views in Chapters 6 and 7.

11. Gewirth uses an argument of this sort, p. 80.

12. Max Stirner, *Der Einziger und sein Eigenthum,* translated by S. T. Byington as *The Ego and His Own,* ed. James J. Martin (Sun City, Cal.: West World Press, 1982), p. 128.

13. *Groundwork,* translated by H. J. Paton as *The Moral Law* (Totowa, N.J.: Barnes and Noble Books, 1978), p. 88. In connection with another formulation of the Categorical Imperative Kant says: "A rational being must always regard himself as making laws in a kingdom of ends which is possible through freedom of the will — whether it be as member or as head" (p. 101). This seems to me his most illuminating expression of the conception.

14. This is the test used by John Rawls in his theory of justice, discussed in Chapter 5. See also Amartya Sen, *Informational Analysis of Moral Principles,* in *Rational Action,* ed. T. R. Harrison (New York: Cambridge University Press, 1979).

15. See, for example, Theorem II of *The Critique of Practical Reason.* The brief reference in my text to Kant's position on determinism takes no account of the central mystery of this position, that he was a determinist about all events; recognized that actions were events; believed in free will; and condemned the "wretched subterfuge," as he called it, of making free will and determinism compatible with one another by ascribing free actions to a particular kind of cause.

16. David Wiggins, "Towards a Credible Form of Libertarianism," in Ted Honderich, ed., *Essays on Freedom of Action* (Boston: Routledge and Kegan, 1978), has interesting arguments against the supposed symmetry and against the Kantian claim that thought cannot be rational if it is caused, a claim that in a vulgarized form is stock in trade with libertarian writers. However, if the truth is that there is an asymmetry between factual thought and practical deliberation with respect to freedom, this will not help to reinstate the kind of argument I am discussing: its attempt to found impartiality on the freedom of practical deliberation precisely depends on interpreting rational freedom in a way that *would* apply also to factual thought, as Kant supposed it did.

17. In discussing this range of questions, I have particularly benefited from the work of Thomas Nagel and from discussion with him.

18. This is part of Kant's own point in the *Paralogisms,* in *The Critique of Pure Reason.* But this transcendental *I,* which is formal in the case of thought in general, is made by Kant to do much more in relation to morality.

19. However, it may not be possible to conjoin every truth with every other, because of the perspectival character of some knowledge: see Chapter 8.

5. Styles of Ethical Theory

1. Scanlon, "Contractualism and Utilitarianism," in Sen and Williams, *Utilitarianism and Beyond,* p. 110. I am indebted at several points to this article.

2. Ibid., p. 116.

3. This can be taken as the defining characteristic of utilitarianism: see Sen and Williams, *Utilitarianism and Beyond,* pp. 2–4, and Amartya Sen, "Utilitarianism and Welfarism," *Journal of Philosophy,* 76 (1979). For some distinctions between forms of utilitarianism, see J. J. C. Smart and Bernard Williams, *Utilitarianism: For and Against* (New York: Cambridge University Press, 1973). James Griffin gives a review of recent work in "Modern Utilitarianism," *Revue internationale de philosophie,* 141 (1982).

4. For complexities that require refinements to this formula, see "A Critique of Utilitarianism," in Smart and Williams, *Utilitarianism,* sec. 2.

5. Strictly, sum-ranking welfarist consequentialism. See note 3 above.

6. For discussion of some effects of this on questions of responsibility, see "A Critique of Utilitarianism," secs. 3 and 5; and Samuel Scheffler, *The Rejection of Consequentialism* (New York: Oxford University Press, 1982).

7. Some utilitarian writers aim to increase a sense of indeterminate guilt in their readers. Peter Singer is an example, and in his book *Practical Ethics* (New York: Cambridge University Press, 1980), he is evidently more interested in producing that effect than he is in the theoretical basis for it, which gets very cursory treatment. As moral persuasion, this kind of tactic is likely to be counterproductive and to lead to a defensive and resentful contraction of concern. This can be seen in research and, at the present time, all around us. For some research, see James S. Fishkin, *Beyond Subjective Morality* (New Haven: Yale University Press, 1984).

8. See John Rawls, *A Theory of Justice* (Cambridge: Harvard University Press, 1971), and the articles cited in note 10 to this chapter. Norman Daniels, ed., *Reading Rawls* (New York: Basic Books, 1975), is a helpful collection.

9. Rawls, pp. 60, 83. There is a final, more elaborate statement of the principles at p. 302.

10. See Rawls, "Kantian Construction in Moral Theory," *Journal of Philosophy,* 77 (1980); and "Social Unity and Primary Goods," in Sen and Williams, *Utilitarianism.* See also T. M. Scanlon, "Preference and Urgency," *Journal of Philosophy,* 72 (1975).

11. Harsanyi's argument is presented in papers included in his *Essays in Ethics, Social Behavior, and Scientific Explanation* (Boston: Dordrecht Reidel, 1976). See also "Morality and the Theory of Rational Behaviour," reprinted in Sen and Williams, *Utilitarianism.* Scanlon, in the article cited in note 1 above, interestingly distinguishes Harsanyi's argument from a genuinely contractual approach.

12. This has a special relevance to population policy. See Derek Parfit, "On Doing the Best for our Children," in M. D. Bayles, ed., *Ethics and Population* (Cambridge: Schenkman, 1976); "Future Generations: Further Problems," *Philosophy and Public Affairs,* 11 (1982); and *Reasons and Persons*

(Oxford: Clarendon Press, 1984). Also J. McMahan, "Problems of Population Theory," *Ethics,* 92 (1981).

13. As presented in *Moral Thinking* (New York: Oxford University Press, 1981). Hare's theory has developed, and I shall refer also to some of his earlier views, expressed in *The Language of Morals* (New York: Oxford University Press, 1952; rev. ed. 1961) and *Freedom and Reason* (New York: Oxford University Press, 1965).

14. Hare has an Ideal Observer of his own, called the "archangel." Firth's theory is given in "Ethical Absolutism and the Ideal Observer," *Philosophy and Phenomenological Research,* 12 (1952), pp. 317–345. For criticism, see R. B. Brandt, *A Theory of the Good and the Right* (New York: Oxford University Press, 1979), pp. 225ff. For remarks on the two versions, see also Derek Parfit, "Later Selves and Moral Principles," in Alan Montefiore, ed., *Philosophy and Personal Relations* (Montreal: McGill-Queens University Press, 1973), pp. 149–150 and nn. 30–34.

15. Hare, *Moral Thinking,* p. 170.

16. John Mackie, *Ethics: Inventing Right and Wrong* (New York: Penguin, 1977), p. 97. "The ruling out of purely numerical differences" refers to the fact that my being me and your being you cannot by itself count as a reason for treating one of us differently from the other. I doubt that even this has anything specially to do with "moral language." For more on universalizability, see Chapter 6.

17. Sen and Williams, *Utilitarianism,* p. 8.

18. "Morality and the Theory of Rational Behaviour," cited in note 11 above.

19. Hare brings out (*Moral Thinking,* pp. 101ff.) that this method in itself need not maximize welfare at all times. Whether it does or not, depends on another issue, how one weighs the now-for-then preferences that are surrogates of known then-for-then preferences, as against other now-for-then and now-for-now preferences. For a subtle discussion of prudential concern for the future, and its analogies to the concern for other people, see Parfit, *Reasons and Persons,* cited in note 12 above.

20. John Findlay, *Values and Intentions* (Atlantic Highlands, N.J.: Humanities Press, 1978), pp. 235–236.

21. Hare, *Moral Thinking,* pp. 95–96.

22. Ibid., p. 96.

6. Theory and Prejudice

1. In this century, G. E. Moore, David Ross (see Chapter 10), and H. A. Prichard were intuitionists. Among earlier representatives of a similar tradi-

tion were Richard Price (*A Review of the Principal Questions in Morals,* 1758) and William Whewell (*The Elements of Morality,* 1845).

2. John Stuart Mill cónstantly attacked intuitionism, in particular for its dogmatism; see his *Autobiography,* ed. Jack Stillinger (Boston: Houghton Mifflin Co., 1964), pp. 134–135. The epistemology of intuitionism was heavily criticized in the 1950s. Besides Hare's *The Language of Morals,* see e.g. Stephen Toulmin, *The Place of Reason in Ethics* (New York: Cambridge University Press, 1950), and Patrick Nowell-Smith, *Ethics* (New York: Penguin, 1954).

3. To be fair, the Trolley Problem, as it has come to be called, was originally introduced — by Philippa Foot, in "The Problem of Abortion and the Doctrine of the Double Effect," reprinted in her *Virtues and Vices* (Berkeley: University of California Press, 1978) — in order to discuss the question of how far the causal structure of a situation may be relevant to moral conclusions about that situation — a question involved in such doctrines as the principle of Double Effect. Examples may be relevant to that kind of question even though they are fantastic. There are other ways in which examples may be relevant just because they are fantastic; a notorious example used by Judith Jarvis Thomson in the discussion of abortion is effective just because of its ghastly unreality: "In Defence of Abortion," reprinted in Marshall Cohen, Thomas Nagel, and Thomas Scanlon, eds., *The Rights and Wrongs of Abortion* (Princeton: Princeton University Press, 1974). For a general criticism of the use of fantastic examples in relation to everyday moral intuitions (though not at the foundational level of moral thought), see Hare, *Moral Thinking.*

4. This is a large and unclear assumption. It plays an important part in the model used by Bruce Ackerman in his *Social Justice in the Liberal State* (New Haven: Yale University Press, 1980): for criticism, see a series of comments on Ackerman's book in *Ethics,* 93 (1983).

5. Rawls, in *A Theory of Justice,* describes the method on pp. 20ff, and relates it to Aristotle on pp. 48–51.

6. Rawls calls it the requirement of "publicity": see *A Theory of Justice,* p. 133 and elsewhere, especially sec. 29. For criticisms in terms of false consciousness, see the references to critical theory, Chapter 9, note 11.

7. Jürgen Habermas' model of human relations that are free from domination makes very strong Kantian assumptions, and also suffers from a demand for limitless explicitness.

8. See, for example, *The Phenomenology of Spirit,* trans. A. V. Miller (Oxford: Clarendon Press, 1977), the section called "The Actualization of Rational Self-Consciousness through Its Own Activity." For comment, see Charles Taylor, *Hegel* (New York: Cambridge University Press, 1975); Judith N. Shklar, *Freedom and Independence* (New York: Cambridge University Press, 1976).

9. Sidgwick's book was first published in 1874; he took it, with many alterations, through several editions. The quotation is from the seventh edition (London, 1907, reissued 1962), p. 382; the phrase "the point of view of the Universe" recurs at p. 420, without the apology. I have written about Sidgwick and the characteristic problems of his kind of theory in "The Point of View of the Universe: Sidgwick and the Ambitions of Ethics," *Cambridge Review*, 7 (1982). Some of the material in this chapter is drawn from that article.

10. *The Methods of Ethics*, pp. 338, 406.

11. These phrases occur in his "Ethical Theory and Utilitarianism," in H. D. Lewis, ed., *Contemporary British Philosophy* (Atlantic Highlands, N.J.: Humanities Press, 1976); reprinted in Sen and Williams, *Utilitarianism*.

12. *Methods*, pp. 489–490. Sidgwick's views are considered by Derek Parfit in his *Reasons and Persons* (Oxford: Clarendon Press, 1984), in the course of a detailed discussion of an ethical theory's being "self-defeating" or, differently, "self-effacing." Parfit's emphasis is on the question whether the fact that an ethical theory has one or another of these properties shows that it is untrue. I am less clear than he is about what this means. The discussion in the present chapter concerns what kind of life, social or personal, would be needed to embody such a theory.

13. Joseph Butler, *Fifteen Sermons Preached at the Rolls Chapel*, sermon XI. What we find in the cool hour is that we cannot justify any pursuit to ourselves "till we are convinced that it will be for our happiness, or at least not contrary to it." Interestingly, it is debatable whether Butler thought that this finding was sound.

14. In my *Descartes: The Project of Pure Enquiry*. For a rejection of the conception, see e.g. the views of Richard Rorty, discussed in Chapter 8. David Wiggins, "Truth, Invention and the Meaning of Life" (British Academy Lecture, 1976), distinguishes between any such perspective and the outlooks appropriate to ethics; though his construction of the latter is more akin to views of John McDowell, discussed in Chapter 8, than they are to the approach of this book.

15. This is not contradicted by the "anthropic principle" discussed by some theoretical physicists and cosmologists, which instead makes the point that certain hypotheses about the universe are excluded simply by the given fact that we exist and can observe it.

16. John Locke, *An Essay Concerning Human Understanding*, I.iii.4.

17. Michael Tooley, "Abortion and Infanticide," in Cohen, Nagel, and Scanlon, *The Rights and Wrongs of Abortion*, and his *Abortion and Infanticide* (Oxford: Clarendon Press, 1983).

18. There is of course another, and discouraging, possibility, which has already emerged in the discussion of indirect utilitarianism: that

the one principle, applied to itself as a practice, gives reasons against itself.

19. For an account of "person" that does not allow Tooley's type of argument, see David Wiggins, *Sameness and Substance* (Cambridge: Harvard University Press, 1980), chap. 6, esp. pp. 169–172.

20. The term seems to have been introduced by Richard D. Ryder, in *Victims of Science: The Use of Animals in Research* (London: Davis-Poynter, 1975). There is a large recent literature on the ethics of our relations to other animals, much of it urging respect for what are called "animal rights." I cannot deal adequately with the subject here. Three points are worth making, in a very summary form. First, there are good reasons for not inflicting pain on animals, but no particular point is made, except rhetorically, by grounding this in *rights*. Rights are a distinctive kind of ethical reason, and they are best explained in terms of assuring expectations (see Chapter 10, on obligations), a consideration that does not apply to other animals. (For a contrary view, see Tom Regan, *The Case for Animal Rights* [Berkeley: University of California Press, 1983].) Second, if the basis is taken to be the simplest utilitarian one of keeping down the level of pain, it is unclear why we should not be committed, as Ritchie pointed out years ago in *Natural Rights* (1894), to spending any time we could spare on policing nature. Last, there is a different line of argument that grounds our relations to animals in a general teleology, which encourages us to see them not as a resource but as sharing the world with us (see Stephen R. L. Clark, *The Moral Status of Animals* [New York: Oxford University Press, 1977]). But I cannot see why, on any realistic view of our and other animals' "natural" relations to one another, it should be thought to exclude our eating them.

21. As a prejudice, it is not altogether unlike one mentioned by Sheridan's Jack Absolute: "I own I should rather choose a wife of mine to have the usual number of limbs and a limited quantity of back: and though one eye may be very agreeable, yet as the prejudice has always run in favour of two, I would not wish to affect a singularity in that article" (*The Rivals,* III,1).

7. The Linguistic Turn

1. For some discussion of this account, see the section on "Good" in my *Morality: An Introduction to Ethics* (New York: Harper and Row, 1972). In "A Reply to my Critics," (see Chapter 1, note 12), Moore agreed that the account given in *Principia Ethica* of the distinction between natural and nonnatural properties was quite unsatisfactory, but he did not give it up altogether.

2. David Hume, *A Treatise of Human Nature* (1739), III.i.i.

3. For various articles on the interpretation of Hume's meaning, see

W. D. Hudson, ed., *The Is-Ought Question* (New York: St. Martin's Press, 1969); also John Mackie, *Hume's Moral Theory* (Boston: Routledge and Kegan Paul, 1980), pp. 61–63, and *Ethics: Inventing Right and Wrong* (New York: Penguin, 1977), pp. 64–73.

4. Hare, *Moral Thinking*, p. 21.

5. I am indebted here to David Wiggins; see "Truth, Invention, and the Meaning of Life" (British Academy Lecture, 1976), and "Deliberation and Practical Reason," in Amelie O. Rorty, ed., *Essays on Aristotle's Ethics* (Berkeley: University of California Press, 1981).

6. The phrase "the linguistic turn" is the title of a collection of papers on philosophical method edited by Richard Rorty (Chicago: University of Chicago Press, 1967).

7. An exception has been Peter Winch, in *The Idea of a Social Science and Its Relation to Philosophy* (London, 1958; Atlantic Highlands, N.J.: Humanities Press, 1970), and elsewhere.

8. Knowledge, Science, Convergence

1. The best-known route for reducing the evaluative to the practical runs through the notion of the prescriptive. That strategy was criticized in the last chapter.

2. See the work of Wiggins cited in Chapter 7, note 5.

3. Richard Rorty, *Philosophy and the Mirror of Nature* (Princeton: Princeton University Press, 1980), pp. 344–345. I have discussed Rorty's views in some detail in a review of his *Consequences of Pragmatism* (Minneapolis: University of Minnesota Press, 1982): *New York Review of Books*, 28 April 1983.

4. There is a confusion between what might be called empirical and transcendental pragmatism. Similar problems arise with the later work of Wittgenstein: see "Wittgenstein and Idealism," in my *Moral Luck;* and Jonathan Lear, "Leaving the World Alone," *Journal of Philosophy,* 79 (1982).

5. Rorty, "The World Well Lost," in *Consequences of Pragmatism,* p. 14. See also Donald Davidson, "The Very Idea of a Conceptual Scheme," *Proceedings and Addresses of the American Philosophical Association,* 67 (1973–74).

6. This has already been mentioned, Chapter 6, note 14. See also N. Jardine, "The Possibility of Absolutism," in D. H. Mellor, ed., *Science, Belief, and Behaviour: Essays in Honour of R. B. Braithwaite* (New York: Cambridge University Press, 1980); and Colin McGinn, *The Subjective View* (Oxford: Clarendon Press, 1983).

7. Notably John McDowell, "Are Moral Requirements Hypothetical Im-

peratives?", *Proceedings of the Aristotelian Society,* suppl. vol. 52 (1978); "Virtue and Reason," *Monist,* 62 (1979). McDowell is above all concerned with the state of mind and motivations of a virtuous person, but I understand his view to have the more general implications discussed in my text. The idea that it might be impossible to pick up an evaluative concept unless one shared its evaluative interest is basically a Wittgensteinian idea. I first heard it expressed by Philippa Foot and Iris Murdoch in a seminar in the 1950s. For the application of ideas from Wittgenstein's later philosophy to ethics, see e.g. Hanna F. Pitkin, *Wittgenstein and Justice* (Berkeley: University of California Press, 1972), and Sabina Lovibond, *Realism and Imagination in Ethics* (Minneapolis: University of Minnesota Press, 1983). For a wide-ranging reflection that owes much to Wittgenstein, see Stanley Cavell, *The Claim of Reason* (New York: Oxford University Press, 1979), esp. parts 3 and 4. Wittgenstein's personal outlook on ethical questions was a different matter: see the posthumous "A Lecture on Ethics," *Philosophical Review,* 74 (1965); Rush Rhees, "Some Developments of Wittgenstein's View of Ethics," ibid.; B. F. McGuiness, "The Mysticism of the *Tractatus,*" ibid., 75 (1966).

McDowell himself draws important consequences in the philosophy of mind, rejecting the "belief and desire" model of rational action. I do not accept these consequences, but I shall not try to argue the question here. Some considerations later in this chapter, about the differences between ethical belief and sense perception, bear closely on it.

8. McDowell ("Virtue and Reason") allows for this possibility, but he draws no consequences from it and ignores intercultural conflict altogether. He traces skepticism about objectivity in ethics, revealingly, to what he calls a "philistine scientism," on the one hand, and to a philosophical pathology on the other, of vertigo in the face of unsupported practices. Leaving aside his attitude to the sciences, McDowell seems rather unconcerned even about history and says nothing about differences in outlook over time. It is significant that, in a discussion of the virtues that mostly relates to Aristotle, he takes as an example kindness, which is not an Aristotelian virtue.

9. The most subtle and ingenious discussion of propositional knowledge I know is that of Robert Nozick in chap. 3 of his *Philosophical Explanations.* Some central features of Nozick's account, notably the use of subjunctive conditionals, had been anticipated by Fred Dretske, as Nozick acknowledges in his note 53 to that chapter (p. 630), which gives references.

10. How rough? Perhaps I cannot read four dots as 4, though I can read six dots as 6. What if I can only read six dots as 6, and everything else as not 6?

11. Alfred Tarski, "The Concept of Truth in Formalized Languages," in *Logic, Semantics, Meta-Mathematics* (Indianapolis: Hackett Publishing Co., 1981). On the present issue, see David Wiggins, "What Would Be a Substan-

tial Theory of Truth?", in Zak van Straaten, ed., *Philosophical Subjects: Essays Presented to P. F. Strawson* (New York: Oxford University Press, 1980). Wiggins' discussion raises a further issue, whether the observer could even understand what the sentences mean, unless he could apply a disquotational truth formula to them. In this he is influenced by Donald Davidson, "Truth and Meaning," *Synthese*, 17 (1967). The fact that there can be a sympathetic but nonidentified observer shows that it cannot be impossible to understand something although one is unwilling to assert it oneself.

12. See John Skorupski, *Symbol and Theory* (New York: Cambridge University Press, 1976).

13. See Wiggins, "Truth, Invention and the Meaning of Life"; McGinn, *The Subjective View,* pp. 9–10, 119–120.

14. A formulation of the distinction between primary and secondary qualities is very nearly as old in the Western tradition as the self-conscious use of a principle of sufficient reason.

15. I have taken two sentences here from my article, "Ethics and the Fabric of the World," to appear in Ted Honderich, ed., *Morality and Objectivity* (London: Routledge and Kegan Paul, 1985), a volume of essays in memory of John Mackie; it discusses Mackie's views on these subjects, in particular his idea that perceptual and moral experience each involve a comparable error. See also McGinn, *The Subjective View,* esp. chap. 7.

16. This difficulty, of finding an adequate theory of error, is encountered by any theory of ethics that concentrates on the notion of ethical truth. When the ethical takes the special form of *morality,* it is connected with a particular deformation, *moralism.* The insistence that a given person is wrong, disconnected from any possible understanding of how it comes about that he is wrong, tends to leave the commentator entirely outside that person, preaching at him.

17. This conclusion is connected to the point made at the end of Chapter 3, that there is a sense in which all value rests in dispositions of character. See also my Postscript.

9. Relativism and Reflection

1. See in particular Gilbert Harman, "Moral Relativism Defended," *Philosophical Review,* 84 (1975); reprinted in Michael Krausz and Jack W. Meiland, eds., *Relativism, Cognitive and Moral* (Notre Dame: University of Notre Dame Press, 1982), a useful collection on this subject.

2. Vulgar relativism, as I have called this view, is discussed in my *Morality: An Introduction to Ethics.*

3. I have offered this idea, with more detail than here, in "The Truth in Relativism," *Proc. Arist. Soc.*, 75 (1974–75), reprinted in my *Moral Luck,* from which I have adapted a few sentences in what follows. As will be seen, I no longer want to say without qualification as I do there (*Moral Luck,* p. 142), that for ethical outlooks a relativistic standpoint, defined in these terms, is correct.

4. For an example of the emergence of a legend — or, rather, several different legends — see J. C. Holt, *Robin Hood* (London: Thames and Hudson, 1982).

5. One very interesting contribution to this large subject is Bernard Smith, *European Vision and the South Pacific* (New York: Oxford University Press, 1969).

6. For the same reason, fantasy not directed to the past has now shifted from exotic peoples to extraterrestrials. Since they can offer no concrete resistance at all to the most primitive fantasies, the results are pathetically or repulsively impoverished.

7. Alasdair MacIntyre, in *After Virtue* (Notre Dame: University of Notre Dame Press, 1981), is interesting on this subject, though he shows a certain weakness for the myth.

8. "When once the veil begins to rend, it admits not of repair. Ignorance is of a peculiar nature: and once dispelled, it is impossible to reestablish it. It is not originally a thing of itself, but is only the absence of knowledge: and though man may be kept ignorant, he cannot be *made* ignorant." Thomas Paine, *The Rights of Man,* part 1.

9. This is discussed by Geoffrey Hawthorn in a forthcoming book on counterfactual thinking in the social sciences.

10. Rawls seems not to have considered the issue in specifically historical terms. For him it would, revealingly, belong to "partial compliance theory," the theory of justice for societies that fall short of the conditions necessary for implementing the full theory.

11. Helpful secondary works are: Raymond Geuss, *The Idea of a Critical Theory* (New York: Cambridge University Press, 1981); Martin Jay, *The Dialectical Imagination* (Boston: Little, Brown, 1973), and also *Adorno* (Cambridge: Harvard University Press, 1984). Critical theory has paid, particularly in the past decade, a just penalty for its obfuscatory style of thought, and for an unlovely combination of radical rhetoric and professorial authoritarianism. But there is something to be learned from it, particularly if some of its insights are deployed in the theory of justice rather than in connection with freedom, which was the Frankfurt School's own emphasis.

12. One important question is how far a universal form of justice can be

given a different content in different societies: this idea is central to the view of justice given by Michael Walzer in his helpful *Spheres of Justice* (New York: Basic Books, 1983). Another question is how we can think the past unjust while knowing that we owe it almost everything we prize. I hope to discuss such questions, and the critical-theory test, in a forthcoming publication based on the Tanner Lectures given at Harvard in May 1983.

13. The best-known and most exciting version of this view was the kind of existentialism that Sartre held for a while after the Second World War, and later came to think as ridiculous as many others had thought it all along. In a less dramatic form, the view has become almost a platitude of much recent philosophy. John Mackie, for instance (*Ethics: Inventing Right and Wrong,* p. 106), was able to say, without finding it at all special, "morality is not to be discovered but made: we have to decide what moral views to adopt," but it is not clear whether "we" means each of us or all of us together, nor, in either case, what we have to do. In such passages, it is probable that a logical or metaphysical doctrine is being misleadingly put in a psychological form.

10. Morality, the Peculiar Institution

1. I touch briefly on some points later in this chapter. Most discussions of free will do not pay enough attention to the point that causal explanation may have a different impact on different parts of our thought about action and responsibility. It is worth consideration that deliberation requires only *can,* while blame requires *could have.*

2. I have discussed the question of conflict in several essays, in *Problems of the Self* and *Moral Luck.* It is important that, if it were logically impossible for two actual obligations to conflict, I could not get into a situation of their conflicting even through my own fault. What is it supposed that I get into?

3. This point is discussed in my essay "Moral Luck," in the book of that title. It illustrates the general point that the morality system lays particularly heavy weight on the unsure structure of voluntariness.

4. W. D. Ross, *The Right and the Good* (Oxford: Clarendon Press, 1930), pp. 21ff.

5. This is so even when the good deeds are part of a general practice that others hope I will join. The point is admirably pressed by Robert Nozick in *Anarchy, State and Utopia* (New York: Basic Books, 1974), chap. 5.

6. The example is of a conflict between an obligation and a consideration that is not at first sight an obligation. It may very readily represent

another conflict as well, between private and public. For various considerations on this, and particularly on the role of utilitarian considerations in public life, see the essays in Stuart Hampshire, ed., *Public and Private Morality* (New York: Cambridge University Press, 1978).

7. Morality encourages the idea, certainly in cases of this kind, but it does not always insist on it, at least in the form that an obligation of mine can be overridden only by another obligation of mine. If some vital interest of mine would have to be sacrificed in order to carry out a promise, particularly if the promise were relatively unimportant, even the severest moralist may agree that I would have the right to break the promise, without requiring that I would be under an obligation to do so (I owe this point to Gilbert Harman). This is correct but, unless the promise is very trivial, the severe moralist will agree, I suspect, only if the interests involved are indeed vital. This suggests an interpretation under which my obligation would indeed be beaten by an obligation, but not one of mine. In insisting that only vital interests count, it is likely that the moralist, when he says that I have the right to safeguard my interest, does not mean simply that I may do that, but that I have what has been called a claim-right to do so: that is to say, others are under an obligation not to impede me in doing so. Then my original obligation will be canceled by an obligation *of the promissee,* to waive his or her right to performance.

8. What counts as being confronted is a real question, and a very practical one for doctors in particular. I touch on the question later, in giving an account of immediacy which does not need the *obligation-out, obligation-in* principle. This is notoriously a kind of obligation increasingly unrecognized in modern cities, to the extent that it is not saluted even by people guiltily leaving the scene.

9. The point is related to the discussion of deliberative questions in Chapter 1.

10. It is relevant to recall, as well, a point made in Chapter 1: the deliberative considerations that go with a given ethical motivation, such as a virtue, may not be at all simply related to it.

11. The reference to contractualism brings out the point that the account is, in a certain sense, individualist. For some further remarks on this aspect, see my Postscript.

12. It is a mistake to suppose that it has to be equally acceptable to everyone. Some may have a greater right than others to complain.

13. This *kind* of occasion? Yes. But particularizing facts, such as that this is the second time (to her, this year), can certainly be relevant.

14. I have made a suggestion about it in "Practical Necessity," *Moral Luck,* pp. 124 – 132.

15. How alike? This touches on an important question that I cannot pursue here, the distinction between guilt and shame. There is such a distinction, and it is relevant to ethics, but it is much more complex than is usually thought. Above all, it is a mistake to suppose that guilt can be distinguished as a mature and autonomous reaction that has a place in ethical experience, whereas shame is a more primitive reaction that does not. Morality tends to deceive itself about its relations to shame. For some suggestive remarks on the distinction, see Herbert Morris, "Guilt and Shame," in *On Guilt and Innocence* (Berkeley: University of California Press, 1976).

16. This is connected with the differing conceptions of the self entertained by Kant and by his Hegelian critics: see Chapter 1, note 6. It is important here to distinguish two different ideas. Other people, and indeed I myself, can have an "external" idea of different ideals and projects that I might have had, for instance if I had been brought up differently: there are few reasons for, and many reasons against, saying that if I had been brought up differently, it would not have been me. This is the area of metaphysical necessity. But there is a different area, of practical necessity, concerned with what are possible lines of action and possible projects for me, granted that I have the ideals and character I indeed have. This is the level at which we must resist the Kantian idea that the truly ethical subject is one for whom nothing is necessary except agency itself. This is also closely related to the matter of real interests, discussed in Chapter 3.

17. The model of a moral law helps to explain why the system should have the difficulties it has with those ethical acts that, as I put it before, are more or less than obligations. It is not surprising that something interpreted as law should leave only the three categories of the required, the forbidden, and the permitted. Kant's own attempts to deal with some problems of these other ethical motives within his framework of duty involve his interpretations (which changed over time) of the traditional distinction between perfect and imperfect duties. On this, see M. J. Gregor, *Laws of Freedom* (New York: Barnes & Noble, 1963), chaps. 7–11.

18. The question of a categorical imperative and its relation to reasons for action has been pursued by Philippa Foot in several papers, collected in *Virtues and Vices*. I am indebted to these, though our conclusions are different. The moral *ought* was one of several targets assaulted by G. E. M. Anscombe in her vigorous "Modern Moral Philosophy," reprinted in *Ethics, Religion and Politics,* vol. 3 of her *Collected Papers* (Minneapolis: University of Minnesota Press, 1981).

19. Of course, much depends on what is to count as having a reason. I do not believe that there can be an absolutely "external" reason for action, one

that does not speak to any motivation the agent already has (as I have stressed, Kant did not think so either). There are indeed distinctions between, for instance, simply drawing an agent's attention to a reason he already has and persuading him to act in a certain way. But it is basically important that a spectrum is involved, and such distinctions are less clear than the morality system and other rationalistic conceptions require them to be. See "Internal and External Reasons," in my *Moral Luck*.

20. This is why I said in Chapter 4 that Kant's conception was like that of the Pelagian heresy, which did adjust salvation to merit.

Index